THE STATE OF THE
CYBERNATION

Cultural, Political and Economic
Implications of the Internet

NEIL BARRETT

KOGAN
PAGE

For Diana, Jenny and Vicky

YOURS TO HAVE AND TO HOLD

BUT NOT TO COPY

First published 1996

Kogan Page Limited
120 Pentonville Road
London N1 9JN

© Neil Barrett, 1996

British Library Cataloguing in Publication Data
A CIP for this book is available from the British Library.
ISBN 0-7494-2054 5

Typeset by Florencetype Ltd, Stoodleigh Court, Devon

Printed in England by Clays Ltd, St Ives plc

CONTENTS

FOREWORD

Writing about the development of the Internet is a bit like trying to shoot a speeding bullet with a bow and arrow. Even as your fingers hit the keyboard new developments occur by the minute. The net is an evolutionary beast moving at an awesome pace creating new opportunities and challenges for all of us. On the one hand it offers access to almost everything on line and, on the other, it can be disappointing and frustrating because it is so slow, chaotic and clumsy. And yet it is all we have, and it may be all we have for some time!

Our real world of physical things and direct human interaction has been constructed over thousands of years. In contrast the telephone network and electronics arrived in only the last 120 years. The construction of the Internet did not start until the 1960s, PCs were born of the 1970s and the first laptop computer arrived with Sigourney Weaver on the flight deck in the film *Alien* in 1979. Only five years ago I could not have been typing this in Edinburgh Airport, with the capability to download direct to the publisher over a GSM telephone onto the net!

Today a new nation is in the making, and it is the cybernation, seemingly unbounded, and for the present, unthinking. I stopped buying books in the UK when I discovered it was easier to go to California (on-line) and make a purchase at USA prices and have them delivered to my home within two weeks. The UK logistics chain is slower, more expensive, and the choice of books far more limited! So I save time and money, and bypass many established institutions and a number of tax collection points. Buying software on-line is even more extreme; I can purchase my bits at USA prices, bypass VAT, and the overheads of a wholesaler and retailer. As more people get on-line they too will see the advantage of doing things in new ways. But how is a national economy to operate if it cannot collect the taxes, cannot see the trade? If suddenly the works of William Shakespeare are not sold for £25 as a bound volume of paper, but as part of a CD purchased on-line for 1.5p – what is the true worth? More dramatically, what if the same bits are given away free on some server without any mention of copyright or reference to the validity of the original source material? But this is the situation today!

Not surprising then we find social, political, banking and legal systems are creaking under the strain of rapid technological change. In one sense the NET really is about the death of geography and coinage – a totally new value chain is in the making. We have to start thinking and debating how we are going to organise ourselves as a global community when we can buy, sell and exchange bits at virtually zero cost from one side of the planet to the other. Trying to hold onto outmoded values and cultures, bounded by the national shore line, will only cause unnecessary tension and even more problems.

Beyond the few examples I have cited, Neil Barrett has addressed a whole range of challenges and difficulties that are being realised and brought about by the establishment of the Internet. One of the most useful messages in this book is quite simple: there is no free lunch. Someone has to pay! The idea that the Internet is free and no-one has to pay for anything is currently prevalent and naive in the extreme. Internet is a parasite propped up by the revenues and investment in telephone networks. The question is: will the parasite eat the host? The likelihood is that the Internet may well become the CB of the global information superhighway whose backbone may emerge from intranets constructed by the interconnection of company networks. Only time will tell.

This book is both timely and informative, with interesting ideas and projections for the future. People in commerce, industry, non-technophiles, and even aficionados of the net will find it an interesting read. It not only deals with the history and the development of the Internet so far, but also with some of the really thorny issues yet to come. The author goes beyond debating, education on-line, marketing, teleworking, advertising and trading, to deal with virtual companies and organisations, taxation and governments. Security and trust, freedom of expression and privacy, the ownership of information and policing are all comprehensively dealt with. Probably the most challenging of topics covered is the need for a mind-set change throughout our society, and particular, in governments and their organs of administration.

In the intervening period between the publishing of this book and the arrival of the information superhighway, the Internet is all we have. It really does not satisfy our requirement for instant gratification and access to everything at a reasonable price – but it is probably close enough for many. This volume should prove a useful benchmark and reference to where the net has come from, where it is at the point of publication, and where it might actually be going. Whether you are a user of the net, or merely a spectator, you will find this book a useful reference and preparation for a great deal of change yet to come.

Who knows – the author may just have shot the bullet!

Professor Peter Cochrane,
Head of Advanced Applications and
Technologies, BT Laboratories
Martlesham Heath
Ipswich, UK
June 1996

ACKNOWLEDGEMENTS

Like many authors before me – and I'm sure most that will follow – I feel something of a fraud. This work could not possibly have been completed without the help, input, comments and material that I was freely and cheerfully offered by a variety of people; my contribution has been simply to stitch what I hope is a coherent whole from the various patchworks. Those contributions have come from far too many people for me exhaustively to list them all: friends and former colleagues from my secondment to the Inland Revenue; from experts in other organisations with whom I worked during my time there, particularly those in HM Customs and Excise, SFO, CCTA and BT; from those at the Henley Centre for Forecasting, who encouraged me to start this book; and from those at the various departments I buttonholed in my trawling for information for the book, particularly the DTI and the OFT. All of them did their best to provide me with helpful, balanced and informative comments; if this is still wrong, it's now all my fault.

Thanks are due in particular to my employer, Bull Information Systems Ltd, who provided me with the opportunity and support to complete the book; the opinions expressed herein represent, however, my own rather than Bull's views on any of the issues covered.

At Kogan Page, Gabi Facer was a cheerful and enthusiastic advocate for the work. My special thanks for her support, encouragement and the chance to publish the book.

Finally, thanks to my family, to whom this book is dedicated. My wife has suffered a distracted and often absent husband as I typed away in a study that was quickly buried beneath a mountain of papers, clippings and printout; and my daughters have had to suffer the double indignity of having a father who is still 'at work' despite being in plain view and who has moreover prevented them from playing *their* games on the computer. It's all over, girls!

NKB
April 1996

PREFACE

Throughout 1995 and the early part of 1996, I was fortunate enough to work closely with a variety of central government and commercial concerns, investigating the continuing political, social and economic trends into the next century. This work was performed to allow those organisations to establish strategic plans for the next decade and an important aspect was the likely prognosis for technology over the period.

In the course of these studies, however, it became obvious that the true concerns of these disparate organisations centred not – as originally expected – on the structural or the party-political issues of the future. Rather, they were most concerned with the cultural and the policy challenges that would arise from, primarily, one technological advance: the *Internet*. This book has grown out of that work: an investigation of the progress, current state and future potential of the Internet technology.

Over a period of more than fifteen years, from when the most basic of 'inter-networks' began to be used in first US and then UK and other countries' universities, the Internet has grown from an essentially academic facility to the status of a cultural phenomenon. In almost a direct reverse of the telephone's development, the Internet has evolved from a social, communication facility, into an infrastructure arguably capable of supporting trading activities. What makes the Internet of particular value – and a particular challenge – is the very ubiquity that this development implies. From academe to corporation, from research student to schoolchild; the burgeoning growth of home PCs and service providers allowing domestic connection to the Internet has ensured that everyone – with PC, modem and telephone connection – can take part in what is, at the most basic level, a global, social experiment.

From a purely technical perspective, the Internet can be defined as the set of standards, protocols and mechanisms that allow a worldwide set of computers – from mainframe to PC – to interact, sharing software and data. However, in the same way that television has come to be more than a set of broadcast standards, the Internet has come to mean much, much more than this.[1] In the context of this book, 'Internet' is taken to mean the following:

> **Internet:** a global pool of information and services, accessible by means of locally executed interface software.

As we shall see, the information and services pool is vast, encompassing e-mail, newsgroups, discussion groups and a host of educational, entertainment or commercially useful data and applications. And 'locally executed interface software' includes applications run on home PCs, with access over telephone lines to the host computers of service providers such as CompuServe, Demon Internet, Microsoft Network (MSN), America on Line and many, many others throughout the world. Moreover, the access is to hosts that may reside as easily in a different continent as in the same building: the Internet is a domain separate from and independent of physical geography; access to host computers – and individuals – in Australia is as straightforward as access to one's nearest city.

The Internet is perhaps the ultimate, large-scale expression of anarchy; not in the sense of ungovernable, free-form violence, but rather in the sense of a society that is not governed by a central authority; more, a society that functions without the *requirement* for a central governing body.[2] There is no single 'owner' of the Internet-supported services; there is no over-arching legislation; there is, perforce, no global regulation of the types of service, of mation and of goods delivered over the world-wide network. In supporting open communication between universities, for example, such 'anarchy' has functioned well; but as traders, service providers, government organisations and crooks have sought to exploit the global reach of the medium, the requirements for such policies, legislation and regulation become increasingly important.

It is this essential conflict between the anarchic, original structure and the governable infrastructure required for trade, and the challenge that such tension poses for the authorities, that forms the central thesis of this book.

A word of warning, however: those looking for an explanation of the Internet arcana, or detailed descriptions of the technological infrastructure underpinning the phenomenon need, alas, read no further. This is not a technology book; this is not a 'how-to' cookbook for wannabe Internet Gurus. Nor will this book show the reader how to 'Get Rich Quick', through using the Internet as a marketing or trading medium. The bookshelves are already well stocked with texts covering both of these areas, from which the reader can get a complete picture. Rather, this is a book which examines the implications for society, for the regulatory authorities, and for consumers and suppliers, of the Internet's continued development and exploitation.

This is a text aimed at policy makers, at business managers and at the 'thinking man and woman in the street'. This is a book for those who want to see a little of the challenges that lie ahead for us all; that want to understand the current thinking of how those challenges will be met; and want a vision of the possible futures – utopian and dystopian – that lie before us.

In writing this book, it has become obvious to me just how quickly the Internet is developing and evolving. In an early draft of the text, I wrote that none of the credit card companies had agreed 'standard' encryption technologies for transmitting order and payment details over the Internet. Before I had completed the first draft, Mastercard and VISA had reached agreement on SET – 'Secure Electronic Transaction'; and before I could change the words to reflect this, American Express had agreed also to use the emerging standard. The speed of progress in all aspects of the Internet is so rapid that I will, undoubtedly, make claims in this book for the state of Internet use and development that will, by the time of reading, have become inaccurate. For this, I can only apologise.

To try and avoid this problem, I have taken examples that are representative, rather than definitive. This book is about the *types* of things that could be done, and the opportunities and problems – cultural, political or regulatory – that would result. It is not intended to be a definitive survey of what exists or is currently done on the Internet. In the various Endnotes and References I have, however, included pointers to information, some of it *within* the Internet, that will allow readers to assess the current state of progress.

In many ways, some of the aspects of the Internet's potential discussed in this book may seem surprising to those who have already used the Internet. To most, the Internet involves long periods of frustration while trying to connect to remote hosts, or the interminable wait as 'busy', cluttered Web-pages are painfully loaded piecemeal. But all current users will also have experienced the joy of finding new, relevant and useful items of information; or valued the easy, global access of e-mail; or followed an interesting Usenet discussion group. As the speed of the network improves – and we all trust and hope that it will – this frustration will not disappear; we will always want the service to be faster than it can be, and to give us ever more useful facilities.

Moreover, with the vast majority of communications on the Internet being in English,[3] the phenomenon is seen as primarily Anglo-Saxon in nature. More specifically, with three quarters of hosts being within the US,[4] the Internet is predominantly a North American phenomenon. While this is true of the current state, the growing number of French, German and other language postings, and the interest and excitement that the Internet has engendered elsewhere, seems set to create a truly global perspective for our 'Cybernation'.

I have called this book 'The State of the Cybernation'. Perhaps a Cybernation is a somewhat surprising idea; we are familiar with the concept of physical, geographical nations, but what is meant by a *Cybernation*?

The Collins English Dictionary defines a *Nation* as '*an aggregation of people or peoples of one or more cultures, races, etc., organised into a single state'*, or as *'a community of persons not constituting a state, but bound by common descent, language, history, etc'*. Thus, UK, US and other sovereign states constitute a nation, but so too do communities based on 'common descent', such as the global Jewish population. A physical nation state might be characterised by territorial boundaries and by the application of a legal, political and economic system within those boundaries – whereas a cultural nation is characterised by a language, religion or set of cultural norms.

As the Internet has been used by more and more people throughout the world, it has carved a unique cultural niche. The initial sub-culture of Internet users evolved a set of acceptable behaviours, a common history and arguably a common identity of beliefs: free speech, protection of civil rights, impatience with naive questions from the newly initiated, etc. A Cybernation – a nation whose communication of commonly held beliefs and philosophies is effected through the Internet or similar mechanisms – already therefore exists and satisfies the second of Collins's definitions. This initial sub-culture has been added to and developed further as ever more people around the world find their way into 'Cyberspace', creating an evolving and essentially self-organising community.

As the system continues to evolve, however, we might see a degree of sovereignty emerging from the Internet community. While territorial boundaries are only loosely relevant in the Internet context, other aspects of 'Statehood' might become applicable: the emergence of a legal framework from the global perspective of 'Right and Wrong' Internet behaviour – so called 'Netiquette';[5] an internally consistent economic framework evolving from the use of digital cash, on-line transactions and Internet-mobile businesses; and a system of politics from the very many discussion and special interest groups supported. Leaving aside the question of physical territories, the Internet communities therefore satisfy at least some of the criteria for nationhood; hence Cybernation.

Physical, 'real-world' nations emerged from the common cause of disparate peoples thrown together within physical territories. The Internet is an Anglo-Saxon phenomenon at present and we do well to remind ourselves of the emergence of the United States, Australia – and long before them, the English themselves – from a chance collection of immigrants, natives and bonded labour. The nations evolved because the peoples *wished* for a degree of self-governance and an independent identity.

Some Internet users have made declarations of Cybernation independence, usually ironically.[6] It is unlikely, in any but the most unexpected of circumstances, that such a declaration would be supported by the users of the Internet on a global basis; and it would be correctly ignored by the 'proper' authorities. Notwithstanding this, the continued evolution towards a potential for 'nationhood' by the Internet community is of interest.

The Internet – and, ultimately, the Information Superhighway – presents our society, the industrialised, 'western-style' economies, with a set of challenges unique in our history. The potential of the Internet is limited only by our collective imaginations; it is therefore effectively boundless. The social and policy challenges it raises are unfortunately similarly boundless. This is a fascinating, sometimes worrying, picture; I hope I have painted it sufficiently clearly.

1

INTRODUCTION

Cars were envisaged originally as carriages free from the encumbrance and the 'natural pollution' of a horse; the phonogram – which evolved into the LP – was developed as an office dictation machine. The steam engine was seen first as a means of pumping water from flooding mines; and nuclear power was thought at one time to be capable of propelling aircraft. We have a long, long history of technological innovation, but a poor record in predicting the use to which that technology will be put, let alone the ensuing implications of that technology's widespread adoption.

We stand now at the threshold not only of a new century, but of a new age: the Internet's popularity heralds the *'Information Age'*. The telephone, television and computer technologies are converging and are helping to support changes in our mode of communication, spending and employment. But the technology itself, and even the first stage implications of the technology are not widely understood. This book seeks to address these issues – not of what the Internet *is*; but rather, what is implied by its *use*.

In time, the Internet is expected[7] to develop into or contribute towards the 'Information Superhighway', a suite of intelligent information services provided to homes, schools, organisations and institutions by means of ultra-high capacity fibre-optic and wireless transmission media.[8] A highway providing information access and computer services on the same ubiquitous basis as the network of high-speed motorway and trunk roads that facilitates rapid travel – ideally – within and between our cities.

However, before our cities and towns were linked by the motorway network we managed through the use of less capacious trunk roads, and before them ordinary cart-tracks. In the case of the Information Superhighway we have the minor roads already in place, in the Internet. As with the road network before it, in some places it may be rebuilt, overlaid or completely ignored; but it is there now and will be used – allowing us to begin to learn about the potential that the Information Age will bring to us all.

The Internet allows services, correspondence and trading to take place in a non-physical realm. The term '*Cyberspace*' was coined to describe this domain of computer communication;[9] a world in which physical, national boundaries become irrelevant; a world in which tiny, back-street shops can market and sell to customers throughout the globe. And a place in which the laws and regulation painstakingly devised over centuries become difficult, impossible or irrelevant to apply; a place which might evolve its own nationhood: a *Cybernation*.

The book falls into three logical parts. The first examines the current state of the Internet: the rest of this chapter discusses the history and users of the Internet; Chapter 2 describes the cultural implications of using the Internet to support global communication; and Chapter 3 examines the several aspects of trading over the Internet. The first part of the book is therefore concerned with what *is* and what *could be* done in the context of the Internet, and the way in which the most basic elements of a Cybernation have been, are, or could be put into place.

The second part of the book then examines the *implications* of a Cybernation in the context of Economics (Chapter 4), Legislative and Regulatory controls, and the challenges implied for Politics (Chapter 5). That is, this part considers the effect that use and development of the Internet could have on the existing 'real-world' institutions supporting it, and the aspects that would be important in the context of a Cybernation.

In the third and final part, Chapter 6 considers the direction that could be taken by the Internet and Information Superhighway beyond the most obvious, current aspects of its use. In this last part, therefore, we consider what could happen as the Internet evolves into a free-standing Cybernation, with an increasing remoteness from the real world.

For those interested in the more technical aspects of the Internet – from security to transmission technologies – the References and Endnotes give pointers to further information sources, many within the Internet itself. Endnotes are shown as superscript numerals; References as bracketed numbers. The Appendix discusses the source of the several references and suggests ways of augmenting the information through access to the Internet published material itself.

While the Internet has, it is true, existed for some two decades, in many ways it is a new phenomenon. Only recently has the potential for the Internet to affect our social, economic and political lives been appreciated. The Clinton administration's and other authorities' enthusiasm for the Information Superhighway has raised the Internet high on the agenda at organisations in the public, private and voluntary sector on both sides of the Atlantic. It has taken several years for the true potential of this infrastructure technology to be appreciated; in many ways we are still limited more by our imagination than by the technology. Only very recently have the key policy and cultural challenges been noticed.

It would be presumptive of any text, at such an early state of the Internet's development, to suggest radical solutions to these particular challenges. This book, therefore, concentrates on elucidating them; on collecting together the themes and arguments that have been presented elsewhere, in a host of discussion sessions, seminars and newspaper columns – and of course within the Internet itself. The points are gathered so as to make them accessible to the general reader in the hope that, from a maze of confusing passageways, a sensible, workable route forward can emerge, allowing us all to benefit from the creation of a Cybernation without damaging, undermining or otherwise harming those 'real-world' entities upon which we all rely.

THE HISTORY OF THE INTERNET

The Internet is, of course, many things to many people. From a technical perspective it is the set of interface protocols that allow disjoint networks, of different types, to exchange information. To the *users*, however, the Internet has become synonymous with the concept of ubiquitous access to global information and communication services, without regard to the real-world location of the computer hosts supporting them. Service providers, such as CompuServe or America on Line, provide their subscribers with so-called 'dial-in' access to host machines and to the range of facilities provided by the organisation for a service fee – together with the cost of the telephone connection itself. Using home PCs and modems along standard telephone connections, users can therefore gain access to the service provider's own network.

In the case of CompuServe, for example, this network includes e-mail services, access to on-line shopping or information services – such as a digital encyclopaedia – and Special Interest Group discussion forums. These services are internal to the CompuServe community, evolving from the initial 'Bulletin Board Service'(BBS)[10], although e-mail can be supported into the wider Internet. This wider access is also supported via CompuServe-provided software, giving a user-friendly mouse-driven interface to a vast expanse of information sources. A single service provider can therefore allow users – at home or at work – to access their own and the broader range of facilities. Other service providers support direct access to the wider Internet community without the parallel provision of their own 'private' domain of services.

There are therefore two distinct models for Internet use: the private or semi-private network – be it corporate or publicly available to paying subscribers – that provides its own, licensed services and information alongside wider access; and the more public, global network. In this last case, users pay for access to the Internet services as a whole and are supported outside of private domains. In this book, CompuServe[11] has been used as an example of the first case and the term 'Internet' or 'Web' is used to specify the second.

However, recalling the definition of the Internet given in the Preface, this book takes *both* types of service provision as instances of the general Internet phenomenon: access to a global pool of information by means of locally executed interface software.

Before moving on to explore the implications and challenges of the Internet, it would be useful to explain a little about the history and workings of the system itself. As discussed above, however, this is not about to be a technical treatise on the mechanisms used, but rather a simple explanation of where the Internet emerged, how it is used and the basic facilities it supports. Those already familiar with the subject may, with impunity, omit this section; those frightened by the technology are, however, assured that it is safe to read on. The Endnotes contain the more detailed technical material for those interested in the 'how' as well as the 'what' and the 'why'.

Early development

As early as 1969, the American government was aware of the immense strategic value of the information held by the then handful of computers throughout the world. Military research projects, but most especially the 'space-race', had led to the accelerated use of computers not simply as overly expensive calculating engines, but increasingly as reservoirs of complex technical data. Two reinforcing ideas suggested the importance of supporting communication links between these valuable resources. In the first place, there was immense advantage in cooperation between the several sites undertaking defence-related research. These sites ranged from the military themselves, through closely associated organisations – such as NASA – to defence contractors and those universities undertaking projects. Each held valuable data of use to other establishments and each had sophisticated facilities that might profitably be shared among the pool of researchers. In addition, a rapid communication mechanism would also support frequent, informal correspondence between the researchers themselves.

Secondly, there was the question of physical security of that data and information. The 1960s was the period of the 'Cold War'; the prospect of a global nuclear conflict was a very real concern. The possible, imminent destruction of all or some of the American – and indeed European – cities was very real. In this context, a means for rapidly and reliably exchanging information between computers – in a mechanism not dependent on the physical movement of magnetic tape along freeways – was seen as an urgent necessity.

In retrospect, of course, this last point was not as realistic as first thought; even a limited nuclear exchange would have damaged the

US telecommunications network beyond the capacity to transmit binary data reliably and quickly; and the communication speeds possible at the time would severely limit the quantities of data that could be transmitted anyway.

Notwithstanding this, the results of the initial experiments in supporting such networks were positive and the first computer communication networks grew rapidly throughout the 1970s. This growth occurred not just within the US, but also in the UK and Europe. Academic and corporate networks grew rapidly and as the numbers of computers increased, the advantages for organisations in connecting the computers together similarly grew.

The initial American experiment was known as the '*ARPANET*': Advanced Research Projects Agency Network. By 1980, this network had grown substantially, and was then divided into two subsidiary networks: ARPANET and MILNET, the military communications network. Each had to be free-standing but there was also a requirement for intercommunication between the two. At this early stage of computer networking, standards for the construction of individual networks had barely begun to emerge; each manufacturer or developer of a given network structure would therefore devise their own schemes for encoding and transmitting information over the connections between computers.

Communication between the computer networks themselves had not, until then, been considered. The agency responsible for the networks – now renamed the Defence Advanced Research Projects Agency ('DARPA') – began work to devise a scheme for communicating between the ARPANET and MILNET networks. The system they devised was a practical, simple mechanism. In computational terms, it is 'cheap'; that is, easy to implement and of relatively low overhead in execution.[12] The connections themselves became known as the 'DARPA Internet'; in time this became simply the *Internet*.

At first this interconnection was limited to the military and defence research establishments, but throughout the early 1980s it was gradually expanded to include a range of non-military networks, thereby expanding the range of available information, and hence the value of the Internet. In 1986, responsibility for the Internet passed from DARPA to the National Science Foundation ('NSF') and by 1990 ARPANET had evolved into NFSNET, and the Internet standards for intercommunication between networks and computers had come to be accepted as the *de facto* standard.[13]

Under the guidance of NSF, the Internet's use and scope grew rapidly, both within the US and abroad. Before this time there had been networks in the UK connected to the Internet – the Joint Academic Network ('JANET') for example, linked UK universities and, through a *gateway*, had connections to the US Internet. Throughout the 1990s, this facility became increasingly available to commercial concerns[14] and, as NSF handed control of the Internet over to the emerging Internet service providers, it became available to private individuals using PCs and dial-up modems. These service providers allow home PCs access to their own computers – so-called 'hosts' – which are then connected to the Internet by wide-area networks, making the facilities available to anyone who cares to take part.

Facilities

What sorts of facilities are provided by the Internet? It supports the transfer of files between computers using 'file transfer protocol' – *ftp*; and it allows users of one computer to access the services of a second using remote login – *telnet*.[15] These are the most basic facilities provided. Most host computers then support more sophisticated services over and above these, such as electronic mail and network news.[16]

Every Internet user has an e-mail address. The computers within the Internet cooperate in distributing mail between themselves, converging upon the target machine and individual addressee. By using this facility, the Internet can support rapid, informal message interchange between any and all users of the system. The implications of this informal communication medium are addressed below.

Network – or 'Usenet' – news is a less personal communication medium than e-mail. News items – 'articles' – are gathered into 'groups' of related items depending upon the topic. Users submit articles, rather like electronic mail messages, to a particular newsgroup. These messages then appear in the list of articles when subsequent users examine the contents of newsgroups to which they subscribe. There are many tens of thousands of newsgroups, however, with topics ranging from the sublime to the ridiculous; from the most esoteric elements of advanced programming languages, to blow by blow reports on TV soaps. Finding articles of value can therefore be a matter of serendipity. Again, the implications are examined below.

The final basic facility is 'Internet Relay Chat' or just *'chat'*, that allows users on the same or remote hosts to communicate directly, terminal to terminal. Characters typed into one terminal appear on the second, allowing a more direct and immediate communication facility. The implications of this simple system are somewhat surprising, as we shall see.

Development

These basic tools allowed the Internet to grow, attracting an active, energetic and enthusiastic sub-culture of users, particularly in the US. The main inspiration for these users came from the potential of the newsgroups, discussing particularly 'fringe' topics. However, mainstream computing continued to view the Internet as remote from their interests: if not exactly irrelevant then at best peripheral. Two developments conspired to alter this view.

The first development was the introduction and rapid dissemination of computer viruses.[17] Primarily malicious in nature, these are programs that 'hide' within other applications, or that propagate through the network by downloading themselves from infected hosts to other systems. From a handful of sites, these viruses spread throughout the network. From that time onwards, all organisations had to become aware of the potential risks associated with the Internet; and coincidentally, the benefits associated with its use. With software to protect from viruses, an increasing number of organisations began to explore the more commercial opportunities presented.

The second development was in tools to 'navigate' and to explore the services provided on the Internet. Initially, as explained, the wider use of the Internet was through newsgroups. Some sites, however, also held files containing information of broad, general interest. NASA computer sites, for example, held digitised image files in standard formats of pictures from telescopes or from satellites; other sites held weather forecasting data, or family-tree records, or even pornography. Newsgroups were used to advertise these files, and users could employ the file transfer mechanisms to retrieve and load those files into their local machines from 'public' accessed directories.

The first navigation tools were developed in US universities to assist students and researchers in locating files containing data relevant for their work. The 'Gopher' facility provided a structured view of the information advertised as available in each host computer known to it. Gradually, a comprehensive record, arranged as a hierarchy of menus, was produced. This allowed users to 'browse' through the menus, specifying the files that may be of interest; these files could then be retrieved using file transfer programs and reviewed locally.

However, the current 'state of the art' is represented by the most sophisticated tool to date: the 'World Wide Web,'[18] usually abbreviated to 'the Web'. The combination of wider access through service providers, support for home PCs, and the user-friendly aspects of the Web is what makes the Internet now of such supreme interest to companies, individuals, and government organisations.

'The Web'

Over half of the machines accessing the Internet are PCs. Web software called 'browsers' runs on these PCs or on high-end workstations and makes requests of server processes on host machines.[19] The power of the Web comes from the graphical, multi-media and highly flexible nature of the system. Information is represented by so-called Web 'pages'. A page is stored on a particular host machine but can be made visible to Web clients throughout the world.[20] Pages have unique addresses, and can therefore be retrieved explicitly.[21] Alternatively, pages can be cross-referenced from others by means of dynamic, 'hyper-text' links. Not all Internet information is held within such pages; some is still only available through the Gopher or ftp mechanisms. Increasingly, however, the most commonly accessed and popular sites have moved to this mechanism.

Web pages are easy to implement, easy to retrieve – but difficult to describe. They can contain pictures, sound clips, or links to other pages; and they are accessed using a mouse, with 'point-and-click'. Links to other pages are represented by highlighted or underlined words. Clicking on the link-word alerts the Web software to retrieve the indicated page. This might in turn contain further links and so on through a complex, web-like structure of information associations.

On high-performance PCs, capable of displaying the colour graphics and sound clips, the Web provides a user-friendly, powerful facility. Even on low-end PCs the Web is of great value. The interface is intuitive to those familiar with Microsoft office applications or similar, and the retrieval is easy to manage. If it has a drawback, it is in the slow speed of such retrieval, although this is a feature of the underlying network rather than the software *per se*.

Web pages can be constructed by anyone having the necessary tools. Corporate, public sector, or private individual Web pages therefore abound throughout the Internet; and they are visible throughout the world. The Web has therefore been described as the 'killer application'[22] for the Internet: the application that took the Internet from a relative handful of enthusiasts, into the domain of serious, commercial and governmental users.

In addition to this, however, the Web has also allowed the introduction of an entirely novel paradigm for the distribution and execution of applications. In this, instead of the Web page containing text or information it presents a *program*, written in a language called 'Java'.[23] Instead of simply displaying an image or text, the local browser includes a simple operating system able to interpret the downloaded program. These programs are, in effect, benign viruses – introduced onto a remote system, the PC, but in a controlled and assured manner.[24]

While this new system provides a simple facility for performing local data checking in the completion of order forms, for example, it also allows a new and exciting approach to the distribution of applications. In a word processor package, for instance, only a tiny fraction of the application's functionality is ever used by anybody, yet all of it is available to each and every user who buys the software. With Internet-distributed applications, it becomes possible to transfer only that part of the software that is actually needed at any one time. The applications therefore remain at the host system or systems, rather than in the connected PCs, and are downloaded piecemeal as required; this paradigm is called 'Networked Dynamic Functionality' (NDF), although the more colourful 'Nomadic Software' (see reference [28]) perhaps describes it better. Software and data move through the network, as demanded by the users, to those PCs where it is required. Central management of the various applications then makes it much easier to ensure that upgrades or the introduction of new software are handled effectively.

In fact, this NDF paradigm has led to a broader debate about the type and nature of local device used to capture the data or to execute the applications. Two schools of thought have emerged, with one proposing the development of 'Internet-terminals'[25] and the other the continued use of PCs. Internet terminals require only minimal intelligence: they are *windows* onto the world of the Internet but with only limited ability to execute software independently and no capacity to capture the transmitted data permanently; this system software in such a terminal is sometimes referred to as a 'Thin Client'. By comparison to such terminals, PCs can capture data *and* can execute software locally, independently of the Internet; but they are expensive. Each has its attractive points and each gives rise to certain drawbacks. However, since the PCs themselves are well established, well supported and growing rapidly in numbers, while Internet-terminals have only recently begun development, the argument would seem currently to be going to the PC school. Moreover, Java can be executed as easily by a 'thin-client' emulator running on an intelligent PC as on a non-intelligent terminal.

PC v Internet Terminal

We can consider several areas in which the PC versus Internet terminal debate might be decided: in the home; in schools, colleges, hospitals or other non-profit organisations; or in companies using the Internet internally – an option we will examine in Chapter 3.

In the home, it would seem unlikely that a pure Internet terminal would displace the PC. Most home PCs use modems that operate at up to 28.8 kbps (thousand bits per second) over telephone lines, although it possible but expensive to achieve speeds of 2 mbps with dedicated and expensive high-speed lines.[26] By comparison, speeds of around 10 mbps are supported in reading applications and data from PC hard disks.[27] Planned developments in the telecommunication structure and in the introduction of fibre-optic cable for the delivery of TV might allow cable modems supporting speeds of around 10 mbps, and in a few decades the widespread introduction of the most advanced telephone networks – ATM (Asynchronous Transfer Mode) – might support a tenfold increase in these rates.[28] But even with these substantial advances in telecommunication speeds and a corresponding dramatic reduction in the cost of the telephone call (see Chapter 2), this would still not act to persuade users to shift allegiance. The domestic PC can be used 'off-line' and therefore brings its own advantages even without considering the Internet connection, and by the time such advances in network technology have been made available the PC's penetration will be very high and the PC itself can be expected to have become even faster in turn. Some manufacturers are, however, beginning to introduce an experimental combination of TV and Internet terminal, that would have the advantage of bringing the computer out of the 'study' and into the living room environment. At such an early stage, it is impossible to determine whether such a product will attain market acceptance *before* the full range of services – video on demand particularly – have been provided.

For those educational and other institutions, a slightly different picture might emerge. In the UK, BT have been encouraged to provide high-bandwidth connectivity at low cost to allow the schools, colleges and hospitals to take part in the information 'revolution'. This would mean that the very high transmission speeds necessary to support the Internet terminal would be in place very quickly. Further, since the terminals are currently expected to retail at about half the price of an Internet-capable, multi-media PC, this gives huge advantages in the case of these organisations, having only low capital expenditure budgets for computer equipment. Of course, this assumes that the essential server structures have been established to provide the downloadable software suites and information, and that they themselves can cope with the large numbers of high-speed modem connections required – server structures that might well be expensive to maintain and run. While the economies of the terminals and even the connections have been explored, the cost of such management has not.

In the case of companies, there are equally convincing arguments for both structures. PCs have acted to liberate user departments from the management of a central IS team; the Internet terminal would have the effect of reintroducing that management. But PCs are expensive and a potential attraction to thieves, while Internet terminals are expected to be much cheaper – although still of course attractive to thieves. A large number of organisations, particularly public sector where the IT budget constraints are very rigid, have begun to explore the *potential* for Internet terminals, while retaining the existing PC infrastructure. Until Internet terminals become more widely available, this will be a difficult call to decide.

In the context of this book, however, whether the Internet is accessed through dedicated, simple terminals or sophisticated PC devices is less important than the observation that the debate is *happening at all*. The argument is about what type of access mechanism will be used, rather than whether or not access will be required. In all quarters, it would seem to have been agreed that the Internet will be an important feature of computing in the 21st century.

THE INTERNET USERS

The bare statistics of Internet usage, particularly the growth, are impressive. From a handful of enthusiasts, the number of user accounts has grown to over 30 million world-wide, with around 150,000 new additions every month. Modest projections put the numbers at over 100 million by 1998, and 200 million by 2002 (see reference [21] for a more detailed breakdown). As important as the growth rates is *who* that growth represents. 'User accounts' may be individual or corporate; in the corporate case, a single account may support 10, 20, even 100 users, and commercial networks currently amount to over half of the networks registered on the Internet. A subset of the commercial networks are the Internet service providers; it is through these that the Internet can be used domestically.

Access to the Internet for individuals is through their workplace, as an aspect of their job; or it is through use of a service provider to their home. This rapid growth rate therefore combines both domestic and work-related use; the statistics, in fact, obscure this distinction. Moreover, the Internet usage in schools, colleges, and government departments is growing rapidly, fuelling the growth in other areas.

However, the current number of accounts reported by each of the Internet Service Providers includes accounts that may well be moribund, or may be duplicate accounts; an individual may access the services from home through CompuServe and also via a company-provided system at work. The true numbers of individuals accessing and using the Internet on a regular basis might therefore already lie close to the 100 million mark; or it may be much less than 30 million. The statistics are very difficult to assess, and estimates published by observers range from 20 million to as many as 100 million.[29] All independent research reports *do* stress, however, the rapid growth rate, with new networks and users added on a constant basis. Commercial subscriptions grow at more than 100 per cent per year, for example.

Because of these problems with the statistics it is instructive to look at the *types* of users that are represented within the figures. In the marketing of technology, it is often useful to distinguish the types of buyers for new developments. Broadly, there are five categories that have been identified,[30] ranging from the *innovators* and *enthusiasts*, through the *pragmatic* majority, to the *followers* and ultimately the *laggards*. Many analysts claim that technologies that are ultimately failures become lodged at the innovator and enthusiast stages; conversely, successful technologies are those that surmount the hurdle of appealing to the more pragmatic majority of users. This distinction of technology buyers applies with equal force to organisations and to individuals.

Innovators are that set of die-hard technophiles who buy, with only a few exceptions, every new idea in a particular field; enthusiasts are those who very quickly follow the innovators' lead. Any new form of technology can find a home, albeit a small one, with this market. Indeed, there are some products that exist wholly within this segment, producing frequent upgrades and modifications to keep the 'freshness' of the product intact and to continue appealing to the enthusiasts' rapidly jaded palates. Sales, even in high volumes, to this segment are not an indication of wider product success and guaranteed growth. Only those products that cross to the pragmatic majority are assured of a continued market.

Pragmatists form the majority of a technology's market. These are the consumers who buy utility rather than novelty; who look for a practical application of a technology rather than the curiosity or niche interest. In crude terms, the first set of buyers of a technology are the 'anoraks' or 'nerds' of the industry – and are usually young males. By the time the product makes it to the high street stores, the older pragmatists of both sexes form a major part of its market. The followers and laggards are then the reluctant buyers, forced by circumstance rather than by fashion, who find the only way of satisfying possibly new needs is through buying the product.

How does the analysis apply to the use of the Internet? Initially at least, as described above, the Internet fell within the domain of the enthusiasts. However, with the facilities of service providers such as CompuServe and the growth in numbers of home PCs it has moved out of this initial area. It was carried forward by so-called 'knowledge' workers, already familiar with using PCs and information sources at work, who saw value in such facilities at home. An increasing number of consultants work primarily from home and so the e-mail and information services are of great value.

From these professionals, the phenomenon has spread further, encompassing now the most unlikely users,[31] from the youngest schoolchild using it to exchange gossip, to grandparents receiving picture files drawn by their young grandchildren using Microsoft 'PaintBrush'. Home PCs can now come with Internet software preloaded; connecting to the Internet and using the Web have come to be a basic element of home PC use for many people.

And at work, many companies are finding that the Internet can provide advantages in terms of marketing and of sourcing information. Now we will consider this use in far greater detail.

Internet penetration

Use of the Internet is therefore growing both at work and at home. Taking the case of the home, it is difficult to establish an estimate of how many homes will have access to Internet services; in the

UK at present, the penetration is about 3 per cent;[32] in the US, 9 per cent. A presentation to the Federal Trade Commission in November 1995, however, suggested that 30 per cent of US homes would be connected to the Internet by 2000;[33] a figure of 65 per cent for the UK by 2005 was predicted separately by the Henley Centre for Forecasting,[34] which would suggest a similarly high rate of growth. These predictions have taken the simplest case; sales of PCs and of modems. However, they suggest that in the UK and the US a high penetration could be supported by 2001 if the current purchasing trends of such enabling technologies continue.

These figures represent the potential market for sales of the basic components for Internet connection, assuming that the products continue to be bought by the same income group – broadly, professional, AB1s. However, with the growth in use of the Internet at school[35] it is possible that sales of PCs – including, increasingly as standard, modems – will accelerate, following purchase by a broader social class. This 'smearing' across social classes was exactly the phenomenon observed with the penetration of satellite TV in the UK and is therefore far from unprecedented.

In addition, there are several active projects to bring Internet access to an even broader range of people, both in the UK and abroad. With the use of the Internet by government organisations there have been plans to make Internet 'booths' available in Citizen's Advice Bureaux, in shopping precincts and in post offices and other public spaces[36]. Additionally, some local councils have initiated Internet-based assistance for job hunters, self-help groups and so forth (see reference [24]).

The actual penetration and use of the Internet throughout the world can therefore be expected, among private users, to be very high by the turn of the century. Estimates range from the 30 per cent given above, to more radical figures such as 80 per cent; in discussion, one enthusiast even put the figure at around 90 per cent for parts of the US, although this may be a bit ambitious! As a rule of thumb, a sensible assumption might be 50 per cent of house-holders having some access to Internet services – either directly, or through the facilities of an Internet booth, or similar – by 2001 across both US and UK. In more 'wired' societies, such as Singapore or other Pacific Rim states, this could be much higher, although the high English-language content has acted as an inhibitor in some countries – notably Japan and France.[37]

It is this important statistic that has lead to the current enthusiasm for using the Internet as a marketing or a trading medium. With the ability to reach consumers relatively cheaply and easily – and on a world-wide basis – it would be surprising if the facilities were *not* exploited to the full by companies and organisations such as charities.

Of course, there is a certain circularity to this argument – reflecting the circularity of the process. More people will use the Internet only if there is a wider range of services available on it; this requires companies to make those services available – which they will do only if there is a market. The current perception is that the existing Internet population, while currently small, is important in spending power and is growing rapidly in number. More and ever more companies will therefore seek to reach that market, and increasingly more facilities, services and products will be made available. This in turn fuels the growth in numbers of users.[38]

In the main, the Internet is still used primarily as a communication medium for e-mail, newsgroups and the Web-page information. However, as we shall see below it can and is being used to disseminate government and commercial information; to advertise and sell products; and to distribute digital 'goods'. As the number of users increases the services and opportunities will also increase. But so too will the legislative, regulatory and cultural challenges that its use implies.

2

INTERNET COMMUNICATION

We live now in a world that must seem entirely alien to someone born near the turn of the century. In 1995 my wife's grandmother died; she was 95. She remembered a world without cars, without telephones and electricity. She remembered a steam powered world and persisted in the belief that Leeds was too far to travel to from York – even while I commuted from there to Paris on a weekly basis.

Our lives now encompass a world in which distance has come to be, if not irrelevant, then certainly of lesser importance than it once was. A world in which our 'village' life has come to encompass individuals scattered not throughout a distinct, geographic locale but rather on a global basis. A world in which our neighbours can be – and increasingly are – defined not by physical proximity but rather by commonality of interest. And a world in which technology facilitates interaction rather than fascinates us for its own sake.

In contrast to my wife's grandmother, our elder daughter is 5. She is already familiar with the computer on which these words are being typed. She is already expert in drawing pictures in PaintBrush and in faxing those pictures to her grandparents in York. She is even sufficiently familiar with the mechanisms to be annoyed that, unlike her 6-year-old friend down the street, her grandparents won't get connected to the Internet allowing her to send the PaintBrush file itself, in all its glorious colour.

If today's world is confusing to our grandparents, how will my daughter's world seem to me, twenty or thirty years from now?

The telephone has allowed us to communicate with our friends and relatives throughout the world; the television has brought us pictures of scenes in real-time on an equally global basis. Perhaps the best, relatively recent example of this immediacy came during the Tiananmen Square protests, when TV pictures brought us the events as they occurred and allowed – through the telephone and the Internet! – similarly real-time protests.

Through the telephone and the television, the world has shrunk – or at least, its topology has changed. We have passing familiarity with the streets of London, Los Angeles and Moscow; we recognise scenes from Hong Kong, Delhi and Sydney – even while the extreme eastern area of Russia remains a mystery. But those scenes are to a greater or lesser extent chosen for us – we are passive viewers of a director's carefully framed video-clip. Only the telephone gives us the more direct choice of venue and that too is limited.

However, with global, Internet-supported communication this control comes fully into our hands. Even at this relatively young stage of the Internet's development, it is popularly held that we can find Web pages that show the scene at Golden Gate Bridge, or from a Weather Satellite – or even the coffee pot in a Californian post-graduate lounge![39] True, our choice of scene is constrained by the available transmission and the display is painfully slow to download – but there is a growing variety of scenes for our choice, if we can *find* them.

And we can use the Internet to *work* on a global basis, sending packages of documents between cities, following the working day as it travels around the world. Big business and the stockmarkets achieve that effect already; increasingly, smaller and smaller concerns can do so. In 1994 I worked on a cooperative project with staff from Phoenix, Arizona; in the UK we worked through our complete day before sending the material to Phoenix for a further working day. Had we had additional staff in, say, Australia, the project could have continued on a 24-hour basis.

Communication was the first, primary role of the Internet – communication between a variety of host computers and then between a variety of computer users; but now, communication between individuals who just *happen* to use a computer – rather than a telephone, say – to effect that exchange of thoughts. That communication will have as great, if not a greater effect on the way we live and work as the internal combustion engine, electricity, powered flight and the telephone had on my grandparents' world.

For our Cybernation, an ability to support communication ranging from private correspondence to publicly broadcast news and current affairs is a vital component; it is perhaps the most basic requirement for supporting *any* community.

The Internet supports this community communication through a variety of mechanisms, the most obvious being the electronic mail and the Usenet newsgroup facilities. Both of these allow individuals to exchange files containing correspondence or data for applications between themselves, globally, at very low telecommunication costs. At the simplest level, a private individual gains access to these facilities through a service provider. For the cost of a telephone call – usually at local rates – the user can connect a local PC to the service provider's host computer. From that point onwards, files and messages can be propagated throughout the world with no additional telecommunication costs, although the service provider may well charge on the basis of message size or numbers of messages transmitted.

As with any other community, the mechanisms used to support such communication then in turn have the potential to impact upon and to change key aspects of our lives: the way that we correspond and the groups of people with whom the communication takes place; the way that we are educated and the scope of information published and accessible to us; and the ways and places within which we can work.

CORRESPONDENCE OVER THE INTERNET

There are already a large number of ways to communicate with distant relatives or friends. Most obviously, one can telephone. In the industrialised, western economies the majority of individuals are accessible by telephone – either at home or at work. However, there are two drawbacks with this approach: firstly, there is the question of expense; secondly, that of time zones. If the relative is particularly distant – say in Sydney, Australia – then the cost of the telephone call may well be substantial. While this might not inhibit the exchange of vital information, it would argue against gossip. As we shall see later, this question of cost may in fact become less of an issue over the following years.

The second problem, that of timezone, is slightly more problematic. In calling Australia, Canada, or the US, there is a limited window of convenience; outside of these handful of hours conversations take place while one or other party would more usually be asleep. To those of us who have had to work under such situations this is far from ideal and many prefer instead to leave recorded messages as 'voice mail'. In these circumstances telephones therefore lose their primary advantage – immediacy.

The alternative to such recorded messages is of course to write – but even in the latter part of the 20th century it still takes several days for correspondence to move around the globe, other than in the case of fax transmissions. And of course the written word – committed and frozen in paper and ink – loses much of the informality. The advent of the telephone removed, for the majority of us, the necessity and therefore the experience of writing conversational letters. As distances over which families and friends may be spread has increased we are in sore need of that ability again.

Of course it is now afforded through that uniquely late-20th century experience: the e-mail message.

E-mail

On the face of it electronic mail is a simple enough idea. Using standard word processor or editor software a file of text is created; this is marked somehow with the address of the person for whom the contents are intended; and system software on the originating and intermediate computers routes the message to the addressee. Upon receipt, the message can be read – again, using standard editor or viewing programs – and if required a response can be sent.

As with standard mail – some people refer to this as 'snail mail' – the file contents can be anything from business correspondence, through love letters and poetry, to hate mail. Where this departs from standard correspondence is in the speed at which the messages can be propagated. While the transmission is not instantaneous, for small files it is very fast: certainly same day; often same hour; and in some cases same minute. By analogy with the real world, it is rather like entering somebody's office, scrawling a message for them and placing it firmly in the middle of their desk.

This analogy, however, bears closer examination, as it gives a very good indication of the nature of e-mail correspondence. Posted letters are collected and distributed within offices and homes at specific hours of the day: breakfast time at home; early morning and early afternoon in most offices. However, the letters might not be opened instantly, they may instead accumulate in an in-tray until the recipient has the time to dedicate to them. Nor, in any but the most conscientious of offices, are they responded to instantly; letters may await reply for several hours, perhaps even days.

Conversely, when one has the ability – and, indeed the close association to allow – entry to another's office to place a 'Post-it' or hastily drafted note in the middle of the desk, the response is significantly different. Most obviously, if the person is present the response to the note may well be instant; certainly attention to the note will be immediate. If the person is *not* present at the time, they will see the note upon their return, perhaps among a pile of other, similar notes. Again, attention and often response is rapid.

In comparison to 'snail mail', e-mail gives immediacy – of delivery and often of response; most people's reaction is to pause on their current work, and to check the contents of the message. Having looked at it, it is then often easiest to respond immediately rather than to postpone an answer. In many ways therefore it is more similar to telephone conversations than to written correspondence, although we shall see that it falls uncomfortably between the two. E-mail gives to strangers that closeness of association to allow messages to be placed firmly in the middle of somebody else's desk: the President of the United States and the President of Microsoft both have e-mail, and both respond – in Bill Gates's case, rapidly and in person – to those messages [2].

The analogy with Post-it notes goes further still when considering the *tone* of the e-mail messages. As discussed above, written correspondence differs from both direct and telephone conversations in the formality of the exchange. In committing thoughts to the written word most people – even in letters to friends – descend to a level of impersonality; love letters, poetry and hate mail are uncomfortable to write and to receive precisely because this formality is stripped away.

However, in telephone conversations we become much less formal. In friendly telephone conversations we find it easy to express our thoughts; and in less friendly conversations we find it much easier to complain. The telephone gives us the ability to express ourselves, on an immediate basis, but without the uncomfortable aspect of having the other person directly in front of us. Direct conversation – face-to-face – is easy with someone we know and like, and for most people difficult with those we don't or with those towards whom we feel antagonistic.

There is therefore a spectrum – from formal, written text, through less formal, 'insulated' telephone conversations, to unprotected direct conversations. If one wanted to complain, for example, most would find it easy to write an icily formal letter, slightly less easy to telephone and berate the customer service representative, and difficult to handle the complaint effectively in a personal meeting.

The telephone therefore sits between the two poles of formality. It has a further advantage: there is seldom, if ever, a permanent record of that conversation – other than in situations where one is immediately aware that the call is being recorded, such as on an answer-machine or VoiceMail system when one's messages are invariably stilted.

Where does e-mail sit on this spectrum? The answer is interesting.

E-mail has the advantages of spontaneity, of informality; many of us have had the experience of 'banging off' a hasty e-mail message, subsequently regretted. However, there is a permanent record of that message. It has the informality of the telephone, the apparent insulation of the telephone, but the permanence of the written word. In early experiments with e-mail, many organisations – particularly universities – reported that the tone of e-mail messages was distressingly strident. Messages would be sent, using words and styles that would not be expected – or even tolerated – in normal discourse.

As organisations and individuals have become more familiar with using e-mail this excessive tone of communication has decreased but there is still a feeling of emotional remoteness in sending e-mail, notwithstanding the introduction of so-called 'emoticons';[40] little figures to denote the intended nature of a sentence.

The final comparison with the Post-it lies in the question of privacy. A sealed envelope marked 'private and confidential, addressee only' is usually treated as sacrosanct. Conversely, notes stuck to office doors can be and are read by every passer-by. As with the other comparisons, e-mail sits somewhere between these two extremes.

The e-mail messages are – in the main – text files. That is, the contents of the message are stored, exactly as typed, in ordinary files on the various computer systems traversed in the message's path to the addressee. In fact, it is not exactly as simple as this; but this will serve as a first approximation. However, the file is constructed at one place, and flows through the network to another computer. At various points through the network the file can be accessed, although this might require high levels of knowledge to do so.[41]

To return to our analogy, it is like asking an assistant to pass a folded message – via a sequence of intermediaries – to the addressee's assistant and asking that assistant to place the message on the recipient's desk. Of course, any or all of the intermediaries may elect to unfold and to read the message. However, in most cases they don't. E-mail is said to be *reasonably* private, in the same way that telephone conversations are 'reasonably' private: it is possible to overhear one or both sides of a conversation; it is possible to 'bug' the telephone lines or, with cellular phones, to listen to the radio signals – as the Royal family now know all too well. In most cases, however, the e-mail messages remain unintercepted, or contain subject matter whose interception would not give rise to problems other than possible embarrassment.

Those e-mail files can be made increasingly more private. Encryption tools exist to allow the files to be encoded in a way that only the sender and intended recipient know how to reverse – so-called 'Privacy Enhanced Mail' (PEM). More, these same tools can ensure that the message is not altered during transit – another problem with e-mail. In the normal exchange of e-mail text such encoding and low levels of privacy are – generally speaking – of only low importance. As we shall see in subsequent chapters, however, with increasing trade over the Internet such privacy and proof from tampering becomes a vital necessity.

Internet Relay Chat

E-mail, therefore, gives the Internet one of its basic characteristics: support for informal, 'off-the-cuff' but permanently recorded correspondence. With increasing use of the e-mail facilities by private individuals for communicating amongst families and friends, and use by commercial and public sector concerns for internal and low levels of external communication, e-mail is beginning to establish a unique role within the spectrum discussed above: slightly less formal than written communication but more formal than the telephone.

The telephone, however, continues to hold a special place in our communication requirements: as BT says, 'it's *good* to talk'; often messages are best communicated either orally or through a rapid, 'real-time' exchange of words. On the Internet, the initial – slightly crude – facility to achieve this is called 'Chat' – or more correctly, 'Internet Relay Chat'.

A user connected to the Internet through his host computer can use the 'Chat' utility to connect in effect directly to a remote PC or terminal, so that words typed locally appear on the remote screen and vice versa. With a simple, individually agreed protocol – '(O)' means 'end of my turn'; '(OO)' means 'end of message', for example – users can hold interactive, typed conversations. So-called 'Cyber Cafes'[42] have been established to support this informal exchange with users gathering in one place, several sites, or even at home, to exchange gossip among a group of like-minded people. As with the more usual 'real-world' situations, romances and arguments can both blossom in these establishments as the users find that a meeting of minds is as easy or as difficult in Cyberspace as anywhere. Some critics have – unfairly – accused such users of living essentially artificial lives, of trying to lead an excessively technology-fascinated existence. However, to those users involved there is little or no difference in conducting a personal relationship through Cyberspace than via the telephone or written word. Pen-pals and so forth have never attracted the opprobrium that Internet users seem fated to receive; in many ways this is perhaps because the critics – rather than the users themselves – have been dazzled by the technology.

However, rather than the sociology aspect, consider the *economics* of these conversations. In the most extreme case both users are at home, connected via PCs and a telephone line – at local charge rates – to their individual hosts. They therefore pay for the local call and a service charge for using the Internet, depending on the applicable terms of their service providers. If one is in Sydney, Australia and the other in London, England, this is a very cheap alternative to long-distance, international call charging.

Of course, the Internet will not *replace* telephone conversations. However, it can support them. A simple device has been developed for transmitting speech over the Internet. Instead of characters or lines of text, this system transmits sound through the Internet Relay connection. At the target machine the sound file is decoded and played through the machine's speakers. Initially, the system was slow and allowed only one person at a time to talk. It was rather like the old-fashioned radio transmissions of the moon landings; users had to be careful not to speak until the recipient was listening. More recent innovations have improved the facility, giving support for real-time, two-way conversations over the network, although at times when the network is heavily loaded the reception can still be poor.

This is a relatively new system, but it has shattering consequences for the existing telecommunications suppliers. As the system continues to improve – and there is every reason to expect that it will – it presents a very real, very cheap alternative to standard long distance telephone calls. If *all* communication can be achieved on the basis of a local call to an Internet service provider why would anyone choose to use, say, BT's international dialling service; or even the long distance service between London and Edinburgh? Moreover, increasing competition between service providers has reduced the cost of local calls – in the US, in fact, many local calls are now free of charge.

Telephone service providers such as BT, Mercury and others, therefore come under increasing pressure on all aspects of their call charging mechanism: from one another on the cost of local calls, which have been traditionally subsidised by the long distance tariffs; and from Internet service providers on the cost of these other calls. This has been described as the 'death of distance': one can already phone anywhere in the world but at a cost that represents not the *true-world* distance, rather the *telecomms-world* distance. That is, it costs more to call London–Paris than London–Glasgow, despite the shorter real-world distance to Paris. This is because in telecomms-world it is necessary for the call to be 'handed' from BT to France Télécom, at a cost.

As the economics of this situation change, observers predict a corresponding change of charging basis by the several telecomms providers. Primarily, a shift from call-charging to service-charging. Instead of paying an amount per minute of call, with different rates for different distances, one would instead pay for the line itself and for any additional services – such as call diversion, call waiting, number-for-life, etc. – offered by the providers.

Of course, as more and more people move from the 'standard' telephone mechanisms to those of the Internet this will in turn place an increased load upon *that* medium. This would then have the effect of depressing the service levels, not just for the Internet-telephone use but for *all* transmissions – perhaps driving telephone users back to BT *et al.* The precise dynamics of this situation are difficult to assess; it is possible that some form of oscillation could occur, with users swapping between the two. Whether and how an equilibrium can be established is at the present time an impossible question to answer; this is an unprecedented development and both the telephone companies and the regulating bodies have yet to determine the impact that change might have. However, pundits such as the *Economist* magazine[12] are confident in stating that a sea-change in the telecomms business is imminent.

The Internet can therefore support a wide variety of person-to-person communication, ranging from the distribution of e-mail to the newly developed Internet telephone service. The cultural implications of this are extended by the impact this capability has on the economics of international and long distance telephone calls. Rapid, low cost, flexible communication allows us to talk with relatives or workmates around the world, to transmit messages or exchange documents, spreadsheets or presentations.

This facility has an impact on the way we carry out our work – the time we dedicate to it, the place at which it is performed, and the location of our employer. It also changes the scope for choosing and communicating with our friends. Only a few short decades ago one was limited to one's nearest, physical neighbours; now one can choose from friends around the world, based not on physical proximity, but on proximity of opinion.

INTERNET DEBATING FORUMS

The Internet supports direct person-to-person communication – through e-mail or by means of the Internet-telephone facility described above – or group communication. Where a set of individuals is interested in a particular topic, they can be collected into a forum, such as the CompuServe *Special Interest Groups* (SIGs) or Internet 'mailgroups'. In this last case, a message sent to the mailgroup is disseminated to each member of the group. This is a quick way of sending an individual message to each and every member of the group. The messages remain private to the members of the SIG or mailgroup, who must be invited to join[43] – there is a degree of selectivity in this case.

An extension to this facility is provided by Usenet 'newsgroups'. Here, messages are sent not to individuals but to a central point. The messages – '*articles*' – are stored and a list of articles is made available to so-called news 'servers' throughout the Internet. Articles therefore have world-wide visibility and are gathered into associated topics of interest, with a hierarchical structure to allow newcomers to locate those topics that might be to their taste. There are tens of thousands of newsgroups, with topics ranging from the bizarre through the childish to the esoteric and the politically relevant. Any and all interests are therefore catered for within the newsgroup structure; and if a particular interest is *not* currently present, starting a newsgroup is very straightforward.

In more 'closed' environments such as CompuServe, the SIG discussion fora are moderated by a specific individual, and support users discussing issues ranging from the problems of difficult children, to cross-stitch and other handicrafts; from UK politics to Global Crises; and from Multiple Sclerosis to Unidentified Flying Objects. Anyone can join these fora, taking part in on-line discussions, submitting news and views, or making material available – such as software, pictures or articles – for other members to use.

A further structure to support such discussions is provided by the CompuServe version of the 'Chat' mechanism discussed above. Users can enter a 'room' and create and distribute messages that are read and responded to by others currently 'present' and involved in the debate. In CompuServe the users' names and their messages are text only, although more sophisticated systems have recently become available on CompuServe and on the Internet, allowing users to navigate and enter into discussions within a virtual world. Other users are represented by pictures – cartoons, called *Avatars* – or by scanned photographs and can be approached and addressed. As with the basic case the messages are currently text only but the relative distribution of characters gives a realistic 'feel' for the dynamics of the several group discussions. And of course as Internet telephony gathers pace it could become possible to talk directly to – or even view through video-phones – the participants of a discussion, although this might remove some of the interesting 'anonymity' associated with on-line discussions.

Usenet newsgroups

Within the broader Internet, there are two classes of Usenet newsgroup: moderated and unmoderated. The moderated newsgroup is similarly run by a specific individual, to whom the articles are submitted; he or she decides whether the article is to be 'posted'. By contrast, unmoderated newsgroups are free-form discussion fora in which anyone and everyone has a right and the ability to place a message. This distinction is similar, generally speaking, to the distinction between chaired debates and open discussions – but with some crucial differences.

Looking at the 'real world' discussion groups first, there is the expectation of an open session in which every participant has the right to speak and express an opinion. Of course this presupposes a number of factors. Firstly, that the individual concerned actually *holds* an informed opinion on the subject under debate; secondly, that they can rapidly form that opinion into articulate and under-standable terms; and thirdly, that they can make the rest of the debating group listen to their views. In practice, even in the most open of debates, there are many whose voices remain unheard – or are not listened to. The speaker may be held in low esteem by the rest of the group – for a variety of reasons, ranging from their age or sex, to their ethnic or cultural background – or they may have difficulty in expressing their view in a clearly articulated manner; or they may simply not have a loud enough voice.

In more moderated debates there is a chairman to arbitrate, allowing as many expressions as possible and steering the ensuing discussion towards agreement. Here, however, choice of contribu-tion is not based upon what they say – they haven't said it at the time they are chosen! – but rather upon reputation, or upon their authority. By contrast, letters to the papers, for example, are published based upon contents and writer. Significant political figures would expect to see their contributions in print, but so too would those making informed, articulate and timely contributions to an ongoing debate.

There are therefore two styles of public discussion fora: moder-ated by an editor or chairman, in which reputation and standing is important; and unmoderated, in which the loudest voice is often the one heard.

In the case of Usenet newsgroups, moderated fora are controlled by the equivalent of an editor, who judges the value of a submitted article to the ongoing debate; in unmoderated fora, which are by far the majority, the submitted article is posted immediately. In both cases, however, the *person* submitting the article is irrelevant, invis-ible: no publication decision is based upon that person's age, ethnic background, skin colour or sex. Physical handicaps, including an inability to speak, are irrelevant. So too is the person's social or professional standing; what *is* important is the content of the submitted article. As the *New Yorker* cartoon has it, 'On the Internet, nobody knows you're a dog!'[44]

Professional standing, in the context of a debate about the person's specialist subject, is – of course – important, but not in the sense of immediately allowing that person a say within a moderated forum. It is important insofar as it is more likely that the contribution will be well informed.

In unmoderated fora of course absolutely no distinction is made about contributors; the article is judged by readers entirely on its own merit. Internet newsgroup fora are therefore democratic, in the sense that any and all interested in having a say have the ability so to do. As with the e-mail case, however, the *tone* of news and forum postings is often strident or abusive – resulting in part from that very anonymity. So-called 'flaming'[45] – the posting of highly emotive or abusive articles – has been a feature of many newsgroups, forcing intelligent discussion into the background. This is similar to public political debates in which those intent on disrupting proceedings can often find a way to do so. Freedom of speech, as enshrined in the US Constitution and in practice elsewhere, must be protected in this and other cases; we will therefore address this in more detail in a later chapter.

In many ways the Usenet newsgroups are like newspapers. Originally, broadsheets were written by the editors using contributions from people who wrote to them – either in the form of letters or articles. Hence of course the term 'correspondent'. Unmoderated newsgroups are like broadsheets in which any and all contributions appear, or walls upon which anyone's graffiti can be scrawled. Unlike newspapers and walls, however, Internet discussion fora have two unique features: they are global in nature and they are continuous.

Global and continuous debates

The global nature of Internet discussions has several aspects to it. Most obviously, articles posted to the Usenet newsgroup or fora are available almost immediately throughout the whole of the Internet community. Articles are therefore visible throughout the world, in every country within which the newsgroup is available; and secondly, articles are readable by every person gaining access to the newsgroup, from the professional expert to the schoolchild.

This means that the contents of the article can be read by anyone. Articles containing sexually explicit text or pictures could be accessed by schoolchildren; there are newsgroups and sites dedicated to any and all forms of erotica, including paedophile material.[46] Articles critical of foreign regimes are accessible within those and other countries; and articles libelling individuals, or revealing cult secrets, or describing precise details of bomb-recipes,[47] are all available. Moreover, while the articles submitted to moderated newsgroups might be checked for relevance, they might not be checked for accuracy. False information can therefore be disseminated – either deliberately for malicious purposes, or accidentally. Unmoderated newsgroups on the other hand can – and do – contain any and all forms of nonsense.

Access to newsgroups therefore implies access to a Pandora's box of views, opinions and information, although, as we shall see, attempts have been and are being made to protect children and others from such ready access. These attempts are being stressed particularly by service providers such as CompuServe, who have the ability to withdraw or to limit access to certain newsgroups for their subscribers. They have also introduced extensive facilities to allow parents to control the type and extent of access afforded for their children on the network. As Chapter 5 describes, this exercise of control has become a *legal* requirement of the service providers.

A further aspect to the global nature of the newsgroups and fora is their visibility. As with e-mail, on-line discussions fall uncomfortably between mechanisms that are known and with which we are familiar. Direct, personal discussions in private allow the open exchange of views in a rapid way. Moreover, participants can often feel free to express in private opinions and views that might not be aired in public. Conversely, in discussion sessions that take place on the radio or TV, participants are always aware of the existence of an audience.

The various forms of Internet debate, however, can lull participants into the illusion of a private discussion among friends. As with the 'real-world' case this can lead to frank exchanges, which may well be defamatory or insulting to other individuals or organisations. The Internet discussions which take place on CompuServe fora or Usenet newsgroups are publicly, globally accessible. The participants may not be aware that a silent audience (they are called 'snoopers') is involved. Moreover, the news articles are stored and are therefore a permanent record of any unwise statement.

As we shall discuss in Chapter 5, this situation has lead to a number of cases in which offended parties have sought to sue the participants, the service providers, or the owners of the host computers supporting the debates. In short, libel is libel; the medium used for the dissemination is not relevant. The exact process of gaining redress, however, is not yet clear.

The second aspect was the continuous nature of the debates. In letters to newspapers there is a period within which such letters are collected, collated and assessed. Duplicate views – and extreme views – are removed before a representative selection is published. With newsgroups the debate goes on continuously around the world, on a 24-hour basis. An article submitted in London at 5 o'clock might, by 9 o'clock the following day, have been debated to death in New York, Chicago, Los Angeles, Honolulu, Christchurch, Sydney, Perth, Moscow and Paris. Debates can therefore move forward on a rapid basis.

Continuous implications

Rapid debates, allowing any and all an equal opportunity to contribute, with submissions universally visible and moderated in only a handful of cases. The cultural implications of such a facility are staggering.

The most immediate implication of the Internet facilities is in the expression of ideas freely and globally – ideas that might be informed and relevant, or ill-judged and in poor taste. In traditional media personal views are filtered by those responsible for the dissemination of the material – editors, journalists and publishers for print; directors and producers for broadcast media. Where the views expressed transgress the bounds of decency, or are defamatory of individuals or of organisations, then there is recourse to an authoritative body controlling that media. As we shall discuss in more detail in a later chapter, however, the position on the Internet is somewhat more confusing.[48]

The second implication lies in articles which are critical of governments. Within the UK there is a greater judicial concern centring on personal libel than on overt criticism of government policy. There have been exceptions of course: 'Shoot to Kill' in Northern Ireland

and in Gibraltar; or the *SpyCatcher* publication.[49] On the whole, however, one would expect to criticise the PM's government with impunity but not to make personal attacks directly on the individual. In other states this is not the case. Oppressive regimes ensure continued power by – at least in part – exercising control over the media. The Internet is more difficult to control and so some authorities solve the problem by brute force, refusing citizens all interaction with the system – despite the benefits that it could bring.

This solution is available to any and all of the states taking part in the global Internet experiment. It is, however, a weak-minded and poor solution, depriving societies of the entertainment, educational and economic benefits that the technology can bring. The best comparison might be with the introduction of the printing press throughout Europe when the Church argued against the technology, saying that it would pollute minds. Nobody now would doubt the advantages accruing as a result of increased literacy and availability of knowledge, and the regulatory and associated issues have been solved – if not perfectly then at least effectively.

The third implication lies in the nature of the debates themselves. It is true that the greatest number of newsgroups are concerned with issues that are – to even the fairest minded observer – essentially irrelevant. Scattered among the trivial, however, are nuggets of pure gold; debates that are timely, informed and – above all – interesting. What gives these debates value is the nature of the contributions and – perhaps in apparent contradiction to an earlier statement – the people involved.

As an example, the issue of abortion versus the 'right-to-life' is a debate that is particularly active. From national medical councils and specialist ethics fora, through university debating clubs, via the print and broadcast media, to the saloon bars and coffee shops – the debate is of interest and of relevance to us all. Moreover, it is of equal relevance in the UK, US, Europe and elsewhere.

Throughout the world there are a great number of discussions, formal and informal, informed and ignorant, about this subject. Internet newsgroups discussing these issues can have contributions from the doctors involved, from parents who have had to make agonised choices, from children whose 'right to life' may have been brought into question, and from a host of other interested parties.

We *all* have a right, perhaps even a duty, to express an opinion on this – and very many other – subjects. We are constrained only by two things: the degree of expertise – professional or otherwise – that we hold; and our access to the appropriate forum.

'Forum' originally meant the marketplace within which all citizens could express a view. The CompuServe fora and Usenet newsgroups provide exactly those facilities on a global basis. The majority of contributions might be from those who have only limited knowledge about a subject – but this is an issue of education, to which we shall return in a subsequent section. Notwithstanding this, the Internet allows broad church debates to be heard and contributions to be made by a wide variety of opinionholders.

This has an implication for the way that states function. Our current pattern of government – and indeed the pattern throughout the civilised world – can be classified as *representative*. Democratic states choose and elect individuals to represent our personal views on all issues important to the governing of our state. In the UK these individuals debate key issues in Parliament, led by the policies of their party and by opinions received by their local constituency organisations. At the very least Internet discussion fora allow many views to be debated and presented rapidly to our representatives; but as – and if – the Internet becomes more widely available, might we no longer need those representatives? Might we in fact be able to move towards a more *referenda*-based style of government? This is a question to which we will return in Chapter 6.

What gives the Internet debates spice and relevance is the nature of the informed views presented in the most relevant of newsgroups. Of course there are newsgroups dedicated to the arcane, the trivial and the childish. But even these have value to those interested in the subject matter. And in each such newsgroup there are always – even in the unmoderated groups – individuals who are particularly well informed. From these individuals it is possible to learn a great deal of valuable information.

USING THE INTERNET FOR EDUCATION

In a sense all use of the Internet is educative, involving access to information. The Internet contains huge quantities of data about a host of topics. Indeed in many ways the problem with the Internet lies not so much in finding as in *sifting* information; in locating the item actually required, among unimaginably huge amounts of other material.

In searching for a particular item of knowledge the information domain can be divided into three simple categories: the *relevant* – that is, the actual piece of information you require; the *irrelevant* – information that is plainly and obviously of no value or is entirely unconnected with your requirements; and the *arguably relevant* – material that must be examined carefully before a decision about it can be made. Ignoring its cost, any search tool is a success based on two simple criteria: how quickly can it create those three sets; and how small can it make the third?

In searching small quantities of structured information – such as an encyclopaedia or dictionary – this task is relatively simple; for larger sets of information it becomes increasingly difficult. But the amount of data available through the Internet is impossibly large and growing rapidly on an hourly basis as more and ever more systems and networks are added.[50] There are a variety of search engines now available that provide a degree of structure over the mass of data and that support enquiries – but finding specific items is often a case of practice, skill in framing search queries, and not a small amount of luck and patience.

In this section we will consider the types of information available before looking at what one can do with it.

The Internet information sources range from material made available by service providers as part of their own services, through commercial databases that can be accessed via the Internet, to academic, corporate or research-project related material offered – freely in the main – by a host of systems. In addition, a large number of electronic publishing exercises are supported on the Internet.

Taking the first category, this is the simplest and most obvious element to users of services such as CompuServe. As part of the monthly service fee, information sources such as on-line dictionaries and encyclopaedia, as well as excerpts from commercial database providers such as Reuters and the weather forecasting bureaux, are all provided. Users can select the information source of interest and use simple key-word search engines to locate the relevant material.

Commercial databases can be accessed similarly, either through CompuServe if the company concerned has an agreement, or via the Web pages if not. In the case of commercial information sources, however, there is a requirement for payment – making the use of such information a tradeable resource. Such transactions – and the difficulties that arise in practice – are discussed in the following chapter and so will be overlooked here.

The most interesting category, therefore, comes in those elements of information made available by means of Web pages. Recall, a Web page is structured 'hypertext' with dynamic links – called 'hyperlinks' – to connect associated pages together. The whole forms a vast, tightly interconnected network of information elements. Some of these pages are produced by companies, some by universities and some by private individuals. All contain *information*, such as pictures from weather satellites, electronic books, journals or newspapers.

It is through these information sources and the combination of newsgroups and e-mail that the Internet gets its educational benefits; conversely, it also gives rise to a requirement for education.

Looking at the facilities and use of the Internet from an educational perspective it is clear that it can support different types of education, raising issues for each. These different types are:

- schooling;
- continuing education;
- re-education or re-skilling; and
- task-specific immediate education.

Moreover, the education can take the form of passive supply of information or more active 'computer-based training'. Since these two categories are similar in nature across all of the education types, we will first consider this distinction and the practical implementations of each.

Passive supply of information

In the passive supply of information, the Internet – and thereby the computer facilities – are used purely as a search engine, as a *window* onto a world of relevant information. Under external guidance, students of all sorts use the available facilities to specify and locate relevant items. This external guidance can come from a project workbook, a form tutor or lecturer, or from one's own sense of curiosity. Having collected the required information, students then collate, arrange and present the material as required.

The nature and extent of that information make this a far from trivial task. Indeed, in many ways the intelligentsia of the next century may well be defined more in terms of their ability to collate and present this information and to synthesise subsequent deductions and inferences from the material, than in their absolute personal store of knowledge.

Computer-based training

In this case, the computer facilities are used in a more active manner. In this, however, I would like to include all forms of education in which the computer is a fundamentally *active* component rather than a more passive retrieval engine. Help and tuition utilities within office automation packages therefore count as such; but so too do fora, newsgroups and e-mail exchanges with acknowledged experts in particular fields, in which the computer is used to support interactive education.

By using the communication facilities of the Internet students can therefore learn from people throughout the world. To take a simple example: for an English schoolchild learning about America the Internet could not only provide encyclopaedia entries on the continent, together with a map, but perhaps also a satellite view of today's weather over California; an image feed from a camera monitoring the Golden Gate bridge; a sound file of native American singing; a video clip of Alistair Cooke lecturing; a listing of relevant textbooks available from the British Library – or even the MIT library; a virtual-reality stroll through Manhattan; or the opportunity to exchange e-mail with schoolchildren in Connecticut learning about England.[51]

This is a powerful, flexible facility. A mechanism that can bring these places *alive* to our children; that will continue the process described above of making the world a smaller place. And of course the Internet can make available the contents of libraries throughout the world; can provide video and sound clips; and can make expert systems and experts themselves available for advice.

If there is a problem with this structure it is that the information has *not* been filtered and judged before being entered into the Internet domain. There is no independent effort therefore to verify the accuracy of the information or the validity of any opinions expressed. The onus for cross-checking and assuring the information therefore lies with the recipient; but of course the mechanism for so doing also lies within the Internet. As we have mentioned above, an important skill in the 21st century will be in the area of understanding and synthesising informed opinion on the basis of the wealth of data available; rather than in the personal possession of vast quantities of information.

Schooling

Schooling was the first type of education on our list that can be supported by the Internet. Ignoring the case in early 1996 where the answers to the Scottish Higher Mathematics examination were posted on the Internet, the example given above is probably one of the best illustrations of the legitimate opportunities presented by the technology. The Internet contains not only information sources of value, but also existing analyses and indices to that material. Those interested in a topic for a particular project, for example, can use the existing search engines, indices and reference material to collect relevant data from a variety of sources. As discussed below, newspapers and journals, together with research papers, discussion groups and even the researchers themselves are all accessible and can all provide useful input to any project.[52]

Set against this, however, is a somewhat darker side to the Internet. As has been discussed elsewhere, the Internet is home not only to useful, educational information but also to vicious political diatribes, offensively racist or sexist literature, pornographic images and much, much worse.

While the Internet can therefore be used constructively, giving our children an ideal opportunity to learn about and interact with an impressive array of information sources, we must also protect them from, and educate them about the risks. But this is a far from easy task. Perhaps the most widely discussed element of this issue is that of access to pornographic material.

In the 'real-world' explicit pornography is difficult to obtain. On the Internet, however, any and all forms are available and accessible. Children that would – without question – be refused access to licensed sex shops can locate and download images with total impunity. For the cost of the connection time and provided that their search through the Web pages – called 'surfing' – has brought them to the right places they can therefore obtain pictures that would not be accessible to them – or even their parents – through any other mechanism.

In a later chapter we will discuss the technical and legal aspects of this cultural challenge. From an educational perspective, however, this raises fundamental questions about training our children. There will *always* be a means by which children will obtain sexually explicit material, whether over the Internet or through some other means; indeed, arguably children in their teenage years are biologically programmed to be curious about sex and sexuality. But the Internet presents that Pandora's box of images from the romantic, through the realistic to the obscene. It becomes necessary therefore to educate our children to regard the perverse images as *being* perverse rather than representative of normal, loving relationships.

There is no simple answer to the question of preventing impressionable minds from discovering unhealthy material on the Internet. Even if there was a simple mechanism, different cultures define unhealthy in radically different ways. To many the softest of 'glamour' images are obscene; to others, even the hardest of hard-core pornography is acceptable. And because of the global nature of the Internet it will always be possible for such images to be distributed – from those who consider them to be harmless, to those who don't.

The very nature of the Internet means that it is difficult to constrain access to *any* information sources. Successful controls on pornography – and other similarly offensive material on the Internet – will therefore have to be established on the local system; this is the approach taken by the major service providers such as CompuServe. We will return to this issue later, in Chapter 5.

Continuing education and re-skilling

The remaining categories of education types are specific to adults and so the issues of protection do not apply with the same force. The first category is that of continuing education; adults whose formal schooling is complete but who wish to learn about further topics, perhaps purely for interest's sake. Currently, this requirement is addressed by colleges and universities; and by night schools, summer schools and correspondence courses. In the case of correspondence courses this may well include provision of video or taped lectures.

The Internet is an ideal medium for supporting this activity. Course notes, transcriptions or recordings of lectures, even reference books can all be made available over the Internet. The background of the Internet in universities and research establishments means that there is a wealth of information about past and on-going research projects – from the search for DNA to the Human Genome project; from the moon landings to the Hubble telescope.[53] This makes the Internet a perfect medium for supporting educational projects and even PhD investigations.

Moreover, e-mail groups can be used in place of classes, allowing students to be gathered from a far wider audience – perhaps even internationally. For those who don't want the formal structure of a specifically timetabled course run by a tutor over the Internet, the material can be accessed on a periodic basis. This last aspect is particularly important in after-work classes since it frees the part-time student from the constraints of a fixed schedule.

Re-skilling or re-education is similar in many ways but is often driven explicitly by the requirements of the student's employer. But again, the student can be freed from the constraints of time and has access to a wealth of information.

Task – specific, immediate education

This category is an increasingly important one. By 'task-specific' we mean education or training in how to carry out a particularly difficult or unfamiliar activity; and by 'immediate' we mean that the education and the task are carried out simultaneously. This might be by personal coaching or supervision in a challenging task.

Take a concrete example. In using a new software application for the first time the user often experiences difficulty in establishing the correct parameters. Through on-line, Internet-hosted connection to the developers it is possible to get the required guidance – perhaps even get them to set the parameters correctly and transmit the configuration file back.

As the Internet increases in speed and capacity, however, it would become possible to support far more powerful facilities. Consider a situation not far into the future, in which Internet connection is via ultra-high speed optical fibre allowing the transmission of video in real-time. As we will discuss below, this is imminent and highly exciting. A UK surgeon is called upon to perform a difficult operation, perhaps for the first time. The operation has been performed successfully, in Canada – but never in the UK.

The Canadian consultant is a busy man, far too busy to fly to the UK simply to supervise this single operation. The UK surgeon therefore needs his colleague's advice but his colleague cannot be present. The high-speed links allow the UK surgeon to transmit real-time images from a head-mounted camera to the Canadian expert, who can advise the surgeon in turn. BT have developed a facility to do just that, 'CAMNET'[30], with a tiny monitor screen to allow the surgeon to see where and how the Canadian consultant would cut or stitch.

The technology can be supported then by Internet-accessed databases, or can be recorded and made available to medical students over the Internet connections. In a German prototype for just such a system, called HOS, 'Health On Screen',[54] minute by minute scenes from a 90 minute operation were transmitted via the Internet to a medical forum, allowing many hundreds of surgeons to observe in real-time a delicate and complicated procedure, and even to e-mail questions to the observing surgical team.

In this last example, to support real-time video the Internet was assumed to have advanced in terms of the technological foundation. At present the transmission speeds are too low to allow such real-time video transmission. Indeed, the delay in downloading images makes even non-real-time pictures painfully slow to obtain; and to download huge files, such as would be required to obtain even compressed feature film videos, is currently unthinkable. However, the entertainment potential of Internet publishing is so huge that this facility can be expected to become available.

PUBLISHING ON THE INTERNET

In many ways, all aspects of the Internet come down to the question of electronic publishing. Newsgroups, Web pages and the explicit provision of applications, text or multi-media are all encompassed. These provide the educational and the entertainment benefits of the Internet. In fact, those entertainment aspects are often difficult to separate from the educational. For many students the Internet is seen as an intrinsically *fun* place to explore;[55] the education potential of the information is almost incidental.

In this section, we will restrict the discussion to that material that can be considered as having been 'published' in the most explicit sense: having been created by an author or authors, the finished material is provided for deliberate distribution within the Internet community in the same way that a book or CD might be distributed through a chain of shops. This is as distinct from the publishing aspect associated with the establishment of a personal home page, or the submission of a Usenet article.

As Chapter 5 discusses, published material within the Internet is covered by copyright, and the various uses to which it might be put are in turn covered by the *licence* provided by the author. In the Internet publishing case, this means that the explicitly published material may be accessed, used or disseminated only in accordance with the copyright owner's rights as the author. The published material ranges from software and computer games, through newspapers and books, to video and CD. In each case, the licensing arrangements will be different, although they fall into a set of broad categories. The material can be put explicitly into the *public domain*, allowing any and all to have free use of the subject matter. It can be copied, re-used, modified or even sold – although this last might be difficult to effect if the material is generally available anyway. Alternatively, the material can be licensed for limiting *lending* rights – as is the case with books, videos and CDs from libraries. In this case, the material is available to the borrower for a limited period, after which it must be 'returned'; in the case of digital goods this might be achieved by deletion, for example. This lending can be on a free or on a charged-for basis – ie, loan or rental.

The material might be licensed as *Freeware*, which is similar in nature to the public domain case, but a restriction applies to the use of the material – say a software application – in revenue generating activities. Or the material might be licensed as *Shareware*, which is similar to the lending case, but the user is expected to purchase the material outright at the end of the loan period, or if the material is to be used for revenue generation.

Finally, the material might be bought outright – although as Chapter 5 explains, copyright restrictions will still apply. Of course, in all but the public domain case, the user can expect to be asked to pay for the goods – either for outright title or a limited access right. This payment question is covered in Chapter 3 in the context of ordering and distributing these digital goods through the Internet. In this section, we will consider the *nature* of these goods, as distinct from the mechanisms and processes by which a user gains access and an author protects his or her rights.

Publishing software

The first category of electronic publishing is that of software: computer games or applications. Computer games have become big business.[56] For many, most particularly children, this is the most important aspect of the computer's role. Internet games differ only very slightly from free-standing computer games, allowing access to games held on remote systems or allowing two or more people to play together over remote connections.

The only novel aspect that the Internet provides is in the distribution of those games and in the manner in which those playing popular games can communicate with one another. Newsgroups, fora and discussion sessions have been established for all of the popular computer games and demonstration versions of new games are freely available. For the price of the download time, prospective buyers can experiment with any new version – often on an unlimited basis – as freeware. This then, the producers hope, prompts the players to invest in the full implementation.

A similar situation occurs with the applications. Early implementations – so-called 'Beta Versions' – are provided as freeware and can be tested by users.[57] Upgrades can also be distributed over the Internet, or the whole package can be provided. Of course in this situation, the expectation is that the user will purchase the goods outright.

Publishing text

Electronic publishing of text presents a more interesting aspect of the Internet, in the production of newspapers, magazines, journals and books. The types of text published can be divided into three sections, which we will consider separately:

1. News articles, whose relevance is time-limited;
2. Background news articles, whose relevance is less limited by time;
3. Substantial fiction and non-fiction works of continuing relevance.

In traditional print media, the first category has been addressed by daily newspapers; the second, by weekly or monthly magazines; and the third typically by books.

Leaving the book category on one side for a moment, journalists and feature writers submit articles usually in electronic form; this might be through e-mail, directly connected terminals or by means of diskettes. This material is in turn electronically processed through a series of computers and ultimately printed onto paper. Electronic publishing, at its simplest, involves merely not printing the words onto paper but rather placing them on Internet accessible host machines. As we shall see, however, there is potential for much more than this.

News articles

This first area of interest can be characterised as 'newspapers-on-line'. There are two subsidiary aspects to this: the simultaneous publication of daily newspapers in paper and electronic form; and access to the continual 'wire' service of providers such as Reuters. Additionally, there are daily specialist news services such as the continuing state of the stock market, cricket scores and so forth.

In the case of simultaneous electronic and paper publishing, while almost every daily and Sunday newspaper has implemented a site, to date this has been seen more as an experimental venture rather than presenting a truly novel way to access a particular newspaper. In part, this is probably because each such access is currently free, and would therefore cut into the papers' revenues were the numbers of users and the service provided to improve dramatically. The publishers do of course attempt to track the readership they are attracting: all those accessing a given site for example are registered, allowing the publishers to understand the scale of interest in any electronically published venture and the types of readers involved. This last aspect is important in understanding the advertising or marketing opportunities afforded by the medium. If the readership in time turns wholly to the electronic versions, both advertisements and reader subscriptions would be necessary to ensure the publishers' continued revenue.

If more and more people do elect to receive some or all of their news in this way, the potential for such publishing will of course develop. In many ways, leaving aside the question of payment, such simultaneous publishing is the least adventurous of the many publishing options, giving the newspaper little or no additional scope for the way in which news stories are presented.

A more ambitious method would be to make *all* journalistic submissions available in something like the published form and to retrieve articles of interest by means of a software agent.[58] This agent could collect material from a wide variety of sources such as the electronic newspapers, wire services and specialist publishing organisations. If the publisher so chooses, even those articles submitted but not printed in the paper form owing to lack of space could be provided.

In the use of agents, selectivity therefore passes to the reader; the tools provide the facility for readers to specify their preferred daily news and current affairs delivery – taking control away from the editors. This change in control will be seen as a recurrent theme in many aspects of the Internet's implications for publishing information.

The potential to use programmed agents to gather news publications is an exciting development, although such systems that exist at present are currently no more than experimental in nature.[59] Should they become available on a general basis, one could potentially ask a search utility to construct a daily newspaper which is *personal* in nature: all general news articles of high importance; all sports news relating to a particular town; anything concerning family or friends; news about the stock market and computer industry; and any Larson, Steve Bell or Peanuts cartoon.

Background news articles

The second area of interest outlined above was 'magazines-on-line'. Here, the material is also only relevant for a period of time – but that time limit is somewhat longer than the daily news services. Weekly or monthly magazines satisfy this criteria; and in traditional print, these publications use the extended time period to allow a more detailed and careful analysis of news and its implications. In addition to the current-affairs publications this category also includes general interest magazines – home improvements, enthusiasts and hobbyists and so on.

As with the daily newspaper case, most magazines that have chosen to take advantage of the Internet have elected to provide somewhat more than the usual paper published format, implementing archives and search routines. The *Economist* surveys (refs [12,13]) for example are available through this mechanism. Again, however, there is the question of potential lost revenues; in the case of the *Economist* surveys, reprints of articles and the original magazine would normally generate income for the publishers; once available over the Internet for free, this income is lost. As Chapter 3 discusses, as the Internet becomes used more widely, such publishing ventures cannot continue to be free of charge.

An important point to note in the case of electronic publishing, however, is the relative – indeed, the *absolute* – low cost of such magazine and newspaper publishing. This provides scope for 'vanity publishing' of magazines and newsletters by anyone and everyone on the Internet, quite separate from the more established and reputable 'real-world'/Internet instances of publishing. In future it will therefore be necessary to practice caution in receiving and using information from Internet-hosted publications: don't believe all you read; although Internet versions of established and reputable newspapers and magazines are of course as reliable as the paper format. At least with these newspapers, magazines and journals the articles have to pass some form of assessment; with vanity publishing this independent assessment is missing.[60]

Books

Fiction and non-fiction books was the final area of interest mentioned above. Most news articles have fewer than 1000 words; most magazine articles fewer than 5000. Downloading articles or even whole magazines and newspapers of around 10 to 20,000 words in total is therefore entirely feasible and very rapid with the present state of the Internet structure. Books are typically around 80,000 words; downloading a whole work – be it fiction or non-fiction – is therefore also currently feasible, although it would take proportionately longer.[61]

The main drawbacks with Internet books centre on the trading and regulation issues: paying for the book; protecting copyright; ensuring that modified versions are not disseminated; protecting against or prosecuting libel. These are all addressed in later chapters. Here, however, we will consider the opportunities that Internet provision brings.

The most interesting potential lies in the way that the material is *presented* to the reader. The skill in writing a book lies not with the collection or explanation of information; rather, it lies with structuring that information in such a way as to be readable. Any collection of associated facts can be linked into a complex network of inter-relationships; explaining those facts – or telling a story – involves providing the reader with a sensible and appropriate path through the network. Books are linear in nature: one starts at the first page and reads through; even textbooks have an element of this linearity, even if chapters or whole sections can be omitted or read out of sequence.

By contrast, text provided by computers can be structured to represent that multi-dimensionality; this has been called '*Hyperfiction*'. Sections, chapters, even paragraphs can all be collected into units; call them 'chunks'. These chunks can be linked into related structures, perhaps in many different ways. As the chunks are presented on screen, keywords can be used as links to other chunks of text; alternatively, dictionary definitions or synonyms can be presented for difficult or technically relevant words or phrases. Using the intrinsic potential of the supporting computer, text can therefore be presented in interesting or more directly relevant ways. And each reader takes from the material those facts or emotions relevant to *their* reading of – ie, their own path through – the book.

Electronic publishing of text, therefore, presents a means of changing the economics of publishing text, the practicalities of distributing news, and the artistic exercise of story-telling.

Video and sound

The final category of electronic publishing was of video or music provision via the Internet. With the present structure of the Internet, transfer speeds can become painfully slow when the systems are heavily loaded. On these occasions even small pictures can take a long time to download and much larger video or sound files would be impractical. At other periods of the day and with ever faster modems and networks, transfer speeds can be acceptable, although files large enough to hold complete feature films or 15-track CDs would still not yet be a realistic prospect.[62] Short excerpts, clips or individual tracks could, however, be transferred even at the present state of the network.

The introduction of extensive fibre-optic cabling and of wireless and microwave transmission throughout the first decade of the 21st century, however, will increase the power of information networks dramatically. This will perhaps increase to the point at which the transfer of files containing the complete video or CD becomes a practicality, certainly in the context of the Information Superhighway.[63]

This book is not in the main concerned with the technical question of *how* this improvement in data rates will be achieved. One point to consider, however, is a reprise to our initial definition of the Internet: information accessed by locally executed interface software. With this definition it is not necessary for that information to be provided on what we *currently* perceive as being part of the

Internet. If BT – say – provides video or music catalogues over its own high capacity lines, the 'locally executed software' could be used to access this service in tandem with (and as easily as) the services of a Demon Internet, CompuServe or an America on Line. As the cable TV companies provide more extensive fibre-optic coverage and as cable modems become available, with transmission speeds of around 10 mbps versus at most 28.8 kbps for standard modems, these too will improve the performance of the Internet.[64]

Either a technical improvement in Internet transmission speeds or a broadening of the definition of '*the Internet*' will therefore make it possible to access or download large files containing, for example, videos or CD-standard music. If this access becomes possible it is unthinkable that the potential will not be exploited. Throughout the following, 'video' is taken as being synonymous with 'video or CD-standard audio'.

The provision of video catalogues over the Internet will have an interesting implication, both for education and for entertainment purposes. To reiterate an earlier point, the trading aspects of this service will be addressed in the following chapter, although in passing we might comment that the system could support sale or rental of either part or all of a CD. We might also note that the trading systems we describe in Chapter 3 could support very low charges, making periodic rental of a single CD track at say 0·1p a time as realistic a proposition as buying the whole CD outright at £15.

The catalogues offering these goods might be expected, initially at least, to represent feature films, popular music and so forth; in other words, a digital version of the ubiquitous video libraries. This, however, begs a number of questions. Will people buy or simply rent these videos? Will the range of videos extend to encompass more than just films? What will happen to existing broadcasters? What will we then view?

At present, one buys a video less because one necessarily wants to *own* that video and more because one wants the ability to enjoy the video as and when desired. Video machines became popular exactly because they supported this basic requirement: of allowing one to record and watch programmes at a time of one's own choice rather than at a time dictated by the broadcasting company or cinema operators. In the case of books, by contrast, there has been a very long tradition of ownership denoting cultural, educational or professional achievement; this is not the case with videos.

While the majority of people therefore prefer to *own* books, borrowing from libraries only where the book cannot be afforded or is required only for a short time, this is not the case with videos. Hence, there is a huge number of video libraries the length and breadth of the country. Music, as distinct from films on video, falls somewhat between these two categories. In both cases, however, what is actually essential is the ability to enjoy the material at a time of one's own choice at an appropriate cost – either by outright purchase, rental or charged-for loan.

With Internet-provided video – an example of video-on-demand – this can be achieved by downloading the video to a local PC. This can then be viewed or listened to locally. Naturally, this will give rise to a requirement for ultra-high performance PCs with TV-quality picture and hi-fi standard sound systems; or a means to transfer the video to tape. If the video can be captured locally in a permanently accessible manner, however, it should be regarded as having been delivered to the viewer: it should therefore be considered as property having been *sold*.

If in time the local system evolves into a combination PC, TV, CD, telephone, etc, so that the video can be viewed locally without explicit capture, or can be encrypted in such a way as to limit the period of accessibility, it becomes possible to consider *rental* as the main delivery mechanism. This does, however, beg an obvious question, that of copyright – examined in Chapter 5. If the video is licensed for rental, locally capturing the material is illegal in exactly the same way that it is against a producer's copyright for CDs loaned from libraries to be recorded on cassette. In the case of the Internet, copyright owners need to be aware of the potential for local capture and renters need to know that such activity is illegal. As we will examine below, encryption technology can provide practical measures to address these concerns.

Turning to the content of the videos, there is a perception that video-on-demand will remain the domain of feature films or at least of those films available in video libraries. If so, however, this merely scratches the surface of the service's potential. Many of the programmes broadcast are available on video. These *could* be made available on the Internet, as could the programmes that make up the basic stock of other terrestrial or satellite TV broadcasting. If these programmes do become available along with the film stock then video-on-demand becomes much more than an entertainment phenomenon; it has the potential to change our lives.

If the Internet video libraries contain more than simple feature film and music offerings it becomes possible – exactly as with the newspaper case described above – to devise one's own personalised TV station. Libraries on the Internet could contain hours of feature films, of science, current affairs, popular soaps or children's programmes. The whole current range of broadcast programmes could be available together with past programmes through a Web page. The home video machine began the process of detaching viewers from the dictates of a fixed schedule; the Internet video library could complete the process.

And of course it becomes possible to 'binge' on chosen programmes: whole weekends dedicated to classic sport or to classic soaps. Moreover, the scope then exists for more extensive provision of 'community' broadcasts: *in extremis* one's home videos could be placed on Web pages; or low-cost transmissions from Covent Garden, or the local football fixtures could all be made available.

As the Internet improves in transmission speed, developing into the Information Superhighway, it therefore makes it possible to free one's viewing habits from the dictates of fixed schedules. In this, however, there are a few cultural implications that must be considered. The most important of these is something of a reprise to the educational issues addressed above.

For the majority of people in the UK our viewing habits were established at a time when there was only a single handful of TV channels. While the range of TV channels is greater in the US and elsewhere, there is still a limitation even if the set is larger. Our tastes were therefore constrained by what was offered and by what we happened to see and enjoy. This might have been as a result of recommendations; of our parents' habits; or of pure serendipity in accidentally viewing a programme. Our tastes are driven by what we have been offered or by what we could manage to find.

By contrast, there is a huge range of novels and magazines published, with vast libraries and thousands of bookshops. One's reading tastes are to a much greater extent a matter of education: a *cultural* issue rather than one of immediate popularity. That is not to say that hyped, 'best-selling' books are not widely read; they are of course. However, the choice of reading matter on a typical underground carriage is far wider than that of viewing matter.

With a change in the delivery of TV programmes, the question of education and of culture becomes relevant in this domain. This is less of an issue, however, for adults with established tastes – and more of an issue for children, particularly young children. We accept as natural that schools educate children to choose and read quality texts; choice of viewing habits is left to the dictates of the schedules. As the range of cable, satellite, 'terrestrial' and Internet broadcast programmes multiplies, this educational issue will become an increasingly important cultural question.

The question of video delivery is therefore similar to that of electronic publishing in that responsibility as well as opportunity passes to the consumer and the benefits partially but not completely obscure substantial issues.

As the responsibility passes to the consumer, however, what will happen to the current broadcasters? In the main the process has already begun: there is already a separation of responsibility for the *creation* of programmes and the *transmission* of those programmes. The Internet therefore becomes only one of several mechanisms for broadcasting programmes – or perhaps *'pointcasting'*, to coin a phrase. As the technology develops to encompass cable, however, and as the advantages of video-on-demand pass into the general culture of programme viewing it is not impossible that Internet and Information Superhighway delivery, rather than delivery through the medium of radio signals, will become the norm. The Internet thus presents an opportunity to broadcasters rather than a direct threat.

In support of this, many computer software, telecommunications and entertainment companies are merging or forming joint ventures to allow them to exploit this exciting market. The biggest push to create an Information Superhighway from the initial Internet experiments will come from these concerns, eager to provide a global news and entertainment service through cable TV and computer connections – and for the revenue that it will bring.

There is, however, a very specific change in viewing habits raised by the introduction and popularity of Internet pointcasting: advertisements. While the more general case of advertising over the Internet is covered in Chapter 3, in the context of programmes it is easy to see that advertisements will come to be associated with the programmes themselves, rather than the gaps between them as now on TV.[65] In this way, retrieving a given video will also involve retrieving the commercial messages along with it as an inseparable module, although intelligent local systems may well be able to 'filter' such explicit commercials. As Chapter 3 discusses, in the Cybernation consumers become *empowered* in their choice both of goods and of commercial messages.

Internet vanity publishing

As well as offering interesting opportunities to established broadcasters and publishers, the Internet also provides the potential for supporting new or amateur ventures. Vanity publishing was mentioned above; this has a long history, in which authors, musicians, painters and so forth pay to make their work widely available. So-called Internet vanity publishing allows very cheap, global publishing facilities to be used by anyone.

Struggling bands unable to get recording contracts or 'gigs' can use the Internet to make their music – perhaps even short video clips – available to 'their public'. Struggling poets can do similar; in fact there is a wealth of poetry (of mixed quality) available throughout the Internet already. Artists can scan their material onto Web pages; sculptors can scan photographs of their latest work. There are established precedents on the Internet for all of these things from already established artists: clips from a Rolling Stones' concert; some of the greatest pictures from galleries and museums around the world;[66] and as already mentioned, poetry.

Internet vanity publishing can go even further. Performance artists, from which there are a wide range to choose, could make their work available on Internet videos. Exhibitionists could even transmit scenes from their own lives onto Web pages – perhaps the ultimate in real-life soap operas or 'fly-on-the-wall' documentaries. Holiday snaps, home videos and so forth could be displayed. There is even an on-line memorial garden ('www.rememberance.com'). Perhaps in time this could evolve into a repository for significant elements of the individuals' recorded lives?

We have barely begun to scratch the surface of the Internet's potential to entertain and inform; although there have been developments to provide such established aspects as music radio over the Internet, it is *more* than a simple extension of existing broadcast or telecommunication facilities – it is a wholly novel platform.

THE WORLD OF WORK

The concept of 'job' has undergone almost continual change over the centuries, coming to mean that part of one's life concerned primarily with the earning of money.[67] Jobs can form a greater or a lesser part of one's total lifestyle; can involve extensive travel or labour at home; can involve working for oneself or a large corporation; and can mean hard physical or relatively light, mental activity. Over recent years there have been a series of trends culminating in a steady change of working patterns, favouring smaller and more focused companies. Moreover, these are companies with increasing specialisation and a requirement for 'Knowledge' workers; and there has been a corresponding appreciation of 'homeworking' in the context of such activity.

These trends have progressed according to their own dynamics, quite separately from the potential opportunities of the Internet. As with the education and publishing cases outlined above, the Internet presents a variety of exciting prospects in the world of work. The perspective taken in this section is that of the workers themselves; subsequent chapters consider the impact of these changes on companies or the economy as a whole.

From the perspective, therefore, of a *worker* the Internet can have implications for:

- the place at which work is performed;
- the type of work performed;
- the location of company and workmates;
- the time dedicated to that work.

Teleworking

An increasing number of people are taking advantage of the opportunity to work from home. In some cases such working has become the norm, with *all* working time carried out in the home; in other cases only a percentage of time is spent at home, with the rest of the time spent at customer premises or in a central office. In the case of so-called 'knowledge' workers, spending the majority of their working lives in the collection, analysis, synthesis or dissemination of 'processed information', home working is particularly popular. Freed from the distractions of the office, home workers are arguably more productive and certainly less stressed given the absence of commuting.

Of course, home working must also include 'piece workers' such as those doing out-working from clothing factories, say; it also includes those whose jobs have *always* involved working from the home: area sales representatives, domestic servants, etc. For the purposes of this section 'home working' will be taken to refer to those whose jobs have been traditionally performed within an office but who now find an increasing opportunity to work from home.

Home working is, however, a special case of a broader social and employment phenomenon, that of *'teleworking'*. In teleworking one's work is disassociated from fixed office premises and supported in locations remote from the organisation's offices. Teleworking can therefore be at the worker's home, at a customer site or in a purpose provided *'telecottage'*. This last is an office, often sited in a rural location, providing generic office services[68] for remote workers from a variety of organisations.

In addition, of course, teleworking can occur in hotel rooms, airport lounges, in cars, service stations: literally anywhere that the employee finds him or herself at the time that work must be performed.

A range of factors support this trend to such remote working practices, summarised in [29]. Office space, particularly in large cities, is very expensive; companies able to operate with only small office provision therefore have an advantage. Office space can be used for those functions that *must* be carried out in fixed, central locations – with other functions carried out remotely. Additionally, commuting time and expense can also be reduced – particularly where the work is performed at home; important during a period of rail-strikes, terrorist attacks and concerns about growing traffic pollution. Thirdly, many studies have shown that – for some workers at least – working away from the distractions of an office improves efficiency. Of course there are management challenges that must be overcome, most particularly the question of maintaining contact with remote workers.

This contact, and indeed the work itself is supported by technology. Two particular aspects are important: telecommunications and IT. Mobile digital phones and laptop computers enable workers to stay in touch on a constant basis and to be able to do computer-specific work anywhere, anytime. Because the digital phones can also support communication with the computers, remote workers can also gain access to the corporate networks.

As such of course, there is no actual requirement for the Internet. Those working for a particular company can keep in touch by telephone – perhaps even by videophone as the facility becomes more popular. Dial-in access to central computer services allows internal e-mail, news and information facilities to be used. Corporate teleworkers can therefore be supported without recourse to the Internet. As we shall see below, internal information and computer services are increasingly converging with the Internet: so-called '*Intranet*' structures. Quite apart from this, however, the Internet can be and is used by these workers; and furthermore, is allowing many more workers to take advantage of teleworking.

At the simplest level Internet e-mail allows messages to be sent between people working for different organisations. This is perhaps the most immediate use, allowing remote workers to contact a greater range of fellows than is available on the purely internal services. Secondly, the information sources of the Internet are particularly wide ranging, allowing remote workers to access not only their own company's internal databases but also a wealth of additional, external data. Thirdly, the Internet can support such work by the increasing number of freelance knowledge workers – consultants – that have resulted from accelerating trends to reduce fixed staff numbers in many organisations. And fourthly, as we shall see, organisations are appearing that are dedicated to trading on the Internet: workers in these new companies can and do use those very same facilities to support their own working patterns.

The Internet, together with the broader revolution in telecommunications and IT provision can therefore support and encourage increasingly remote working habits. It can also support work for companies that are themselves increasingly remote from their marketplace and their employees. Anticipating slightly the themes of Chapter 3, it is entirely possible for companies based outside of the UK to trade and employ workers in our country. Using Internet communication facilities, UK domiciled workers can perform functions over computer links to these remote organisations. This might involve writing English instruction manuals for German dishwashers, or software for Indian computer manufacturers, or a host of other activities.

UK workers can therefore use the Internet to support their work for remote organisations; and can moreover use the Internet facilities to maintain social contacts with their remote fellow-workers. One drawback, however, of this phenomenon is the extent to which such Internet-supported remote working intrudes on one's home life. Many home workers report difficulty in balancing home and work lives; the Internet will not help but rather will exacerbate this problem. This is particularly the case when UK workers are involved with, say, Canadian companies and the problems of time zones are considered.

While it is true that e-mail can provide a means to alleviate the problems of divergent time zones, in working life it is often the case that immediate – or at least, very rapid – responses are required. Core working days of nine to five thirty become increasingly difficult to maintain when head office core time does not overlap with the core time of workers. To some this would appear as a distinct advantage – allowing one to work hours of one's own choice; to others it could put intolerable strains on domestic arrangements. Additionally, with an expectation that work can and is performed without regard to location it becomes as practical to work on the beach, through the weekend or during holidays, as at any other time. Other employment factors add to these issues and these will be considered further in the context of Internet trade and the change in company structures and sizes in Chapter 3.

In the pure context of working patterns, however, the Internet does present an exciting and interesting further potential: *virtual reality*.

Virtual reality

Virtual reality software provides a realistic rendition of a computer-generated set of scenes: a virtual *world* or environment is represented within the computer and the user is presented with a graphical perspective of that world. The user is also presented with a means to 'move' within the environment, either by keyboard commands, mouse, joystick or 'dataglove'; and the scenery is viewed either through headset, goggles or a flat screen.

In the Internet, a standard for defining such virtual worlds has begun to emerge: VRML – Virtual Reality Modelling Language.[69] Real-world or purely imaginary scenery can be rendered within the system and in the best of these the user is given a 'first-person' perspective: it is exactly as though they themselves were indeed walking, running or flying through the environment. The scenery can be produced artificially or can be wholly accurate. Hence, archaeologists have created – and made available on CDs and the Internet – realistic virtual reality scenes of temples, cathedrals and so forth.[70] Alternatively, first-person combat games allow players to fight one another through a pretend environment – a medieval dungeon or futuristic space station, say. In these multi-user games one or more additional players is connected over Internet protocols with the same virtual environment. Each player therefore appears similar to a computer-generated character in the game but is instead controlled by the commands issued from a remote terminal or PC.

In a working context this gives the exciting possibility of producing artificial versions of an organisation's office.[71] Remote workers could then 'move' through a realistic view of their workspace, passing desks that might be occupied by their equally remote colleagues. A remote worker might, for example, have a representation of his or her own desk; coming into the office could then involve moving through the virtual world, approaching and clicking on one's desk. The software could then provide access to the company's own computer systems – after authentication checks – allowing the employee to begin work.

More exciting still, approaching a representation of a fellow worker could allow interaction exactly as with the 'chat' example discussed above. Clicking on the colleague might for example open a direct videophone channel to that person, allowing real-time conversation; alternatively, a message could be posted on their desk – appearing as e-mail. Files, represented by handfuls of paper folders, could be exchanged. Two or more virtual workers could go off to the coffee lounge or smoking room together for more informal discussions. The social isolation from office discourse felt by many remote workers could thereby be alleviated or even removed completely.

And of course there are even further possibilities. In the virtual reality office one's colleagues need not be represented by 'stick figures' but by realistic representations of the true person. However, this representation can be what the employees themselves *want* to project. This is an important point: at its most basic, handicapped workers could represent themselves as being as able bodied as their colleagues; or they could represent themselves in, say, their wheelchair but not constrained by its presence. In virtual offices, stairs and closely crowded desks need not therefore inhibit wheelchair access. People could show themselves as black, white, male, female; or as androgynous, colourless creations. The physical body behind the virtual worker therefore becomes irrelevant; to reprise the cartoon: 'On the Internet, nobody knows you're a dog!'

From the perspective of the organisation itself, the virtual office has further potential. Representations of the company's major suppliers and customers could be placed *virtually* adjacent to the office: walking out of the office allows one access to a corridor along which suppliers are accessible on one side and customers along the other. Visitors could be greeted by digital receptionists and business meetings carried out electronically.

Ambitious; futuristic? Of course. But in Chapter 3 we will consider the *actual* state of Internet trading; and in Chapter 7 we will return to this virtual environment of the future.

SUMMARY

This chapter has examined the most basic requirement of our Cybernation and the most fundamental aspect of the Internet: the ability to support communication between individuals or groups. The key points from this analysis are that the Internet correspondence and discussions are as rapid as direct or telephone conversations, but are essentially anonymous – encouraging the exchange of highly emotive discussions. They are also recorded and therefore bear permanent witness to any such indiscretions. The discussions are also global in coverage, encouraging contributions from individuals of varying expertise, located around the world. Groups interested in a particular topic can include people from cultures having a very different notion of the acceptability, morality or legality of a given issue – and provide scope for educational benefits and a challenge to our ability to protect our children.

In essence, the Internet therefore presents our society with a particular difficulty: to benefit from the services provided while ensuring a maintenance of the basic set of civil and other rights we afford ourselves, examined in Chapter 5.

The Internet is in many ways more significant than the introduction of the printing press or of television and radio. It is a global, freely accessible medium with which all those with basic communication mechanisms can enjoy *interaction* rather than passive reception. Perhaps the most colourful simile for the Internet is of a global toilet wall: anyone's graffiti can be seen and responded to. But even this is not totally accurate: the Internet supports free-form communication and debate; can support the rapid exchange of news and opinion around the globe in a matter of moments; can support new types of company and of workers; and can provide mechanisms to facilitate marketing and trade of goods.

3

INTERNET TRADING

The change in commerce and trading styles throughout this century has been every bit as staggering as the changes in person-to-person communication. I remember going shopping with my mother. We lived in a rural village: milk, butter, cheese and eggs would be delivered to our home directly from the local farms. Bread came from the bakery at the end of our street and meat from one of two local butchers. Flour, potatoes and other vegetables came from slightly further afield but would also be delivered to the house on a monthly rather than a weekly basis.

For the more unusual items the Co-op (pronounced 'Kworp' in my village!) was also at the end of the road, stocking a cornucopia of goods, from knitting wool to towels. Twice yearly we would catch the train from the nearby station, for the unimaginable excitement of a journey to the big city and to what then seemed the largest department store in the world. And payment was in cash for all but that twice yearly shopping trip.

In what seems to be a few short decades those shops have closed – or have retreated to the immense, sprawling shopping centres that we have imported from the US. Economies of scale allowed the 'supermarkets' to compete with and eventually supplant the covered markets of my childhood. And the ongoing banking revolution has led to credit or debit card payments for all but the smallest of purchases. My daughter believes that 'plastic money' – the credit or debit card – is for buying things and that coins exist solely and exclusively to be tossed into the fountain at the middle of our shopping centre.

These visible changes are tangible evidence of the deeper changes in our society and in our economy. Commerce is performed on a global, perpetual basis – with digitised credit transferred at the speed of light along world-wide networks linking stock markets, banks and traders. And the companies themselves have grown to specialise in particular 'core' activities – with ensuing reductions in staff numbers. But yet all these radical changes have taken place *before* the revolutionary impact of the Internet has been felt; what further changes will result from its introduction, acceptance and widespread use?[72]

In the previous chapter, the potential for cultural or social change of Internet communication was described. These changes will be felt in the way that we gather our news or interact with our friends and workmates. Arguably, however, the impact of these changes on the economy will be far greater: on the way that companies operate; on the way we buy goods; on the way we perceive advertising; and on our general levels of *wealth*.

All trade – between retailer and consumer; supplier and manufacturer – revolves around communication in its broadest sense. Communicating messages about the goods themselves: their utility, unique selling points; communicating orders or requests for information; and communication in the sense of transporting those goods to market. Where the Internet can help in the communication of correspondence or of political opinions it can also support this trade communication.

To be successful in this arena, the Internet must first support marketing information. This can take the form of explicit advertising of information about companies and their competitive advantages or handicaps; or of more general information about a particular type of product – access to consumer reports on dishwashers and so forth.

The basic measure of marketing success, however, is the *sale* of the advertised goods: an order from consumer to retailer, or manufacturer to supplier. This order informs the supplier of the requirement to be filled and results in the delivery of two things: the goods themselves and an invoice. The invoice results (one always hopes) in payment, which in turn results in a receipt, that for many goods also represents a guarantee that the supplied product is 'fit for the purpose'.

This is therefore the basic chain of the trading process: marketing, order, delivery, invoice, payment, receipt and customer service. Some or all of this chain can be transferred into the domain of the Internet.

Moreover, the Internet could support the complete trade process – or substantial parts of it – for many different types of companies. In the previous chapter some obvious areas were discussed: electronic publishing, videos and music for example. The Internet can also help to generate new kinds of trading company, and can change the basis upon which existing companies carry out that trade. Here, trade is being used in the most general sense, to mean the buying and selling of a company's products; these might be the expertise of their staff, in the case of consultancy organisations; or books, magazines and journals; or cars, lorries and aeroplanes.

This chapter therefore considers the aspects of the trading process that can be transferred into the Internet domain – so-called 'Cyberspace'. In the first section, marketing is considered, followed by an examination of the nature and types of goods that can be traded partially or wholly over the Internet.[73] Later sections then consider the way in which some companies will be able wholly to remove their 'real-world' footprint, allowing them to exist purely in Cyberspace.

INTERNET-BASED MARKETING

The marketing functions range from positioning a company and its products with respect to any competitors, through the collection of market-segment information, to producing advertisements and product literature for use by sales staff.

The Internet can be used for each and every part of this process. Moreover, as more and more people come to use the system, expertise in Internet marketing will become ever more important. It must be recognised, however, that there is a danger in all forms of Internet marketing. In Chapter 1, the historical background to the Internet was described; recall, the system emerged and was popularised initially by a sub-culture of users. This sub-culture developed a well understood but non-articulated set of Internet-accepted behaviours: the term 'netiquette' is often used to describe this. Overt marketing is frowned upon. Stronger: overt marketing is *punished*.

Clumsy attempts at Internet advertising, referred to as 'spamming' for some inexplicable reason, have given marketing in this environment a particularly poor reputation. Posting advertising messages to all newsgroups; slogans and messages attached to otherwise innocuous or even irrelevant postings; all of these have collected their critics, even resulting in a 'blacklist' of advertisers from whom Internet users are encouraged not to buy. The authors of the blacklist even go so far as to give suggestions for a number of mechanisms within the Internet that can be used against such advertisers. The most famous – or infamous – example of spamming is that of the American lawyers Canter & Siegel whose deliberate and celebrated stratagem resulted in a stream of abusive messages and the withdrawal of their Internet access by their then service provider when their computer became overloaded.

In this case, however, the offence is obvious. Such blanket, direct marketing is the digital equivalent of the impersonal collection of random junk-mail that we all suffer daily. In the Internet context, however, it is even more objectionable: many users have to *pay* to download newsgroup articles that might be of interest. We would all be indignant – quite justifiably – if the postman expected us to pay postage on the daily delivery of junk-mail. Those who would try to benefit from the Internet's global reach must therefore be sensitive to the concerns of the 'natives'.

However, marketing activities in the broadest sense *can* be performed, supported by the Internet, that run no or little risk of transgressing netiquette. The marketing can be thought of as running through a spectrum from 'passive' to 'active':

- Collection of technical, product, competitive or consumer information;
- Establishment of 'virtual market stalls';
- Proactive dissemination of advertisements.

Collecting information

The first and most basic task of a marketing department lies in the collection of accurate information: about the desires and expectations of customers; about the activities and offerings of competitors; and about the relative competitiveness of different products. This information is available to the marketeer through a host of different mechanisms. Current customers can be canvassed for their opinions; trade journals and the general press can be monitored for relevant news stories; competitive products can be purchased and compared. Standard 'real-world' marketing has developed a wide range of solutions to the central problems of helping customers to buy products.

At the simplest level the Internet provides rapid access to information sources provided by marketing-service organisations. In the main, these are organisations that have provided information to marketing departments for many years, either in the form of periodic newsletters and reports or through direct, dial-up access to the organisations' databases. The arrival of the Internet allows such services to be accessed by means of Internet-supported connections. In itself, this is hardly revolutionary.

The Internet does, however, present certain unique features in the collection of broader information: the same medium allows access to these commercially-offered databases as well as access to on-line consumer reports and technical forums discussing topics that might have broader implications for the marketeer's industry[9]. Simple, generalised search utilities, similar to those discussed in the context of personalised newspapers, would allow a marketeer to collect, analyse and present information from a particularly wide range of information sources.

There are very few such sources of interest to a marketing department that are accessible solely and exclusively via the Internet itself. Perhaps the only such set of information arises in the context of newsgroups, where discussion topics are of relevance. These are considered to be distinct from the technical forums mentioned above and feature consumer discussion – ie, general discussion groups among non-professional but interested parties. Marketeers could choose periodically to scan newsgroup articles to register discussion of important, relevant issues.

As an example a marketing department of a car manufacturer might choose to observe discussion in a number of forums covering topics ranging from autosport through environmental concern to the features of particular cars. They might even elect to initiate their own discussion group, dedicated to their range of cars. Would this have any value?

The answer is, probably not. Recall from Chapter 2, the newsgroups are open to any and all – without regard from whom the submission has come. Articles could be posted by disgruntled customers, salesmen from the competition, schoolchildren – anyone, in fact ('On the Internet, nobody knows you're a dog!'). But for a marketing department it is important to know who the submission is from: purchasers or recommenders; tyre kickers or the merely tiresome.

Even worse, the newsgroup would certainly be observed by competitive organisations even if they didn't choose to make malicious, mischievous or distracting submissions. The visibility of the medium, advantageous in other respects, would be disastrous in this one.

In the context of collecting information therefore, while the Internet presents a unified access mechanism to the information, it presents very little that might be considered new and important. It is in the other areas that the Internet presents novel and interesting potential.

Taking first the CompuServe-like case, such 'private' domains provide a range of shopping services available through an electronic mall or 'Cybershop'. These are remote shopping services in which many of the Internet-related problems we address below have been addressed. CompuServe, for example, can boast 10 years of on-line shopping with no credit card-related fraud or thefts. Because shoppers are all CompuServe members by definition, their account numbers and addresses are known; and conversely, the users know that the shops are providing a service that has been agreed with CompuServe themselves. Records, flowers, software and a range of other goods are advertised and purchased through the CompuServe mechanisms that serve as an on-line catalogue and are then delivered through standard postal or despatch mechanisms.[74]

While the private domain of CompuServe – or American-on-Line, Prodigy and others – is perceived to be relatively safe for on-line shoppers,[75] the more public, general Internet domain is less so. We will therefore concentrate on these aspects throughout this and subsequent sections unless specific reference is made to these services.

Setting up a 'market stall'

The most obvious, uniquely Internet-facilitated marketing device is the Web page – the digital equivalent of a market stall. Web pages can be created in a very straightforward manner, although the precise mechanisms are beyond the scope of this book. The Web page can, however, be established within the World-Wide Web on one's own or a service provider's host machine.

Ideally a company's 'home' page – their domain or virtual 'point of presence' – will have the same name as their company. Company names are protected in the 'real world'; in the Internet context this protection is not as immediately obvious. Several organisations exist to register company names throughout the world, ensuring that the name cannot be used by other companies or individuals, perhaps deliberately, perhaps inadvertently. This is discussed further in Chapter 5. The establishment of this home page, however, ensures that the company has an identity within the Internet, that the identity cannot be used by somebody else, and that it can be located by prospective customers.

Depending on the company, the Web page can then carry a host of relevant information. Taking the case of the car manufacturer, the page could contain brochure-style pictures of the cars within the manufacturer's current range. More, each picture caption could – if viewers 'click' on it – link to further information: more detailed pictures, technical specification, optional extras, price range, addresses of dealers; anything and everything that the manufacturer would want to have said about the car can be presented.

It needn't stop there. In addition to providing an on-line brochure for the complete range, the Web hierarchy can also provide details of the manufacturer themselves: company reports, share price performance, location of manufacturing sites, charitable donations, current rankings in various autosports. Anything that the marketing department would like to make visible about the company can be placed within the collection of Web pages. Most of the major car manu-facturers have already established just such systems, with Web pages ranging from simple text to complicated pictures – Ford in America, Vauxhall in the UK and Peugeot in France are particularly good examples.

This is similar in nature to distributing glossy brochures, taking out television advertisements and putting information in the press. It has, however, certain unique features – primarily, those who access the various Web pages can be recorded by being asked to complete an 'entry form' or registration for example. This is an important difference when compared with, say, a two-page spread in an expen-sive magazine. A car magazine can provide the company's marketeers with some general information about its readership: circulation, type of buyer, and addresses of subscription holders. This is, however, fairly crude; and it doesn't indicate whether those readers did in fact actually read the advertisement or not.

By contrast, the Web page access is known to a precise degree. The e-mail address, for example, of each and every person accessing the page can be recorded; in the case of a hierarchy of pages, the type of interest by that person is also known: did they look at the estate cars or at the boy-racer range? Did they get as far as the price and dealer information or just look at the pictures? The Web page access beyond the top-most level – in which the most generic of information is held – can give a precise indication of the interest shown by each and every digital 'passer by'. As such, Internet marketing is more like marketing at a trade show than in a maga-zine. This ability to record and analyse access is particularly important given the wide range of people accessing the Internet; the most 'popular' and attractive Web pages might well attract high numbers of digital visitors, but in most cases these will be just 'passing by' – the tyre kickers, attracted by pretty pictures. Some Internet advertisers have suggested that a good guide for a Web page would not be the *total* number of visits, but rather the number of third or even fourth time visitors it attracts: does the Web page have a continuing attraction, or merely a novelty value?[76]

In other areas the 'market stall' of the Web page can be used to present a very wide range of material. The Web page structure could bȩ used by retailing organisations to present an on-line catalogue of the goods in their various shops; and as the speed and capacity of the Internet improves these catalogues can become ever more sophisticated. At present large quantities of pictures and sound clips take a long time to download to the local PC, particularly at times when the Internet is heavily loaded with other users. As the Internet develops, more extensive video clips – in time, as we discussed above, complete films – could be accessed through the service.

A retailer could therefore provide a market stall of Web pages that allows a 'virtual shopper' to browse the complete range of their goods. Full descriptions, price ranges and video clips of models illustrating the several types of lingerie on offer, for example, could be a feature of shopping in the 21st century.[77] An on-line music megastore could allow shoppers to select and listen to snippets from the complete range of CDs stocked or to view selected previews from videos; of course, in time those videos and CDs themselves will be available directly over the Internet.

The Internet market stall can, as we have seen, be supported by the Web page structure. Many organisations have already begun to experiment with such structures; we can be confident in expecting many more such. However, as the Internet develops it will present steadily more sophisticated mechanisms for achieving this effect. As we saw in Chapter 2, distributed virtual reality systems developed from the initial gaming versions could become useful in the context of remote working. A similar mechanism would of course support digital shopping: the presentation of an artificial, ideal shop – free from the crowds and through which virtual shoppers could move, selecting and examining items of interest, perhaps even interacting with virtual store assistants. We are admittedly a long way from this; but it is a natural progression from the current state.

Proactive marketing

In these two facets of Internet marketing the interaction with the consumers themselves has been somewhat remote; in the first, information is collected about or from passive consumers; and in the second, the 'market stall' is laid out ready for their inspection. In neither case is the marketeer involved in what one might think of as 'proactive' marketing. However, in the final category the marketing department use the facilities of the Internet to support a more direct approach to consumers.

As noted above, the provision of advertising on the Internet must be very carefully handled – but there is no doubt that the Internet, or rather the PCs and terminals that connect to it, present an important new medium. Any and all media – from newspapers, through TV, to roadside hoardings – have been populated by advertisements. Anywhere that a potential consumer's gaze may linger has been used, apart from PCs and terminals. In a way this is surprising; PC users are predominantly the well-paid, young to middle-age, professionals – even though this distribution will change over the next few years as PC use becomes more ubiquitous.

To be successful in this context of course, the advertisement must work. There are two aspects to this: the advertisement must be *viewed*; and it must then *persuade* the viewer to buy the advertised goods. At the most basic level there is no difference in the Internet or PC context and the success of advertisements on TV or in the newspapers. The key difference lies in the transference of that advertisement to a viewable location.

In the case of newspaper advertisements, the reader buys the paper and accepts the inclusion of the advertisements as an integral element of the medium. In the case of TV commercial breaks, there is broad cultural acceptance of the interruption implied. We may skip over the advertisement, or boil the kettle, or passively view the subject; but in all cases we accept that the advertisement has a *right* to be there. This is not the case with advertisements on the Internet, as the earlier discussion of netiquette made clear, other than potentially for advertisements linked to 'video-on-demand' programmes served over the medium.

The only area in which such intrusive adverts *have* become accepted is within the many 'search engines' that must be used in locating relevant information within the Internet. As has already been mentioned, the wealth of information available within the Internet is truly phenomenal. To find a particular item or locate a company's page it is necessary either to know the address of the page directly, in which case it can be entered immediately; alternatively, a search must be performed. Search engines are built into the popular browsers – Netscape, Explorer and Mosaic – and these build up indices and references.[78] While a search is being performed, however, some of these programs display advertising banners capturing the attention of the patiently waiting 'Internaut'.[79] The heavily US-oriented nature of these advertisements can be an irritation for the UK user but other than this they are entirely inoffensive.

Leaving to one side, however, marketing which centres on the passive, market-stall approach of simple Web pages or their equivalent for people to *choose* to view, and the simple banners within search engines, more active advertisements must somehow populate the users' PCs; they must be smart advertisements,[80] *'smartverts'*. This could be achieved in one of three ways:

1. The advertisement could *invade*.
2. It could be explicitly *downloaded*, as a known component of some other Internet entity.
3. The advertisement itself could be *collected*, again explicitly.

In each case, the advertisement can be a program of some description – that modifies the appearance of the Windows desktop to include a company logo, or associates a slogan or jingle with an action in Windows, or introduces a 'commercial break'-style screen saver. As with more traditional advertisements the range of message types is broad: they can be boringly informative or amusingly catchy; they can even be staid or risqué – or positively obscene. Anything in fact that catches a viewer's attention.

In the first case, the program could be contained as a part of a virus or a hidden element of some other application: a so-called 'Trojan horse'. The virus is 'caught' by the user accessing software or data on an already infected system, allowing the program to be transferred to their own. In all likelihood, however, while such invasive advertisements are a *practical* possibility and may even be attempted, they are unlikely to be successful in persuading people to buy goods. A real-world equivalent might be having your door kicked down, and a crudely printed sheet of paper advertising something thrust into your hand! Few if any of us would welcome this, let alone then spend money with the company concerned.[81] Moreover, spreading viruses – even relatively harmless ones such as these – is restricted in the UK by the Computer Misuse Act and would therefore be illegal, as Chapter 5 discusses.

The second point is a more practical possibility, with advertisements accepted as an explicit part of a desired program or set of information. As an example, companies could offer to sponsor the upgrading of a particular application.[82] Users of the application are offered the upgrade free of charge provided that they accept a set of advertisements from the sponsoring company. These can be explicit statements of sponsorship – 'This program brought to you courtesy of . . .' – or can be a package of messages on the desktop, screen saver and so forth.

The third case is equally practical and quite interesting. In this case, the advertisements themselves are downloaded in the full knowledge that they *are* advertisements. PC implementations of witty TV advertisements would be an immediate and successful instance of this. Advertising campaigns already feature snappy and memorable slogans; newspaper and hoarding series; multiple commercial break stories – often with a short 'reminder' advertisement at the end of the break; and simultaneous release of the background music as a single. The addition of smartverts to this general range would be an obvious next step. Some companies have already begun producing such screen-saver adverts – the most popular being the Guinness example;[83] we can expect many more such as the relationship between consumers and advertisers changes in the light of Internet developments.

These changes influence a particular aspect of advertising: *legitimacy of presence*. In other media – print, TV, etc. – the legitimacy of an advertisement's presence is not questioned. Advertisements on the Internet or downloaded to one's PC are less well accepted. As mentioned, in some Web browsers the search utilities display commercial messages, but in most cases one would not expect to receive an advertisement unless it is explicitly requested. Advertisers must therefore accept that consumers have become *empowered* in the Internet context. A wealth of consumer information together with an ability to exercise choice over the advertisements received empowers consumers to be much more than passive receivers of commercial messages. The problems of retaining TV viewers' attention through commercial breaks are as nothing against the problems of attracting viewers to an explicitly commercial Web site – perhaps through the provision of games or free software.

With the exception of the first category, these proactive advertisements would support Internet marketing without transgressing legal restrictions or the sensitive boundaries of netiquette. They would allow the marketing departments of any company – of any size – to take advantage of the unique opportunities presented by the Internet. The prospects are of course exciting; any new medium is exciting in the context of transmitting commercial messages. Quite apart from netiquette and the risk of upsetting the natives, however, Internet marketing carries a number of significant risks – commercial, cultural and regulatory.

The most obvious such risk is that of identity: does the 'market stall' *really* belong to the company that it claims to represent? A clever pressure group, for example, seeking to discredit a particular company, could easily create a Web site purporting to be from the company itself. At the topmost level the Web pages could be accurate and enticing, with more detailed pages representing the company in an ever poorer light. Consumers finding the site would, in the cleverest case, be left with a poor opinion of the company concerned, without in fact realising that the information was not presented by the company itself. This notion is carried further in the context of fraudulent trading, which is considered in Chapter 5.

In addition to this the company has the worry of whether or not their Web pages will be *found*. Prime sites on the high street or shopping mall do not transfer readily to the Internet;[84] companies must advertise their Internet addresses within the currently available media. The size of the Internet makes the accidental discovery of a given site very unlikely; users must search for the relevant locations or know the addresses explicitly, perhaps from non-Internet advertising or publicity. Of course if Internet-hosted media – personal newspapers and video-on-demand, as described in Chapter 2 – gradually supplant the more traditional forms, organisations may have to become even more proactive in publicising their Internet sites.

However, there is the regulatory issue of the content of the advertisements themselves. Most immediately, there are no global regulations that control the types of advertising message that can be placed over the Internet. UK advertisers work in a 'self-regulation' domain; other countries exercise greater or lesser influence over advertising messages or the goods which can be advertised at all: some countries ban all forms of tobacco or even chewing gum advertising for example, while others are far more relaxed. The global nature of the Internet therefore makes conflicts of style and of regulation highly likely. The furore over the Benetton advertising in 1994 and 1995 for instance, illustrates the differences in acceptable styles of 'shock' advertisements between Italy and the UK. France has a much looser approach to nudity within advertisements than the UK; and even the UK's approach is looser than that of the Arabic nations. The cultural clashes to which these different styles will lead – even without consideration of netiquette – will need careful attention.

This is of course quite separate from the question of policing misleading advertising. Where advertisements are placed by companies outside of the UK, EU or other established regulating authorities what practical measures will it be possible to take?

Many of these problems can be addressed by the use of Internet 'Electronic Malls' – or digital shopping centres. Where a company is marketing its services or goods from within a reputable Internet location[85] – or, say, from within CompuServe – then consumers can have a high degree of confidence that the organisation has been 'vetted' and that there is at least some recourse in the event of any problems.

Within the Internet itself, netiquette has led to mechanisms such as blacklists, 'mail bombs' and automatic diallers all being used by individuals to exercise an internal policing influence over the nature of commercial messages supported within the medium. This is of course a further example of the essentially anarchic nature of the Internet, and while such solutions might be applauded by some, they give rise to serious concerns on the part of the authorities. The UK Treasury and other government departments, for example, were at one time concerned that such mail bombs and 'flame wars' might be carried out directly against *them*.

In general, judicial and regulatory authorities dislike such 'vigilante' approaches to the policing of anti-social, illegal or unacceptable behaviour. We will address all of these issues in Chapter 5.

ORDERING GOODS OVER THE INTERNET

The Internet can support the advertising of goods and the provision of virtual market stalls or shops set out to allow prospective customers to browse through the goods on offer. Sophisticated electronic brochures can be provided and a careful record of interested parties can be maintained. It can also support the process of ordering, invoicing and paying for those goods; it can even, as we consider in the next section, support the delivery of certain goods. In this section, however, we will limit the discussion to the mechanisms and challenges associated with the *ordering* process.

We use the term 'vendor' for the organisation selling a product or service by means of the Internet; and 'purchaser' for the individual or organisation buying the goods. For the sake of clarity, in this section the purchaser is assumed to be a private individual, shopping from a home PC connected to the Internet; and the vendor is assumed to be a 'normal' shop having an Internet presence. It will be recognised, however, that the mechanisms described apply equally to institutional purchasing from supplier organisations. While organisations in the retail sector have used Electronic Data Interchange (EDI) successfully for many years, this has been in support of communication between *themselves* and their own suppliers; similarly, banks and building societies have used private, secure networks to transmit credit and other information around the world in a digital fashion. The change that the Internet brings, however, is the potential to extend these facilities to the communication with *customers* and with private citizens directly and on a global basis.

At the most basic level, to order particular goods a series of steps must be completed:

1. the general category of goods must be determined;
2. a vendor must be located and chosen;
3. the specific goods required must be identified; and
4. the vendor must be informed of the goods and quantity required.

In addition to these most fundamental of purchasing actions, there is also the requirement to effect a *contract* between the purchaser and the vendor; the vendor must agree to accept the requirement for delivering goods suitable . to the advertised purpose and the purchaser must accept the associated requirement to pay for those goods. In 'real-world' transactions with which we are already familiar these steps are well understood; indeed, to spell them out as I have done here seems almost artificial. But in Internet trading, as we shall see, these fundamental processes are far from straightforward.

In the first step described above, a purchaser identifies a need that can be satisfied by the Internet-traded goods. This can be as a result of advertising – Internet-hosted or not – or through some other process. In any case the influence of the Internet on this process is at best peripheral. Where Internet trading becomes important therefore is in the next stage: identifying a vendor. The marketing activity detailed in the previous section allows a vendor to establish a presence of some form within the Internet domain. Knowledge acquired by purchasers outside the Internet – from standard advertising, etc – would allow the vendor's Web pages to be located; or the purchaser can search explicitly for the company by name, where the domain name has been registered; or the purchaser can use a search tool to hunt through the myriad of pages representing organisations selling examples of the chosen category of goods.

To take a specific example, as a result of advertising the purchaser may have decided to buy a newly issued CD of some popular music. The Internet Web pages for music shops can then be searched for and retrieved, giving the details of prices, shop locations and so forth. The search could be performed on a very specific basis, naming the required shop, or on a general basis. Of course, in this last case a list of all (or at least the first 100) Internet-advertised music shops will be returned, including those throughout the world. With most search engines the bias of information returned is strongly towards the US, although this can be influenced if required.

The purchaser is therefore presented with a series of Web pages within which the goods are offered for sale. From these a choice of vendor will be made. In 'real world' shopping this choice might be made on the proximity and accessibility of the shop or supplier; on the friendliness and courtesy of the sales staff; or on a host of other aspects. In all cases, however, it will be constrained by the available options: shops which have been visited; suppliers who respond to tendering invitations. In the Internet case vendors will be located on a very wide basis – in local towns or different continents. While choices can still be made on 'real-world' terms, the visibility of global pricing of particular goods presents the purchaser with far more information than is available in touring the nearest shops.

To return to the music shop example; as we said, the search routine run in the UK can be expected to return a list of US music shops as well as UK ones. In the US, CDs are cheaper – generally a CD will cost the same in dollars as it does in sterling in the respective countries. Armed with this information the purchaser is free to negotiate with the UK vendor, or simply to buy from the US and have the CD imported. We will consider the question of distribution of goods in the next section. At this point, however, it is important to realise that *global* advertising supports the global *visibility* of prices.

This visibility of prices for identical goods, all of which may be ordered through a simple mechanism over the Internet, allows competition not simply between vendors in different countries, but also vendors of different sizes and natures. The Internet presence of a small, specialist music store can be every bit as impressive as that of the largest conglomerate – perhaps even more so, since the established organisation will not want to impact upon its 'real world' sales, an important point to which we will return in due course. Moreover, the visibility could empower purchasers to exploit price differentials between suppliers; the Internet therefore can ensure that the purchasers of goods buy them in an 'ideal' market: one in which the price for the goods is fixed in terms of the amount a customer is prepared to spend. This will have an impact on aspects of the economy, although given the low value of such goods it is likely to be only a minimal one at present.

Armed with the competitive information the purchaser therefore makes a choice of vendor. The next stage is to effect the order itself. The Internet presence of the vendor may be in the form of a simple, alphabetic list of titles stored in a file; or it may be a series of Web pages – in effect, a catalogue – or possibly in something more esoteric, such as a virtual reality shop as described above. In whatever form, however, the purchaser is presented with a means of selecting the goods required. To complete the transaction the purchaser must then inform the vendor of the number and nature of items required and give his or her own details. This is usually achieved through the completion of an order form.

These forms are stored as part of the Web pages and can therefore be transmitted to the local PC for completion; or in the non-Web situation, the forms may be ordinary files that must be completed. In the simplest case, the purchaser completes the form locally, typing name, address and order details into the appropriate parts of the form. Once complete, the purchaser 'clicks' on a send button within the form to transmit the information to the vendor. In more complicated Web forms, verification routines written in Java can be embedded in the page to ensure that only valid order details are entered.

In either case, having completed the form the purchaser transmits it to the vendor, thereby effecting the order itself. Once the order form is received by the supplier, the order has been established: the supplier accepts the responsibility for supplying the named goods; the purchaser, responsibility to pay for them.

The analogy of course is with mail order shopping, in which the purchaser completes a hand-written form and posts it to the vendor. There are, however, a number of crucial differences between the two types of order. Firstly, the mail order form can contain payment details – a credit card number, cheque, money order; even cash itself. Secondly, the form can be *signed*. Both of these aspects can be problematic in the Internet context; and the Internet carries a further series of novel differences from more standard purchasing mechanisms.

In those standard mechanisms, there is usually no doubt that the order form will be received by the vendor. While most organisations stipulate that 'proof of post is not proof of receipt', the expectation is usually that the posted order will not go astray or be somehow damaged in transit. In the case of face-to-face and even telephone orders this is also a valid assumption. In the case of orders transmitted by computer, however, there is always the risk that the one or more computers in the transmission path might fail, thereby preventing the order from reaching its destination. Alternatively, a computer connection might fail during the process of receiving the order; or in the process of acknowledging or even fulfilling the order.

In the case of the established EDI and banking networks described above, the whole process of ordering and acknowledging an order is taken to be an *atomic* whole; either the complete process succeeds, or it fails entirely. So-called 'Transaction Processing Monitors' ensure that the processes are performed in a reliable and consistent manner. In the Internet case, this atomic nature of the transaction is not guaranteed,[86] although the communication protocols do ensure that a transmission once started will be completed, allowing recovery in the event of intermediate computers failing. These protocols do not, however, guarantee that the transmission state will survive a failure on the part of the system that has *started* the file transfer.[87]

Methods of payment

Taking first the question of payment, many vendors currently expect the purchaser simply to provide their credit card details, unless the purchaser is already an account holder. The establishment of an account with a particular vendor can be effected through 'real world' mechanisms and is therefore reasonably safe – although the problems of authority described below will still need to be resolved.

In the most general case, however, the purchaser needs to provide the vendor with payment details over the Internet. These can be written in the appropriate part of the electronic form exactly as with the mail order case and transmitted to the purchaser. This is the simplest situation but is of course fraught with peril. Most obviously, the file transmitted through the Internet is held on a number of intermediate machines. As with the case of simple e-mail described in an earlier section, the file can be read, the credit card number stolen and used elsewhere illegally. From the perspective of the credit card companies, ordering goods in this way is tantamount to writing one's credit card number on a globally visible noticeboard, allowing any and all passers-by to copy and use the number elsewhere.

A growing number of tools to address this issue have been made available, attempting to solve the problem through encryption. In the context of the Internet these tools and mechanisms are all currently at the status of proposals and experiments; no *officially-sanctioned* encryption for public Internet communication yet exists.

Either the whole order form, however, or just the credit card details can be encrypted in some fashion so as to ensure that the information can only be read by the intended recipient. This is an important element of the second point mentioned above, that of *signing* the form. This signature in paper documents is taken as indicating that the form is firstly genuine; and secondly, authorised. 'Genuine' means that the form has indeed been completed by the named individual; 'authorised' that the form would be accepted in a court of law or similar as representing that individual's intent – so-called 'repudiation' security[16].

Where the purchaser has an account with the vendor or with a trusted third party such as a bank or CompuServe this guarantee of authority is *still* required: someone else may have attempted to use the account holder's computer without permission.

In the domain of electronic order forms there are a series of concerns that must be addressed: firstly, the form may not be genuine – it may not have been issued by the individual from whom it purports to come; secondly, it may have been intercepted and read by some third party – to obtain for example the credit card number; thirdly, it may have been intercepted and altered – to give a third party's address for delivery of the goods for example; and finally, it must represent legally acceptable authority. This is of course a question of confidence as much as a question of technology.

There are four parties therefore to be considered in the question of Internet ordering and payment. Firstly, there is the purchaser; and secondly, the vendor. In completing and delivering the order, purchaser and vendor must feel confident that the communication between them is secure: that it is not intercepted, overheard or subject to third-party intervention. In the case of mail-order or telephone ordering this assumption is now commonplace; in other than the most extreme of cases one does not expect post to be intercepted or telephones to be 'tapped'.

Within the Internet, purchaser and vendor can effect such private 'point-to-point' communication through the means of sophisticated encryption tools. A growing number of these are becoming available and fall into two categories: in the first, the packets that are transmitted through the network are themselves encrypted; in the second, the initial file is first encrypted, and then the packets are transmitted. One is therefore a system-level encryption, the second a user-level method.

Two of the most popular Web browsers – Netscape and Mosaic – now have system-level encryption mechanisms built into them. Each has chosen to adopt a different program; indeed each uses a different *type* of program. Mosaic encrypts data before passing it to the lower level routines for translation into data packets – 'SHTTP'; Netscape encrypts those packets themselves – 'SSL'.[88] Where browsers are not used or where an additional level of encryption is required, such as in the exchange of e-mail, a package called 'PGP'[89] has become popular – although it should only be used outside of the US in those circumstances where it has been licensed. In addition to these, there are a growing number of other encryption tools; new releases of Windows 95 from Microsoft for example are currently planned to include support for generic encryption tools[90] for use over the Internet along with their *Explorer* Web browser.

Each of these encryption methods relies on the use of 'public keys' and the maintenance of private, secure keys by users.[91] Public keys are distributed or lodged with a trusted third party – such as the Internet Service Provider, a bank or credit card company perhaps. They provide two main advantages: firstly, the messages if intercepted cannot be read; secondly, both parties can be assured that the transmission has been sent from and received by the persons named. The public key encryption is used for the distribution of automatically generated, one-time keys that are exchanged between the two parties to the secure transaction.

The purchaser can therefore be assured that the order has not been intercepted or altered. The vendor can similarly be assured that the order has not been amended once transmitted. We said, however, that there were *four* parties involved in this transaction: the vendor and purchaser were two; the other two are the *payment* organisation – the bank or credit card company – and the *judicial authorities*. The payment organisation must be assured not only that the order has not been amended or accessed but that also it was initiated by the card or account holder from whom it purported to come.

So while the vendor and purchaser can be confident in an encryption tool, be it at system or application level, it is necessary also for the credit card company to be satisfied. The best way to achieve this is through the use of a mechanism that has been approved by the credit providers. Mastercard, VISA and American Express – the three largest such providers – have proposed just such a standard public key mechanism, called 'SET': Secure Electronic Transaction. Although the banks and others have not yet all agreed to follow in the adoption of such a standard, it can be assumed that they will do so in due course, or propose a superior mechanism in their turn. Moreover, this standard must be agreed on a world-wide basis for the full advantages of secure Internet transactions to be felt. Despite this progress, however, advice to credit card holders from the companies themselves is at best superficial, at worst absent; at the time of writing, leaflets from credit card companies and banks that include information about credit card security do not for example even *mention* the Internet.[92]

Assuming that the vendor and purchaser are using an encryption technique endorsed by the credit card company, the final assurance necessary is that the order was issued by the holder of the credit card itself. This is relatively straightforward to achieve. In the simplest case it is only necessary for the company to maintain a record of individual cardholder's public key – a 'certificate' – along with the other cardholder details. The private key – in effect, equivalent to the current PIN numbers we all have to remember – remains exclusively private to the individual. Payment can then be guaranteed by the credit card company where the stored public key of the named individual can be used to decrypt the order details – which could only have been generated by the holder of the private key – and where address and other details are consistent.

Once credit card companies, vendors and purchasers have been satisfied of the reliability of the encrypted transmissions it is necessary also for the judicial authorities to be similarly reassured. This is to ensure that in the event of a dispute between any of the other three – say, a purchaser disclaims responsibility for an order which is, as far as the vendor and credit card company are concerned, apparently valid – then the police, lawyers, judge and juries must have a legal position from which to proceed. If a standard mechanism has been agreed and implemented broadly – certainly within the UK and ideally more widely – then this legal position can be established far more easily.[93]

The Netscape, Mosaic, SET or other mechanisms[94] *may* emerge as acceptable, international standards; they are being used in practice at present but have not yet gained official, international acceptance. Insofar as they might become *de facto* rather than *de jure* standards, they follow the same path as the transmission mechanisms themselves used within the Internet; these gained practical acceptance many years before the official standards committees gave their blessings – to a much less successful alternative, as it happened. In the case of encryption, however, this acceptance is likely to be much easier; firstly, there is a strong drive to gain this acceptance so as to allow the Internet's commercial exploitation; and secondly, although the programs themselves are not accredited the basic algorithms (RSA and DES, for example) on which each one is built have been.

So far this discussion has been on the basis of credit card payment. In 'real world' purchasing it is also possible to pay for goods through a *debit* mechanism: a cheque or debit card payment against a bank account or similar. An identical encryption and transmission routine would address this requirement with debit card numbers in place of the credit card. However, it will be similarly necessary for standard mechanisms to be determined and agreed upon; for simplicity it would be better if these mechanisms were the same as those used by the credit card companies and by all other payment organisations.

The final type of real-world payment is that of physical cash, which has interesting potential in the Internet context. So-called 'Smart Cards' have been used to store a digital encoding of money. That is, an encoding of the money *itself* rather than of a reference to a stored credit bank account or credit provision service. In return for a payment of cash – transferred from an account, say – a digital record of the quantity of cash is stored in memory chips embedded within a credit card-size piece of plastic. This record, protected by a range of security software can then act as a 'digital wallet' allowing individuals to purchase goods at shops equipped with devices to read and transfer the digital 'coins' from a card to a till or other card.

Within the card an encoding protocol is used to store a record of the cash and a similar protocol is used to support transmission of that record between cards. Digital cash is analogous to real world cash: it is anonymous. Notes and coins do not maintain a record of whose wallet or purse they lie within or have passed through since having been issued by the central banks. Digital cash is similar; once issued onto a digital wallet the cash can be transferred freely and without reference to a third party. Unlike credit or debit payments, therefore, digital cash is both mobile and untraceable. In particular, the digital cash could be mobile within the Internet using the encoding and transmission protocol not between card and till but between a PC-connected device and similar mechanism at a vendor's site.

This would complete the picture of Internet-supported ordering of goods, allowing payment of the goods to be direct and immediate; it would therefore remove the 'authorisation' aspect since no third party payment would be involved, but not the worries of order form alteration in transit. It has, however, significantly wider, regulatory and economic implications that will be addressed in Chapters 4 and 5.

The Internet can therefore support mechanisms for advertising, ordering and paying for goods. In the description above it has been assumed that the purchaser pays for the goods at the time of ordering; of course in some circumstances payment is not on order but on receipt of the goods – or rather of an invoice. This invoice can be similarly distributed over the Internet and payment is exactly as in the cases outlined above.

DISTRIBUTING GOODS OVER THE INTERNET

There is, in principle at least, no reason why any and all different types of goods should not be marketed and traded over the Internet. In practical terms, however, as with other forms of distance and catalogue selling, certain goods and services are not suitable for such trading. This is not to say that the companies involved in any types of trade cannot profitably use the Internet to support their marketing or advertising activity but rather that some goods are not suited for *selling* in that domain. Personal services – such as hairdressing, chiropody or so forth – might be advertised over the Internet but the transaction itself would not be supported. Nor would such services – relying on proximity to the purchaser – be of particular interest in the broad, global context of the Internet.

Those goods which can be bought and distributed from some central location to a purchaser will, however, find a ready market in the Internet. There are three categories of such trade and distribution that can be considered:

1. Goods that are distributed through some other, 'real-world' medium to the purchaser.
2. Goods that are distributed wholly over the Internet.
3. Goods that are distributed partially via the Internet and partially through some real-world mechanism.

In the first category, while the advertising, ordering and perhaps also the payment for the goods is effected over the Internet the purchased goods are then distributed by some other means; this is the mechanism used by traders within the CompuServe shopping model. This might be parcel post, distribution from a local shop or collection from some local point. Clothes, tools, equipment and so forth bought by mail order are the exact analogy with this Internet example. These are goods that cannot wholly or partially be transformed into an electronic, digital form for transmission – pending the invention of a 'Star Trek' matter converter! The distribution aspect is therefore in this case not of great interest in the Internet context, although some couriers have implemented Internet gimmicks, such as DHL's 'Package Tracking', to allow customers to monitor the progress of their parcels around the world.

In the second case, however, the Internet is used to effect the complete distribution. Certain goods are digital in nature or can easily be transformed: videos, software, music or books would all come within this category. Once the order and payment have been processed these goods can be transmitted in an encoded, compressed and error-free format to the purchaser's PC or local system. As with the ordering and payment case described above it is necessary for the purchaser and vendor to be assured that the transmission is valid.

This has several aspects: firstly, the purchaser must be confident that the vendor has *transmitted* the goods; secondly, the vendor must be confident that the goods are destined to the appropriate *address*; thirdly, vendor and purchaser must be confident that the goods are not *intercepted* or *garbled* in the process of transmission; and fourthly, the vendor must be assured that the goods have been *received* by the purchaser.

In standard mail order transactions these stages are entrusted to the Post Office or courier mechanisms: the courier signs a receipt acknowledging collection of the parcel from the vendor and committing to its delivery; the purchaser signs a receipt to acknowledge delivery of the parcel at his home or office. In the Internet case these stages are handled by the software within the intermediate hosts through which the digital 'parcel' must pass. As with the case of the order therefore it is necessary to ensure that the digital delivery is not intercepted by any of the intermediate stages.

Unlike physical goods, digital goods can be copied – precisely and exactly – at any stage of the transmission. Continuing the example from the earlier section of ordering a music CD, the content of this recording could be transmitted to the purchaser over the Internet rather than delivered in the form of a physical disk plus packaging. This is a file transmitted between hosts within the Internet and intended for the purchaser. An intermediate host could therefore simply take a copy of that file: they have then a copy of the CD contents without having paid for or ordered the goods. Moreover, this copy is every bit as good as the 'correct' copy and can in turn be used as a 'master' from which other copies can be created.

To avoid this problem, as with the ordering case the goods can be encrypted using the public key mechanism mentioned above. In this situation only the intended recipient – the purchaser – is able to decrypt and hence *receive* the goods.

This encryption mechanism could ensure and guarantee reliable transmission of the file to the purchaser. The vendor could then be confident that the goods concerned have not been illegally copied – ie, stolen – by some intermediate party. In addition to this, clever encoding and encrypting can also provide a number of other features – for example, limiting the number of accesses allowed to a particular file or limiting the time period over which the file can be used.[95]

This is a particular advantage when the file represents digital goods loaned from a library or a computer program available on trial. Alternatively, it can support the sale of 'single-shot' elements of binary data, such as the sale – at a very low cost – of one play of one track from a CD chosen from a catalogue. Even if the purchaser makes a copy of the file, the encryption techniques prevent its re-use without the purchase of an additional key. Chapter 5 discusses this aspect in more detail in the context of protecting copyrights.

Unlike the case of the order and payment forms, however, there are some further difficulties associated with the transmission of digitised goods, most obviously the size of the file within which the goods are transmitted. To understand why this might be a matter of concern it is necessary to understand a little about the transmission mechanisms employed within the Internet. A file might contain the text of an e-mail message or it might contain software or data; to the hosts and networks that make up the Internet this distinction is broadly irrelevant: the file is considered to be simply a collection of characters that may or may not be interpretable by the receiving software. To transmit the file it is subdivided into the appropriate number of equal-sized units, referred to as 'packets'. Along with part or all of the file to be transmitted the packet contains an address of the machine and user to which the information is destined.

Depending upon the size of the original file it may take only one packet to encode it or it may take very many. One single sentence of characters would possibly fit within a single packet; a file such as the text of this book would require several hundred. Each packet of the file is numbered in sequential order and is transmitted in sequence from the vendor's host machine. This host may be directly connected to a set of – perhaps several hundred – other similar hosts. Each of these is running system software to receive and forward the packets transmitted to it, allowing those packets to flow through the Internet gradually coming closer and closer to the target machine. At each stage, however, the neighbouring hosts can be expected to have to handle packets from very many other transmitted files. These packets cannot be processed instantly; they must therefore be placed within a queue and processed in turn. The length of this queue will vary from machine to machine depending upon the amount of work the host must handle at any one time.

A host connected to a set of neighbours is kept informed of the length of processing queues on each of them. At any point in time therefore it has a picture of which neighbours are lightly loaded and which are working heavily. The packets of the files will be transmitted normally to the neighbour which is most lightly loaded. Because of this feature distinct packets from a large file can be expected to flow through the Internet along individual and quite different routes, arriving at the target machine in a jumbled order. At the receiving system therefore the sequence number on the packets must be interpreted so as to reassemble the original file – a process that cannot complete until each and every one of these packets has been received.

A second characteristic of the Internet is important here. Each individual host and constituent network is owned and managed independently of any other and while the operators of those networks have agreed to cooperate in transmitting packets between themselves there is no commitment to quality in that agreement. There is therefore no assurance of how long this may take: seconds, hours or even days. The transmission of several hundred thousand packets might therefore take a very long time, particularly if some of the packets inadvertently travel through heavily loaded or particularly slow parts of the network.

For small files such as the encrypted order form this transmission characteristic is seldom relevant: individual packets usually flow very quickly from point to point and there are no or only a few subsequent packets to be waited for. With larger files this becomes increasingly important, leading to very long delays in the transmission of large quantities of data. Where the purchaser is connected to the Internet by means of reliable channels this might not be a concern; but where the connection is via slow, unreliable and possibly expensive telephone lines this can cause difficulties. Connections to the host computer may be 'noisy', having the effect of scrambling parts of the transmission; or the connection may be lost during the transmission.

There are therefore two important aspects for consideration: firstly, the file may take a long time to be transmitted to the local PC, with a corresponding expense; and secondly, the file may not be transmitted accurately. To address these issues the Internet hosts use a variety of encoding mechanisms over and above the encryption example described above. Firstly, the file can be 'compressed' allowing a reduction in size of the file of anything from between 90 per cent to 5 per cent.[96] This allows much smaller files – and hence fewer packets – to need transmission. Secondly, clever downloading software can allow the transmission process to recover and continue from such problems caused by noisy lines – but it may still take a long time. Transmission times of around 50 minutes for a compressed file containing a computer game for example are typical, and probably represent the maximum period acceptable.

For very large files, the problems of slow and expensive connections will continue to dog the distribution of digital goods over the Internet. With no overall global authority to regulate service provision within the Internet, vendors and purchasers depending upon Internet transmission of goods are relying on a medium that comes with no guarantee of service level. Parcel post or delivery by couriers comes with a guarantee and agreed penalty clauses: overnight delivery means just that or the repayment of fees. Within the Internet individual networks do not provide such repayments or assurance of delivery. Technological developments by constituent network operators will improve the transmission performance but not in a guaranteed and reliable way; only global regulation or pan-Internet service levels can achieve this, and these are very unlikely in practice.

Transmission of goods over the Internet, while currently slow, is a practical alternative to real-world, physical distribution. There is in principle absolutely no reason why compressed files of CDs, videos, software and books cannot be downloaded from vendor's host machines to the purchaser's local system, other than the connection cost and time associated with such delivery. This is of course assuming that the encryption mechanisms described above are employed so as to protect the goods.

The final category of distribution types described above is an attempt to balance the benefits of Internet distribution against the currently high downloading costs. In this type of distribution both Internet and other distribution mechanisms are used. This can be achieved in a number of ways. As an example, consider the distribution of a complex and expensive computer game.

One mechanism would be to make a simplified version of the game available free of charge on the Internet and invite interested parties to download and sample the game – perhaps requiring 30 to 40 minutes of transmission time. Those who enjoy it and want to see more – further episodes of an adventure game perhaps – can then buy the complete software via Internet-transmitted orders for example and have a CD-ROM delivered to them through standard postal services.

Alternatively, the simplified version and the complete program could be distributed free of charge by means of magazines or even junk mail targeted at households known to have multi-media capable PCs. The simplified version could be readily available, with the complete program 'locked' in some way. Those who want to order and pay for the full game could do so over the Internet and in turn receive not a huge file but rather the key with which to unlock the other aspects of the CD.[97]

Both of these mechanisms use the Internet to its advantage but rely on external solutions to effect the distribution of large quantities of data by means of CD-ROMs or similar. Related techniques can allow free use of complete programs but for a limited period of time; thereafter, enabling keys must be ordered and downloaded to allow continued use of the software.

These techniques are necessary only because of the current limitations in the speed of downloading large files from the Internet. As this improves – and it is expected so to do as individual networks become increasingly dominated by fibre-optic technology and other similar higher capacity media – then the hybrid distribution can be expected to become less prevalent. Of course once the file containing the digital goods has been received and decrypted it must then be accessible to the purchaser. In the case of software – applications and computer games – this is very straightforward: the goods are already resident where they are required. In the case of videos or music this is not the case and the file must be transferred to the appropriate device – or more integrated PC/home entertainment units marketed to the Internet-connected consumers.

Services via the Internet

In this section we have chosen to concentrate on the distribution of goods over the Internet. In addition to these of course it is possible to provide *services* by means of the Internet. Estate agents for example can use the Internet to market and sell houses – perhaps even including a virtual 'tour' of the property; travel agents can book seats[98] and hotels – and perhaps also provide virtual tours of destination resorts; lawyers and solicitors can provide advice by means of the Internet; accountants can use the technology to support communication with their clients and with the authorities.

Banks can extend their services from high street and telephone to 'Cyberspace', although security worries have made banks – particularly in the UK – reluctant to embrace this potential.[99] And many alliances have been formed between telecommunications and entertainment providers to bring the *content* of video on demand, orchestral works, great pictures, etc, into the Internet domain; Bill Gates for example has formed a separate company, Corbis, to buy the rights to the on-line versions of many of the world's greatest art treasurers.

In addition to these services there has been a growing interest in gambling over the Internet. Bookies in one country – say, the UK – receive and process bets on sporting events or similar in other countries – say, Japan. In the case of Japan and the UK, there is a significant level of difference between the two countries' approach to gambling, allowing UK-based companies to offer such services from a 'haven' of sorts. In Chapter 5, we will look at this issue of havens more closely.

VIRTUAL COMPANIES

The aspects described in this chapter create a growing fervour for the *Internet company*. Pushed by the Department of Trade and Industry in the UK and the White House in the US, for example, it has raised the prospects of supporting trading patterns on a global, high-technology basis. All companies, government departments, even charities are receiving enthusiastic, messianic messages about the benefits and opportunities of the new medium – this despite the concerns outlined in previous sections. There is no doubt that the growth of the 'virtual company' is likely – perhaps even unstoppable. There are several aspects that this might take:

- companies can *trade* within the Internet;
- the Internet can be used to support post-sales *customer service*;
- companies can use the Internet to communicate and *purchase goods* from their own suppliers;
- companies can use the Internet to support their *own workforce*; and
- companies can access their *internal information sources* and services by means of Internet-tools.

Before looking at these aspects, we will first consider with whom those virtual companies might trade and interact.

While the Internet can, as we have discussed, support marketing, trading and distribution of goods and services, it is important to consider the types of consumers and suppliers it can reach. There are two aspects to this: those that are currently available, and those that can be expected to emerge over time. At present, although a great many commercial concerns are already – or have plans to effect – marketing via the Internet, only a very small number have implemented full shopping and distribution services. Similarly, only a small percentage of consumers buy goods via the Internet.[100] In part this is influenced by concerns over the security of such transactions; in part by the limited numbers of people currently able to access the Internet from home; and in part by the restricted types of goods made available today.

The present numbers of consumers and suppliers on the Internet are therefore stunted; perhaps at the level found in the mail-order business when initial attempts began. The growth projections for the Internet's use by individuals – prompted as much by communication and information access as by potential trading facilities – is very well established: the Internet's use will grow very dramatically through the following decade. As we discussed in Chapter 1, projections of half of every UK or US household having Internet access directly or indirectly early in the 21st century are not overly ambitious. These users will find a means to exchange messages rapidly; access to a multitude of discussion forums; and access to a wealth of information sources, games and reference texts. They will also find the marketing and advertising material distributed by the companies.

Distribution of goods wholly through the medium of the Internet is dependent upon increases in the transmission speed and quality of the constituent networks. Some of these will definitely improve; others might not. Fully effective distribution mechanisms are therefore not currently assured. The reliable ordering and purchasing of goods and services, however, is dependent upon growing consumer and supplier *confidence* in the technology currently being made available.

When first introduced, credit cards were the subject of consumer concerns: would the waiter use the card to order goods for himself; was the carbon from the payment slip likely to be recovered from the shop's garbage; would the credit card company honour an unsigned, telephone order? With growing familiarity we have come to take as natural the use of telephone credit orders for such things as flowers; and a range of additional security measures have removed many of our other concerns. Of course credit card fraud exists; indeed, it is a serious worry.[101] But it is *understood*: by the credit card companies; by the police and judicial authorities; and by the consumers and suppliers themselves. Provided we use the credit card in an 'acceptable' manner we can be confident that legitimate purchases will be honoured, illegal ones prosecuted and our liability limited to reasonable levels.

A similar process will occur in the context of Internet trade. Service and Internet-software providers now make a wide range of facilities available to support such shopping. As discussed above, the credit card companies themselves are gradually growing in awareness of this issue. Because of these advances, and with a growth in supporting services, increasing interest on the part of suppliers and a growing population of Internet users – particularly high-earning professionals – one can confidently expect Internet shopping to increase in importance from the current low levels of involvement. Who are these shoppers and from whom will they buy?

In the case of both shoppers and suppliers one of the most interesting characteristics in the Internet context is the global nature of
the medium. The shoppers and suppliers can be in different continents: the medium supports the facility for a transaction to be
performed between Australia and the UK. And this is without regard
to the time of day, or day of the week: a virtual shop on the Internet
is able to trade on a continuous, transnational basis.[102]

In the case of the individual shoppers, there are further characteristics that are of importance – primarily, that the shoppers are
users of PC technology; they are currently therefore likely to be in
the high earning, professional bracket. There is an assumption,
however, that use of the PC – or equivalent – will be an important
aspect of working and social lives through the early part of the next
century. Indeed, some commentators have likened this to the growth
in importance of cars; non-drivers are at a significant disadvantage,
certainly within the US and increasingly within the UK and elsewhere. Access to, and familiarity with PC technology is expected to
become a central part of many jobs.

Of course, this might sound somewhat worrying to those who are
not computer literate; perhaps that should be so. After all, while
one can currently claim – in some cases proudly – a degree of
computer-illiteracy without fear of stigma, one would not expect
similarly to claim an inability to read, drive, use the TV or telephone. But yet in the world we can see developing over the next
decade – and certainly thereafter through the early 21st century –
computer technology will become a central part of one's world.
Telephones are becoming ever more sophisticated, as are televisions;
even where individuals do not have home computers almost all
now have these basic utilities.[103] Even in the unlikely event that
the Internet itself somehow implodes (this is not impossible as we
shall see later) then information services via TV and telephone that
are already well established, will continue and grow in sophistication.

To return to the thread of the discussion. Because of this growth
in computer use – perhaps even dependency – the medium of the
Internet and the potential market for sale of goods will grow dramatically to cover more social classes, throughout the world. Internet
traders can therefore reach a very wide, disparate collection of

shoppers; and those shoppers in turn are provided with access to a global range of shops.

This, as we have discussed above, gives shoppers advantages in terms of collecting price and supply details from a range of potential vendors. Armed with relatively comprehensive data, shoppers can then exploit the shopping medium directly or use the data to make more informed choices. How will these shops work?

The cyberstore

The mechanics of supporting Internet trade have been described in the preceding sections. These processes allow companies to communicate and trade with consumers throughout the world using an electronic shop of some description as their 'point of presence'. In the 'Cyberspace' world this presence is effected by means of Web pages giving details of the company, its goods or services and a means of communicating with the organisation.

In many cases this is simply an additional aspect to an existing physical presence; the company may have a series of high street shops and an Internet shop to service those consumers available through that medium. In the case of, say, a chain of music megastores, the company might have shops throughout the UK. Each contains a comprehensive sample of the CDs, videos and software that the company offers, although larger shops – 'megastores' – are better stocked than their smaller cousins. The Internet version – which we shall call a 'Cyberstore' – can have the *complete* range available. Moreover, this can be represented as a virtual reality implementation of the largest, flagship megastore. Consumers can then move through the cyberstore using the mouse or keyboard to direct their search. Shelves full of goods can be displayed and the shopper can select and sample goods – perhaps simply by 'clicking' on the image of the CD.

As the Internet speed improves these goods can be bought and paid for over the Internet and then downloaded to the local system. The consumer has browsed, chosen, bought and collected the goods from a cyberstore without leaving his or her home. This has a number of implications: the shopper has not travelled to the shopping centre using public or private transport; and one less shopper has visited the local megastore. Moreover, the shopper, in electing not to visit the shopping centre has not added directly to the shopping centre's economy: no petrol was bought and burned; no car parking space was paid for; no food or drink was purchased from the cafeterias; no impulse purchase was made from nearby shops.

Should more and more people elect to shop in this manner at least some of the music chain's stores might find a reduction in the number of shoppers visiting local branches in favour of the more comprehensive cyberstore. And since the cyberstore is cheaper to run – there are no staff costs, office space, cleaning bills, maintenance in terms of heating and lighting, no requirement to maintain restocking processes, etc – it would not be unexpected for the company to want to move wholly into this Cyberspace.

A single Internet-based cyberstore could therefore potentially serve a much wider range of consumers than a chain of smaller, less well-stocked shops in the UK towns and cities. Moreover, the cyberstore is visible on a global, perpetual basis, allowing trade around the world. Other than the costs of maintaining the host systems and installing new CDs, videos and software as they are released, the cyberstore would be much cheaper to run. The chain of shops could therefore become a 'virtual company'. In so doing it would have reduced its requirement for staff, premises and the range of supporting services it was previously using.

In the case of music, videos and software, this is a relatively obvious series of steps that might be taken. The process can apply equally well, however, to a vast range of other concerns. In an earlier section we discussed the case of a car manufacturer able to use Web pages to provide a series of more detailed aspects of the organisation and of the goods offered, and able to finely judge the degree and type of interest shown by each passer-by.

Armed with this information, the manufacturers can target that potential purchaser in a very precise manner. Most particularly, the organisation doesn't need to wait for the prospect to visit one of their showrooms; instead a more direct approach can be made. Moreover, the wealth of other information available to the manufacturer and sourced via the Internet could give them precise details of the prospect's current car – its age, mechanical condition and any recent problems; they could learn whether the prospect has recently had a new baby, or inherited some money – subject only to the restrictions of the Data Protection Act. An offer can be presented to the prospect to take a test drive in the car of interest, secure in the knowledge that the prospect is in the market for a car and knowing exactly what *type* of car would suit the prospect and their circumstances most exactly.

Again, the company has moved a significant part of its operation into the domain of the Internet, in this case at the expense of a local garage or dealership for the manufacturer concerned.

In both of these situations the companies concerned would undoubtedly find benefits in such a virtual status. However, it is important to recognise that neither situation is likely in practice.

Agreements between car manufacturers, and local dealers would restrict such encouragement for obvious competitive trading mechanisms, and a nationwide chain of shops employing many hundreds of staff would find great difficulty in simply withdrawing from the 'real world' in this manner. That having been said, virtual status does allow such organisations to trade internationally; conversely, it allows other organisations – operating from other countries – to compete with *them*.

Virtual companies – that is, *wholly* removed from real-world presence – are more likely to occur therefore in the context of small start-up operations seeking to minimise establishment costs, or in smaller national companies wishing to start to trade internationally – again, with low costs. In many ways this is one of the most worrying aspects in the context of virtual companies. Established, well-run and successful high-street or big name shops will continue to operate within the real world, perhaps augmenting their service through cyberstores. Even where such concerns operate transnationally there would be an expectation that effective book-keeping and maintenance of records will continue and that the organisations will retain a 'real-world' presence in addition to their Internet point-of-presence. Newer organisations, however, tempted by the ease with which they can compete with those big names in Cyberspace will then move into this sphere, potentially with smaller numbers of staff and much less efficient accounting, auditing and record keeping. Moreover, these newcomers can potentially operate from 'havens' that are inadequately regulated in comparison with the UK, US and elsewhere.[104]

In this context, we have considered organisations that are providing goods to private consumers: virtual shops. Other types of companies can also move into a virtual domain, taking advantage of the global aspect to provide services. An obvious case might be an estate agent, providing information on homes overseas; or an employment agency holding and making available CVs.[105] Such services are not geographically limited and would therefore make sense in the Internet context, with the organisations needing no – or very limited – 'footprints' in the real world.

Customer service

In addition to the trading of goods and services from virtual companies it is also possible to effect customer service functions via the Internet. In this case, while the whole company need not be virtual in nature the department concerned may be.

The most obvious and apparent aspects of customer service are *communication*: listening to and understanding complaints, problems or basic information from consumers and purchasers; collecting relevant response material from internal sources; and then providing that assistance, guidance or instruction to the outside world. Most organisations provide some form of customer service function, from the most basic aspect of answering telephone or written queries to complex, central help desks. The Internet presents an alternative mechanism for providing such assistance.

More than this, the information sources that the customer service staff draw upon can also be made available directly to customers. Using the Web browsers or specialist tools, users can search through databases and files of hints, work-arounds or other sources of customer service advice.

At the most basic level, the Internet can provide a means for exchanging communication between purchaser and trader: e-mail of correspondence; or return of faulty software, videos, etc where those have been distributed through the Internet mechanisms. At a deeper level, however, the Internet presents broader potential for the *location* of customer service functions. The telephone has of course

why on earth would you want to
do this - just quote the version Number

already brought such changes: directory enquiries serviced out of Scotland; centralised enquiry desks for all calls to help lines; even automatic call routing to cheaper operatives overseas. The Internet presents scope to extend this further still, moving to virtual departments with staff working from home, telecottages – even for other companies.

This touches then on the third category: communication with suppliers. Such electronic communication – EDI, for example – has been a feature of manufacturer-supplier relationships for many years and has gained in popularity, effectiveness and applicability. From Japanese car manufacturers, through American computer companies to British engineers, all have learnt to exploit and benefit from the advantages of closer working with suppliers, supported by IT and communication facilities.

Virtual offices and virtual office *blocks* present further opportunities for easy, intuitive Internet communication with a much wider range of organisations of all sizes and locations, entirely within the abstract Cyberspace. In this context, the physical location of the supplier is irrelevant providing that the relationship between supplier and contractor is effective. Here, however, it is important to recognise that the consumer protection mechanisms applicable to the Internet – discussed in Chapter 5 – apply to *consumers*, not to the purchasers of contracted services or goods; in this last case, it is necessary for the contractual arrangements to be well established and clear, particularly where the companies concerned are in different countries.

Virtual suppliers – particularly of services which can be delivered over the Internet such as programming, writing, translating and so forth – will be at a great advantage in the coming years. The scope for easily managing the relationships through such devices as virtual offices, video phones and global e-mail will accelerate the use of the services – and in turn the use of the Internet itself. Should the Internet's use by *consumers* falter, for whatever reason, the continued use by companies in relationship with their suppliers can be expected to continue undiminished.

In a similar way the Internet can assist in supporting a company's *own* workforce, where they work remotely from the company concerned. This can include those who work away from a fixed office on an occasional basis, to those who always work remotely – perhaps even in different countries. Many organisations have been tempted by this potential, seeking to move certain functions and jobs away from central offices, thus allowing freedom to the workers.

There are problems, as with any such change: uncertainty over management methods; difficulties in monitoring and motivating remote employees; the pollution of domestic and work times. In many cases this represents the relative novelty of this working arrangement for most people. And of course the companies themselves are often at fault – looking at what *jobs* could usefully be performed from home rather than at which *workers* could work from home. Domestic situation, worker personality and job-type should *all* be considered as key in making home or teleworking a successful part of an organisation [29] – before the scope for Internet assistance in the process is assessed.

The Intranet

In many ways the aspects discussed above are obvious developments from the existing Internet status: it can support most of a company's functions that are externally facing simply because it is itself a communication medium and therefore externally facing in its turn. Communication with consumers, suppliers and workforce are therefore facilities that are ideally suited to such a global and pervasive mechanism. The final category mentioned above, however, is slightly more surprising. In this, *internal* functions are increasingly supported by Internet mechanisms. In practice of course such a development should not be unexpected; many analysts believe in fact that the true success for the Internet will come from such internal use rather than by home shoppers and the like.[106]

In the case where a company communicates with its customers through the Internet, perhaps advertising and receiving orders through the medium, it is necessary for the advertising to be issued from, and the orders to be received into an internal information management system. Marketing and product development must communicate with one another, and product development must undertake an element of research activity in the construction of new products. And orders received into the organisation must be propagated to the order fulfilment departments, with relevant statistics provided in turn to the marketing function. Internal and external worlds therefore communicate and cooperate in a variety of ways, assisted in part by the Internet.

If external communication therefore is effected by the Internet – with simple distribution, correspondence and general communication mechanisms – the next step is to use the Internet internally: an '*Intranet*'.[107] To provide security for the internal processes and information stores a so-called 'fire-wall' system[108] is required, ensuring that unauthorised access to internal machines is not possible. Intranets then use the externally available software, processes and protocols to manage the internal e-mail requirements and the information hand-offs and analyses.

This has advantages and disadvantages. The Internet software is relatively inexpensive. Indeed, a lot of the programs are offered free of charge or are distributed freely in their early state for testing and assessment by the broader Internet community. This, for example, was the case with the early versions of several popular Internet browsers such as Netscape and even of the Web server software itself. In addition, the programs are often intuitive, easily learnt and used; moreover, where the company has Internet connections the programs are probably already in use by those employees accessing the Internet directly. Internal information sources can therefore be structured as Web pages accessed by Internet browsers; e-mail, newsgroups and facilities for distributing files around an organisation can all prove of value.

Set against this, however, is the almost perpetual state of flux within the Internet. The global nature of the Internet, its background in academic and research organisations and the types of users to whom it still plays host, ensures that a rich variety of software emerges naturally within the network. Often for no commercial gain widespread collections of enthusiasts develop and disseminate programs. These might be games or essentially trivial; or they might be new and exciting forms of Web browser. Because collections of enthusiasts can span the globe, cooperative work on these programs can occur on a rapid, 24-hour basis. Unlike the more stable development programmes of established software manufacturers, the Internet supports software 'hot-housing' – of programs that may emerge and gain in popularity before essential support, maintenance or guarantees of quality can be considered.

This feature means that – unlike the case with those established software vendors – Internet 'product development timetables' are obscure; indeed, such timetables do not exist. Instead programs can emerge almost spontaneously, allowing IT staff in the world at large little or no warning. As an example, the first Web browser was Mosaic – that was used and appreciated by a wide audience. Within a short period – much less than a year – an alternative, Netscape Navigator, appeared and in turn gained popularity, offering facilities not found within Mosaic.[109] Many users turned from Mosaic to Netscape. What might emerge next?

Development plans for Netscape itself are known – the company publicises these details exactly as does IBM or Microsoft – and in fact they have their *own* Enterprise intranet strategy, working with organisations such as Informix. But the next great application may well emerge from a 'garage' somewhere, eclipsing these programs.[110] IT managers prefer the absence of surprises – and prefer to be able to control their users. This allows them to establish stable operating platforms whose characteristics are well known. A justification for using Internet applications internally, however, is that they are the *same* as the external applications; if new and exciting applications emerge outside their doors the IT managers will be faced with users demanding access to *those* in preference to the 'old-fashioned' software of only a few months before.

This may not be a problem. IT managers and staff currently have to plan for the programmed upgrading of all their software. Adopting Internet software in favour of, say, Microsoft or Lotus suites simply means accepting a different – possible obscure – upgrade programme. Moreover, that upgrading process is likely to be driven *by* users rather than *for* the users, as they demand access to the newest application. In the context of this book, however, this must be accepted as a cultural change taken on the part of the IT management of those organisations – and there are an increasing number – who have chosen to look to the Internet for their *internal* support. And of course Microsoft themselves, and others, such as IBM with Lotus Notes, are turning to the Internet, developing and delivering their *own* solution sets.

INTERNET USE BY OTHER ORGANISATIONS

So far, this chapter has considered the use of the Internet to support *trading*. Communicating with customers, advertising and the process of paying for goods – all of these are features that must be handled effectively in the Internet context to allow such trading to be performed comprehensively. Once these mechanisms have been developed and exploited for trade, however, they can also be used by a variety of other, non-profit organisations. Indeed, the current state of the Internet already provides sufficient functionality to support much of this requirement.

Several types of non-profit organisation might be considered in this context, from central and local government, through to charitable and voluntary bodies and pressure groups with a set of specific concerns. In addition of course, the facilities can be used by terrorists, vandals, and organised crime. In the context of this section we will restrict the discussion to the *legitimate* use of the facilities; Chapter 5 considers the issues of illegal activities.

In the first case, both central and local government have a similar set of concerns and activities. They must distribute and collect information from citizens; they must inform the public of their activities; they must provide their staff with access to their own and other information sources; and they must provide mechanisms for communicating with the staff, each other and other organisations. Almost all government organisations have made some attempt to exploit the Internet facilities.[111] In part this is not surprising: the popularity of the Internet is been driven to a degree by the enthusiasm and the rhetoric of central government in support of the Information Superhighway. All of the major parties have expressed support for these developments, although the practical aspects differ markedly between them. Politicians have gained e-mail addresses; press releases are made available over the Internet; and leaflets, brochures and publications are advertised or disseminated through these mechanisms. In the UK, Parliament itself has a series of Web pages to allow the public access to information about Bills under consideration and the introduction of various Acts.[112] Each of the major parties has a Web presence, and many individual MPs have begun to embrace the communication potential that it offers. A similar situation exists in the US and elsewhere.

Looking first at local government, the major initiatives in this sphere have been in supporting features such as self-help or discussion forums for the unemployed. Many councils have provided facilities to allow the disabled or the economically disadvantaged to gain access to IT; some councils have even gone further, using the Internet to furnish those individuals with training, counselling or merely the scope for extended discussion groups. These 'community-net' projects [24] in the UK and the US provide an important voice within the group – often for those who would not otherwise have access to or the encouragement to use such facilities. Supported by local government, local business and local academics or enthusiasts, the existence of such access mechanisms are vital if the Internet is to become more than simply a 'toy' for the professional worker.

In the case of central government, the major departments have also begun experiments although security worries remain a concern, most especially for those departments which hold personal information: in the UK, the Inland Revenue and the Department of Social Security in particular. These and other departments use the Internet currently for one primary purpose: the distribution of press releases and smaller publications to citizens, along with general information about the individual department's mission and basic processes. However, many are also moving towards a position of establishing an e-mail presence for their board members and senior staff – allowing, for example, communication between the department and those ministers who have these facilities already available.[113] In addition, this Internet presence would also allow the departmental staff to use the vast range of information available on the Internet in the course of their work; this will not, however, encompass private information or information that might be considered sensitive. This use of the Internet is supported by the CCTA – the UK government's own communication consultants – and HMSO. In itself, this is not an exciting exploitation of the technology; in fact even the press releases are only made available the *following* day rather than on the day of release. In the US, the equivalent departments are somewhat more advanced than their UK counterparts, with politicians' speeches, departmental objectives and relevant government publications all available.

As the security concerns relating to Internet use are alleviated, however, more radical application of Internet technology can be envisaged. In the context of trading on the Internet, purchasers must complete, authorise and transmit order forms to the traders. Moreover, as we discussed, these order forms must remain private and immune from intervening parties. In the case of the Inland Revenue for example, such facilities could be used for the completion of tax forms – although this is not currently envisaged as part of their established plans. Analogous mechanisms could be used by other departments: Internet communication with traders for VAT processing by HM Customs and Excise; Internet supported payments to DSS claimants – although as the department themselves admit, there is currently a significant gap between a typical DSS 'customer' and a typical Internet user. The Internet booths and similar facilities provided by local government initiatives might help to bridge this gap. In the case of taxation of small and medium-sized companies paying corporation tax and VAT, the Labour Party have in fact outlined proposals for using the Internet to support an 'Enterprise Zone' for such rapid and cheap communication with the local offices involved.

In all cases the Internet provides a direct, accessible and easy facility for the public to express their opinions to – or even of – the departments and their local offices. And the Internet facilities can then be used by those departments to support their own staff's communication and information retrieval requirements by the use of intranet systems – protected of course by stringent firewall and other security processes.

This description of Internet use has been UK-centric; of course, all of these aspects can be and are employed in the US and elsewhere. The IRS distributes vast quantities of advice to those completing tax returns; the US armed forces provide a wealth of interesting information about various units' history and activities; even the White House has a Web presence, publishing major speeches and publicising events.

In the case of charitable and voluntary organisations there are two key aspects:

1. communicating the *necessity* for assistance to a broad population; and
2. receiving that assistance or the payment of donations in turn.

The first challenge, however, of the Internet's use in this domain is
the requirement to pay for the Internet services. Richer, popular
charities may well have the money available to spend on such services
– in the same way that they can afford newspaper advertising space;
others might not. A growing communitarian spirit within the Internet
community has given rise to the community-nets mentioned above
and these give some facilities; in other cases company sponsorship
provides the vehicle for accessing the medium, giving further scope
for Internet advertising.

Assuming that the charity or voluntary concern can gain this
access, the Internet presents them with an exciting range of opportunities. Access to a wide, global population; scope to transmit
messages in a more complete manner; and an efficient payment mechanism. Of course this facility is not essentially different from that
of the newspaper advertisement case but the extent of the readership is potentially much wider. As Internet facilities develop it will
be possible to provide many more video or sound clips within Web
pages, giving the scope for very effective 'marketing' of a charity's
message.

This same is true in the final case, where the message is transmitted by a pressure group. In this situation the requirement is to
deliver a comprehensive message about a particular aspect of society,
life or an organisation. Greenpeace, for example, use many forms
of media to alert global citizens about global environmental concerns;
Amnesty International ensure that as many people as possible know
about infringements of human rights. In these and similar cases the
objective is akin to that of the charities: to gain membership and
thereby donations, subscriptions or contributions of assistance. More
direct pressure groups deliver petitions and information to government ministers or draw attention to detrimental road developments,
or declaim the transportation of live animals.

In all cases the Internet presents a powerful medium for their use.
In the context of newsgroups, however, the strident tone of many
was commented upon in the previous chapter; in the case of many

pressure groups this high emotional content is particularly obvious, often distracting from and therefore damaging the essential message that the pressure group would like to transmit.

SUMMARY

The spread of the Internet within companies, government and other organisations – together with a growing use by private consumers – leads to the exciting and challenging prospect of virtual companies. Marketing, selling and distributing goods and services wholly or partially within a non-physical realm, such organisations and consumers can be geographically quite remote, trading by means of digital credit, debit or cash transactions. The whole requires the support of a sophisticated, acceptable and authorised mechanism for encrypting and reliably transmitting the information relevant to the particular transaction.

As has been examined, there is little in the Internet that could not in practice be achieved by other, more mundane mechanisms. It has always been possible to buy goods from companies other than those most immediately local to a consumer; it has always been possible to take money out of the country; it has always been possible to work for foreign companies. The novel aspect to the Internet lies not in *what* it can support but rather in *who* is supported. Private consumers can buy on a transnational basis, perhaps unconsciously. Small, essentially local concerns can trade with states of whose legal and regulatory framework they are completely unaware.

It is this transnational and essentially 'other-worldly' aspect of Internet trade and communication that gives rise to the greatest of the Internet's very many impacts; that produces the 'Cybernation'. With an ability to effect communication amongst its 'citizens' and a marketplace within which trade can occur, the most fundamental aspects of the Cybernation are in place. This will then produce an Internet economy which will in turn have an impact upon the existing and established economies with which we have the most familiarity.

In following chapters we will consider these issues, looking first at the effect that Internet ubiquity could have on the economy of the various countries supporting the Internet.

4

ECONOMIC IMPACT

Over the centuries, the foundation upon which the world economies are built and interact has changed dramatically. From trading on the basis of cooperative barter on an individual or a nation-to-nation basis we have moved to a tokenised system [6]. Our coinage and notes were initially representative of real, physical objects denoting wealth: silver in the case of the UK – hence 'pound sterling' – and gold in the case of the US. 'I promise to pay the bearer on demand . . .' is a symbol of *confidence* in the reality backing beautifully decorated slips of paper.

As trade has been carried out on an increasingly global basis, however, this attachment to physical wealth has gradually weakened. Banks and others moving money between nations no longer need – in all but the most exceptional of circumstances – to move bullion; digital signals are transferred. Money – *wealth* – has been digitised: coins and banknotes are no longer abstract representations of physical objects; they are themselves a physical instance of an even more abstract representation of wealth – binary, electromagnetic signals. And information itself has come to be seen as property – associating value with stored data.

From atoms to bytes: the basis of our economy has changed. But to date the movement of wealth over computer networks has been the purview of the banks and of the various government authorities. Moreover, it has been very carefully regulated. The Internet, however, brings the potential to change this.

Changes in the way that people work and are paid for that work; changes in the way that companies carry out their activities; changes in the relationship between consumers and suppliers. The Internet brings the potential for a series of structural alterations in the mechanisms and processes that underpin the economies of the industrialised, western states. More, by changing the *way* in which trade, consumption and expenditure can be effected, the relationships between developed and developing economies will be impacted. Competition will move to a new basis, with the access and ability to exploit Internet potential becoming an increasingly important factor for countries and for individuals, giving rise to a whole new category of the economically disadvantaged.

The Internet allows companies of any size to carry out transactions and trade in goods entirely within the abstract 'Cyberspace' domain. As such, this trade is performed on a basis that is independent of geography; companies can therefore be trading on a transnational basis with the same ease as they trade on a local basis. In fact there might be no way for them of *knowing* that trade is local or transnational.

More than this the 'trade' can be carried out by individuals, buying or being paid over Internet connections to economies and nations with which we might or might not have treaties and agreements. An increasing ability to move credit or goods between countries across a medium that is difficult to monitor and regulate will lead to a series of impacts on the way that national economies are managed.

In this chapter, the economic implications of the developments described in Chapter 3 are examined. As more and more companies find and exploit the means of investing abroad and as organisations respond to a host of dynamics leading to smaller enterprises, an increasing amount of international trade will be performed by transnational small companies – perhaps even individual, sole traders. This will affect the mechanisms whereby a country's economy is monitored and the ability for nations accurately to judge levels of wealth and of purchasing power.

These effects will be felt most directly by the authorities in terms of the collection and management of taxation revenue from direct personal tax, indirect expenditure taxes and duties payable on imported goods. While the detailed issue of managing these aspects

– or of policing illegal activities – is postponed to the following chapter, this chapter examines the potential scale and qualitative impact of the activity.

In the final parts of this chapter the issue of digital cash – as distinct from credit – is considered, particularly the means by which digital cash can be moved throughout the world by individuals.

First, however, we will consider the *direct* impact of the Internet's economic aspects in terms of the cash it generates or consumes immediately.

THE ECONOMICS OF THE INTERNET

The Internet will, as we have seen, impact upon many areas of our lives; it will impact also on several aspects of the way the economy is managed and monitored. An area that must be considered, however, in the context of this impact centres on the question of the commercial aspects of the Internet itself. Big business – and rapidly growing small businesses – have chosen to concentrate resource, effort and investment in the Internet. There is money to be made and money to be spent in the establishment of Internet services, over and above the question of moving credit, orders and goods over the medium. A recent analysis for example gave a figure of £35m for the UK Internet market with a current growth rate of over 200 per cent per annum; analysts expect a market of nearly £1 billion in the UK alone by the turn of the century – and for this to be barely 6 per cent of the world-wide Internet market [21].

To understand the way in which this complicated Internet market operates we will first consider the way that the Internet itself works. At the most basic level, Internet traffic must flow along real-world, physical networks. These can be fibre-optic, copper cable, microwave or satellite transmissions. At this level of consideration the exact nature of the stream of bits flowing along the real connection is broadly speaking irrelevant.

In the UK, BT owns mile upon countless mile of these connections. But they no longer hold a monopoly position of the cables themselves. Energis run network connections along the countrywide national electric grid; cable TV operators own an increasingly complex network of fibre-optic cable with an unimaginably large bandwidth available to carry TV programmes, voice transmission and data; even the cellular telephone operators own a network of radio data transmission facilities. In the US, AT&T, Cable and Wireless, MCI *et al* all are in a similar position; as are France Télécom in France and Deutsche Telekom in Germany, etc. All these companies are in the position of owning the property rights to the basic tarmac surface of the Information Highway. In addition to these, there are the several 'backbone' networks of the Internet: the academic, research or government networks that run over cabling that is either their own or that is leased from the network owners mentioned above. This is the most fundamental level of the Internet, at which profit-earning companies exploit the requirement for the Internet traffic to flow along real-world connections alongside voice and other data transmissions.

In many cases, however, these basic-level connection providers are less interested in the Internet *per se* than in the provision of bandwidth to customers. BT, for example, *do* have an interest in providing Information Highway services – indeed, the Labour Party have made a deal with BT to that effect; that they will establish low cost, high bandwidth connections to schools, hospitals, etc,[114] in return for a lifting of restrictions on their activity should Labour come to power at the next election (1996 or early 1997). While BT would not want to lose out to the cable TV providers in this 'information/ entertainment' market, their primary interest is in *voice* traffic; this is their core business, as it is the core business of the several other telecommunications operators throughout the world.[115] Conversely, the cable companies – who are already important in the US and are growing rapidly in the UK – have a more general interest but it is in the provision of *their* services, rather than the general services of the Internet.

In the early years of the Internet the US government and academic concerns around the world drove the development and support of the Internet. As the NSF and others have pulled back from direct involvement this drive has passed to the commercial operators, with only the most distant of direction from government. In this sense, the commercialisation of the Internet – an anathema to the Internet 'old-timers' – is a vital necessity if the service is to continue and develop. It is for this reason – to which we will return in the next chapter – that the ability to regulate and to manage service levels within the Internet has become important.

While the telecommunications giants own the highway infrastructure itself, access to that highway – the 'on ramp' as it is often called – comes from the Internet Service Providers. These are the companies that make money by the explicit sale of Internet services, rather than by the more fundamental facilities of the switching and cables themselves. These ISPs fall into two tiers; the topmost level are the largest of the providers, who sell bandwidth on their range of leased lines to both multinational companies and to the lower tier of regional or smaller ISPs.

In the UK for example the majority[116] of the leased line capacity is bought from Unipalm PIPEX, the European market leader; much of the rest comes from EUnet. In 1994 to 1995 PIPEX's turnover was £17.7 million. In late 1995, it was acquired by the American ISP giant Uunet, whose turnover rose from $4 million in 1994 to £24 million in 1995 even without allowing for the inclusion of PIPEX's business. At this end of the Internet market high growth rates[117] and high profitability abound.

While PIPEX *does* offer a dial-up service for home users, its main market is a commercial one, providing Internet access services to companies. The domestic Internet direct dial-up market in the UK is lead by Demon Internet, although there are very many hundreds of other service providers of all sizes and types – from the small local service providers in particular regions, to more specialist, community services. At this end competition is fierce – and of the 2000 world-wide ISPs only the large ones can expect to survive as independent companies over the next few years. Demon themselves for example were valued at almost £27 million on their stock market flotation in 1995 and managed profits of £355,000 on a 1995 turnover of £2.76 million. But their figures – including a monthly growth averaging 8 per cent, comparing very favourably with PIPEX's – are in marked contrast to the majority of other access providers who show little or no profit; one of the largest US ISPs is Netcom, for example, who showed a loss in 1995 on a turnover of $52 million.

For the majority of home users access to the Internet services is not through the growing numbers of dial-up ISPs but rather through the more structured BBS offerings of CompuServe – the UK market leader – and others such as America-on-Line, Prodigy, Europe-on-Line, and now also Microsoft Network (MSN). These are the equivalent of the neatly laid out suburbs off the Information Highway. Carefully tended, well protected areas in which users are furnished with access to services and shopping facilities that have been thoroughly checked. These dial-up, private bulletin boards (BBSs) have grown to incorporate Internet access – first through e-mail and access to the Usenet newsgroups; more recently, direct access through browser software. As these services have developed into seamless offerings they can provide a range of advantages to their users, most particularly the experience and guarantee of quality that comes from their longevity. The majority of ISPs for example are less than five years old; many are even younger. CompuServe by comparison is over 10 years old, with a healthy and growing base of users.

From the perspective of the Information Highway these companies therefore represent the basic infrastructure and on-ramp service provision. Through access to these facilities users are furnished with access to the global highway. Having got there, however, users must be able to *travel*. In the context of the World-Wide Web this is achieved by means of a range of software tools falling into two principal categories: browsers and search engines. These are the equivalent of cars and lorries within which real-world travellers progress along the highways and byways. Unlike the real-world case, however, many of these tools are *free*. It is as though cars and lorries were just waiting for passers-by on the hard shoulders and service stations; pick one you like and drive it for a while. If the owner starts to ask for payment, simply swap to another. In the real world this seems absurd; but this is exactly how the tools are used, abused and distributed over the Internet.[118]

While there is a great deal of money to be made in basic service provision there is therefore little to be made in the provision of software itself to end users; provision to companies for use *internally* is likely to be the biggest growth area for these software vendors.[119] Analyses of the vast ocean of information – the equivalent of designing and selling road-maps – *is* valuable but even that is seldom uniquely available from paid-for sources. Private individuals with a passionate interest in almost any subject matter have made indices and directories available for free.

There are of course some profitable value-add services that are associated with the Internet; a recent analysis suggested that in the UK alone sales from related industries peripheral to the Internet itself would be over £65 million in 1996: consultancy in terms of establishing successful advertising or corporate home pages; analysis of Internet opportunities for organisations; security services in ensuring that corporate systems are protected from the attention of Internet hackers; sale of space on host computers and the insurance and other services that go with it; name registering services – even the sale of company names themselves. In this last case, there have been recent warnings that many companies around the world have not yet registered their company or product names as Internet domains thereby allowing others to do so. These names must then be *bought* from the Internet owners if the company wishes to establish or to protect its Internet position.

In the main, however, the anarchic nature of the Internet and its idealistic history has made it difficult to earn significant revenues by establishing uniquely Internet-related services within the Internet context. For any one person offering a service for sale there are likely to be a large number of others able, willing and eager to offer the advice, service or software tool for free.

In addition to this there is of course the *content* industry: those organisations that are planning to make the images, books, sound and video offerings available within the Internet as paid-for goods. Entertainment giants and telecomms giants throughout the world are entering into broad, multi-million dollar deals[120] to enable them to offer the programmes, feature films, and art exhibitions that the Information Superhighway will demand.

Returning to our analogy of real-world travel, we have the basic infrastructure, access roads and vehicles available. These vehicles, however, in travelling cost money: fuel, wear and tear, perhaps even tolls. The comparison with the Information Highway is particularly interesting. We have mentioned before that the structure of the Internet makes it as cheap to transmit e-mail – or even voice through

Internet telephony – to Australia as it is to London. A local call is usually sufficient to provide global communication facilities. In real-world terms it is as though travel was effectively free, drivers and passengers simply needing to pay a basic access fee and then travelling without regard to distance or duration. How is this possible? Who is *paying* for the transmission of data?

The answer is fairly straightforward but has a number of aspects. Firstly, all those who have any form of Internet access are sharing in paying for the global service. Secondly, one should perhaps not ask, Why is the Internet so cheap? But rather, Why is voice telephony so expensive?[121]

Leaving on one side the recent telecommunications developments, traditionally voice telephony was performed over dedicated lines. As one dialled a number a series of connections was established between the two telephones. This connection – technically, this is known as 'circuit switching' – is maintained for the duration of the call. This is a wasteful use of the available bandwidth; for much of the time in normal conversations the line is carrying silence – the pauses between words. Telephony charges were established on the basis of the economics of such processes; long distance, long duration calls were charged heavily because they tie-up more of the network services.

In computer communication these expensive line resources are used far more efficiently. As we have already discussed 'files' of information are broken into smaller units called 'packets'. Moreover, the file itself may already have been compressed – in voice transmission for example the pauses between words can be filtered out and reconstructed when the file itself is reconstructed at the destination. Instead of using a dedicated line for the duration of the call it is only necessary to establish a connection long enough to transmit each packet in turn. And through the network these packets can flow individually, using the network in the most efficient manner possible. This is called 'packet switching'.

While voice transmission can now also be managed through packet switching, digital mechanisms rather than the original analogue signals, the pricing remains fixed on the older systems. In comparing prices with the Internet case therefore we are not comparing like with like; notwithstanding this, it is of course possible that pressure of comparison with the Internet case will act to drive down the cost of long-distance telephony. And given that the telephone companies are coming under increasing cost pressure on local call charges from other service providers – including mobile phones – the 'death of distance' seems a very likely prospect, as discussed in Chapter 2.

However, the transmission itself is paid for by all of the Internet users. Most Internet traffic is carried over leased lines; this is ignoring for the moment the 'local loop' connection to the domestic PC and its modem. Companies who take leased lines pay for them on the basis of expected bandwidth requirement, rather than on the basis of actual usage. CompuServe, Demon Internet, Prodigy *et al* charge their users a subscription rate that allows them to pay for the line access requirements that they forecast. Domestic connection to the services is then on the local loop from home to the telephone network and then to the host computer of the service provider. This is why use of CompuServe for example costs a fixed price for the service and a telephone charge dependent upon the time use of the facilities in the UK. In the US this can be even cheaper since many telephone customers are not charged *at all* for local calls; in the UK at least one ISP has started to offer access through a 'freephone' number.[122] Some ISPs *do* charge a variable amount depending upon the number and size of e-mail messages carried – although many don't and the cost is usually only a nominal one.

The price of bandwidth is falling rapidly as fibre-optic cabling becomes more and more accessible. Set against this in the Internet context the requirement for bandwidth is mounting rapidly. The multi-media aspects of the Web means that many more pictures, sound clips and even video clips are being transmitted, rather than strings of simple ASCII characters. This can be seen as a race of sorts; will the requirement for bandwidth exceed that available before the network provision can catch up? At certain times of the day the Internet performance is particularly poor; this shows that the bandwidth isn't keeping pace. However, the Internet is being constantly upgraded and the belief is that fibre-optic and compression technologies will allow the bandwidth to satisfy expectations.

But somebody must *pay* for this expansion on a global basis. Just as somebody must pay for the disk space and computer resources that are used to store the unthinkable quantity of information contained in the many tens of thousands of Usenet newsgroups, e-mail articles and Web pages. Because the basic backbone of the Internet has been traditionally funded by government and academic institutions this has not previously been an issue; but with the increasing commercialisation of the services the expectation of the authorities is that future funding – for both maintenance and expansion – will come from the private sector. As we have said, an anathema to the 'old-timers'; but commercial interests – advertising, sale and distribution of goods to an eventual mass market – are the only way in which the Internet will survive and evolve into the Information Superhighway.

While there are only limited opportunities for directly Internet-related profits other than in the provision of service access – and even that is likely to fall in price in response to intense competition and commercial practices – the prospect for the Internet to effect real-world economics is very great. We have already mentioned the likelihood of Internet telephony. In this clever encoding, compression and transmission technologies are used to allow individuals to converse over Internet-supported connections. Even IBM, perhaps the most conservative in nature of the IT organisations, have plans to develop and market a sophisticated telephony tool, possibly even incorporating video.

This will impact severely upon traditional telecommunications but then will also place a greater burden on the Internet infrastructure to carry the increase in traffic. While this is likely to lead to an oscillation as customers move between the two systems in search of performant services, it is also likely to impact upon the profitability of the various telecommunications providers. And it is these very providers who are essential to the future development of the Internet infrastructure since the basic cabling is theirs. But their response may well be to improve network offerings for their *own* information or entertainment services; BT for example would like the ability to compete directly with the cable TV companies in the provision of 'Video on Demand' and other entertainment services.

Because of this dynamic some analysts have constructed scenarios in which a 'son of Internet' emerges as the basic Internet performance deteriorates due to overuse.[123] This alternative system would be provided by the large telecomms and cable TV providers, offering significantly improved, quality guaranteed performance but with a cost premium – and hosting their own services as well as the basic transmission of data packets. Organisations such as government or large commercial concerns who are planning to buy the next generation of telecomms provision (ISDN and ultimately ATM) could be expected to prefer the improved performance, leading to the development of a parallel network.

Of course since the 'Internet phenomenon' as defined in this book is about access to global information from local PCs, whether this is effected through the current Internet or through a more performant alternative run by telecomms or cable TV operators is essentially irrelevant. All western economies have now become so dependent upon global computer networks and the ability to transmit data rapidly and reliably that Internet or 'son of Internet' – or Information Superhighway – would all be embraced.

TRANSNATIONAL SMALL COMPANIES

While the Internet's direct economic impact is likely to be primarily connected to the issue of service access provision, as we have described elsewhere there will be a number of other effects. These arise from the use of the Internet in favour of, or in support of real-world activities by companies trading throughout the world. From the commercial perspective the Internet presents a trading and employment domain that is independent of physical geography. Within the Internet it is as easy for Californian record shops to compete in the UK as it is for the UK shops themselves; moreover, that competitive ability holds true throughout the world. Within the Internet the physical location of one's business and even of one's employees and customers becomes much less important.

In real-world economies, however, there is a significant level of investment by organisations overseas. Japanese conglomerates invest in Hollywood production companies and in Welsh and Scottish manufacturing plants; UK engineering firms perform work for Indonesian customers; and newly developed economies on the Pacific Rim invest aggressively around the world. The globalisation of economies is well established[124] – in particular the sensitivities of regional economies to global perturbations over which they have little or no control. As an example, much of the Japanese pension funds are invested overseas in London, New York and elsewhere. Should those monies be repatriated – say to support the rebuilding of Tokyo following a massive earthquake – the impact throughout the world would be substantial. News and information from overseas can therefore have significant effects upon national economies.

As a communication medium, it could therefore be argued that the Internet would add to this sensitivity of globalisation. In practice of course this is unlikely to be the case; the Internet *does* present a global medium – but no more so than the existing TV and journalistic media with which we are already familiar. The Internet's interest lies more in its ability to support such globalisation of news at a *personal* rather than at a corporate or national level. As such, in terms of communication of news, views and events, the Internet is unlikely to have any greater impact than existing media.

Because the Internet supports global companies – of any size – it is more likely that it might have an effect on the levels of foreign investment required. At least in part, foreign companies are encouraged to invest in local economies in order to gain legitimate footholds. Japanese companies for instance invest in many British concerns. While this certainly gives access to a skilled workforce – in engineering for example – it also gives access to wider markets in Europe. Such foreign investment therefore confers a degree of legitimacy for Japanese businesses to trade outside of their most immediate markets. The same is true in many other fields.

The Internet, however, supports such foreign trading without the necessity for the company itself to have any presence – other than perhaps a distribution mechanism – in the country in question. And for those goods such as video, software *et al* that can be distributed electronically even such a loose association is unnecessary. Might the Internet therefore act to retard levels of foreign investment?

In some cases such investment may be reduced, but this is unlikely to have a major effect on national economies. As was discussed in Chapter 3, only the smallest and newest of companies is likely to move wholeheartedly into a virtual state. The more established transnational concerns might well augment existing activity with a virtual presence but will also still require or desire the physical shops, plants and distribution facilities. The Internet is therefore unlikely to impact on levels of overseas investment in any but the most peripheral of ways. And it is those major concerns that are the least likely to move wholly into Cyberspace that are most likely to be carrying out such foreign direct investment.

A greater impact is likely to be felt in terms of the size and nature of companies that are carrying out such transnational trading. Over the past decade a series of structural shifts have occurred within the economies of both the US, UK and many other developed countries. Increasing competition from low overhead economies in the developing world and the Pacific Rim have forced the developed economies to concentrate on value-add service and tertiary industries at the expense of basic manufacturing and other primary production.

A globalised economy allows and encourages basic engineering and production activity, for instance, to be carried out overseas and then exported to the target market. World Bank projections for example show that exports from newly developed or developing economies will overtake those from the developed nations – defined as the OECD members – around 1998. The cost overheads in many recently emergent economies are significantly lower than that of the US and UK – or most particularly Germany.

This has led to a number of shifts in emphasis: from manufacturing to service and value-added service industry; from full-time to part-time and self-employment; from local economies to globalised economies. These trends are of course driven by factors quite independently of the Internet; but the Internet will be used by these self-employed workers or by the service and slimmed-down manufacturing companies that result.

Driven by external competition and by the search for internal efficiencies most companies have focused on so-called 'core competencies'. As with many such changes this approach was led by the Japanese in their car industries, producing a complex network of specialist companies orbiting and servicing one another and the giant car manufacturers [5]. While this might have started in Japan, however, it has spread far and wide. Taking just the car manufacturing example, BMW buys 80 per cent of car parts from third party organisations; and at least 50 per cent of manufacturing is outsourced by many of the large American industrial giants in other fields [3]. The whole structure is linked by effective use of IT and IT-supported manufacturing controls.

This has had a number of impacts. Firstly, the average sizes of companies has changed quite markedly throughout the last 15 years. In 1979, companies of over 500 staff accounted for over 40 per cent of the total private sector UK employment; conversely, 33 per cent was accounted for by companies with less than 50 employees. By the turn of the century this is predicted to have changed dramatically: 27 per cent employed in the larger companies versus nearly 50 per cent in the smaller. A similar pattern is emerging in other countries.[125]

Secondly, looking more closely at the smaller companies, there is an even more marked change when one considers the sole traders or partnerships: in 1979, these accounted for almost 7 per cent in the UK; by 2000 the figure will be over 15 per cent. Coupled with this there is an associated change in the nature of employment, moving rapidly towards part-time and self-employed labour in preference to the full-time employment pattern of previous decades. In 1984 for example nearly 70 per cent of employment was full-time; by 2005, this is projected to drop towards 50 per cent. A significant change not simply in working patterns, but also in income expectations and even the ubiquitous 'feel good' factor.

This therefore gives a picture of the economic environment within which the Internet will be used: a shift in emphasis from manufacturing to value-add service industries with a marked change in the size of those companies, favouring many more smaller concerns employing a more 'contingent' workforce. And the continued globalisation of economies will continue to favour the trends towards transnational trading by those smaller companies. More, government – both in the US and UK – is positively *encouraging* the use of Internet or Information Superhighway by companies of all types. While the larger organisations will see many benefits – such as using the Internet facilities internally for example – by far the greatest benefit is going to be felt by the smaller traders and specialist companies trading transnationally.

The Internet will therefore be used by a growing pool of small businesses, employing contingent workers or subcontracting activity to other, similarly small concerns. These businesses – primarily value-add service oriented – will use the Internet as a cheap, flexible and global means to communicate, advertise and trade on a world-wide basis. This will allow extensive competition to be supported within the Internet between such small, perhaps only loosely audited businesses and their larger brethren.

In terms of numbers of companies, this is particularly difficult to assess. The basic facilities for using the Internet will be in place for all but the most technologically naive of businesses: PCs, telephone connections and access to the services are the most fundamental requirement and certainly all businesses currently use the telephone and almost all use some form of PC, either directly themselves or via the services of their accountants. In 1995, there were some 1.5 million businesses registered for VAT in the UK – a figure that had changed only very slightly since 1994 and is expected to remain reasonably stable over the period to the turn of the century. Increase in self-employment – between 300,000 and 400,000 in the UK for the period 1994 to 2001 – will occur but the overall numbers of traders is expected to remain at around the 1995 figures.

This gives potentially a large number of small companies in the UK able and willing – indeed encouraged[126] – to use the Internet facilities to trade on a transnational basis or to employ workers in a contingent fashion, perhaps working from home. A similar pattern can be expected in other countries, giving rise to an emerging, international community of small businesses, strongly focused in niche or specialist fields, using the Internet either to reach consumers directly or to support their transnational operation. The Internet developments described in the first part of this book illustrate the ways in which these businesses – or even departments of larger companies – could operate in Cyberspace, giving rise to an active, healthy and essentially self-contained Internet economy.

IMPLICATIONS FOR TAXATION AND CUSTOMS DUTY

The Internet economy will impact on the world's 'real' economies in a number of aspects, some of which have already been mentioned. Firstly, the effect of globally transparent prices through Internet marketing will be felt by consumers able to act in a more empowered manner. While there might be, for example, very good reasons for price differentials between US-sold and UK-sold music CDs, these might be more difficult to maintain when *all* purchasers have access to both equally. Secondly, the direct Internet economic issues – revenues from service providers, telecomms companies and so forth – will flow into the several economies, benefiting shareholders, taxation authorities and consumers alike. Thirdly, increasing transnational Internet trading will have an influence – albeit only a small one – on a country's balance of trade with other states. This last is affected more by heavy items such as major manufactures, foodstuffs, foreign exchange dealing or such invisible assets as tourism or professional services, than by those goods such as music or software that might be sold over the Internet, at least initially.

However, the Internet economy *will* have an influence over a given country's government economy; the income and expenditure of the government itself. Government expenditure is on items such as health, education or social security; government income is from taxation or duties. We saw examples in the first part of the book of the way in which the Internet could bring benefits to the health or education fields, making a world of information or access to expertise available through a simple mechanism. As far as the delivery of social security is concerned, many local and voluntary organisations already use the Internet to help job seekers, the handicapped or the disadvantaged to benefit from technology.

A greater impact will be felt in the area of taxation or of duties[15]. These fall into several simple categories:

- direct, personal taxation;
- direct, corporation taxation;
- indirect, expenditure taxation;
- importation and customs duty.

In the case of personal taxation, this is collected either through continuous calculation mechanisms such as Pay As You Earn (PAYE in the UK) or through an adjustment mechanism associated with the completion of an annual tax form. In the US most taxpayers expect to complete and submit tax returns on a yearly basis, perhaps assisted by accountants or other agents; in the UK, those on higher-level incomes or with complicated tax affairs that cannot be handled directly by their employees in PAYE receive and complete forms. The UK is, moreover, moving towards a regime known as 'Self Assessment' (SA) – although it might more correctly be called 'self calculation of liability' – that will place a greater burden directly on the taxpayer, perhaps in turn leading to a requirement for assistance from professional agents.

All taxation systems already make allowances for the fact that some taxpayers might work overseas for some or all of a period; that taxpayers might be paid salaries from foreign companies, perhaps into local or to remote bank accounts; and that double-taxation agreements – in which foreign nationals or overseas workers are not taxed twice, once by the host and once by their own nations – must be operated efficiently. The starting assumption for taxation regimes is, however, that such a situation is the exception rather than the rule. In the UK, PAYE is the basic taxation mechanism and is expected to cover the majority of employed individuals.

The self-employed and those with complex employment or income patterns are handled in a slightly different manner and must complete tax returns – perhaps in addition to the PAYE return made by the company. An overseas worker, or self-employed consultant, or simply somebody with investment income, must therefore complete a tax form. As was discussed in an earlier chapter this tax form could be issued, completed and returned via Internet-supported mechanisms provided that the basic security mechanisms are in place and are trusted. US tax authorities use the Internet to distribute tax forms and information; UK authorities to distribute only information; no tax authorities yet trust the Internet mechanisms to support the return of forms themselves – although the UK *has* experimented with electronic lodgement over non-Internet networks from companies filing corporation tax returns.[127]

As the changes outlined in the previous section develop, however, some of the assumptions fundamental to the operation of the UK taxation systems may come into question. Most obviously PAYE represents a proportionately greater burden on the operation of smaller companies than on large ones. From the perspective of the Inland Revenue, PAYE is a particularly efficient mechanism for collecting personal tax; the bulk of the work is done by the employer. With smaller companies and with a greater use of part-time or self-employed workers this 'burden of compliance' may become excessive.

To ensure that the correct levels of taxation are assessed and collected this would therefore require more people to move into the SA pool. The operational efficiencies of PAYE, however, would be lost as more and more people had to be issued with forms, provided with customer service and those forms had to be recovered, audited and entered into the departmental information systems. Operating a taxation system such as SA – even allowing for the assumption that high numbers not only do their own calculation of liability but that they do it correctly – is an expensive venture. Efficiencies in the distribution, customer service and collection of forms would therefore be essential.

In many other fields government departments have mimicked the mechanisms used in the private sector; indeed, in some ways they can be accused of following 'cargo cults' in applying poorly understood private sector nostrums to public sector problems that are only superficially similar. Both in the US and the UK for example taxpayers or social security claimants are called 'customers' and private sector customer service practices are applied despite the fact that there are significant differences between customers – who have the right of choice – and for example taxpayers, who haven't!

Notwithstanding these limitations, as the Inland Revenue's operational problems in applying a mechanism such as SA grow it is reasonable to assume that they will begin to use the private sector techniques. Specifically, they might choose to follow the introduction of Internet-enabled customer service and information distribution to their 'customers', allowing increasingly efficient systems to be applied. As with the private sector case this will rely

upon the introduction and widespread acceptance of security mechanisms to guarantee reliable transmission that can be authorised and
proof from challenge.

On the personal, direct taxation front the Internet is likely to bring
more advantages than problems. While it is true that the Internet
could support overseas employment and overseas earning in a simple
way, the taxation authorities have mechanisms to manage such
affairs. The Internet might support many more people carrying out
such activity but the processes, procedures and legislation required
to handle them are already in place. Of course individuals could do
such paid work without declaring it on their tax forms; they might
even choose to be paid in untraceable, digital cash – we will consider
this issue in the following section. But from the perspective of the
Inland Revenue this does not present a *new* problem – simply a new
aspect of a well-known one.

An interesting additional potential that the Internet brings,
however, is that of *'virtual communities'* – possibly global associations of individuals using the Internet to support their community
life; we will consider these in more detail in Chapter 6. Outside of
the Internet, private communities have already appeared, in some
cases on a limited basis, in a particular area. These have given rise
to LETS – Local Exchange Trading Schemes.[128] Here, individuals
cooperate and trade with one another using a non-cash based,
tokenised economy which is similar in nature to a barter system.
Many of these in fact emerged from baby-sitting 'circles' or similarly local cooperative ventures. Scheme members undertake work
or provide goods or services for one another on a closed, private
basis without recourse to money. This has proven particularly
popular in areas of high unemployment or low income, where the
cash resources that an individual or family does have might be
severely limited.

From the tax perspective, many members of such schemes have
assumed that the token economy is outside the taxation system;
while local agreements might well be established with a particular
tax office, in the UK such schemes *are* in fact taxable. The token
might represent perhaps one hour of somebody's time spent
gardening or painting a house; in which case, the token economy

can be taxed on the basis of cash equivalence for each token, taking an hourly rate for that person's time as the exchange rate to be applied.

On small, local schemes such an economy is likely to be of only low absolute value; they have therefore tended to be overlooked by the authorities concerned. The World-Wide Web, however, present an opportunity for such communities to be supported on a much wider basis, using secure Internet transactions in place of the physical token exchanges for the private barter of goods and services; these schemes can then become of much greater cash-equivalent value. The point remains, however, that from a purely UK perspective, the Inland Revenue can be expected to treat such tokens as personal income for UK residents involved in the scheme and to assess a taxable cash value associated with the transactions. Detecting that such a scheme is in place, however, might well be a non-trivial task.

For the taxation of companies – corporation tax in the UK – a similar picture emerges. Corporation tax is payable by companies registered in the UK, on profits exceeding a threshold value; it is also payable on profits by companies that are *not* registered in the UK but which trade through a fixed agent or subsidiary in the UK. Taking the most extreme case, that of a wholly virtual company operating entirely within the Internet, there are two situations that might arise: firstly, the company could be a UK registered company; or secondly, it might be registered overseas.

In the case of UK registered companies there is a requirement for that company to have a registered office, a company secretary and at least one director, and for it to publish its company accounts. That the company trades wholly or partially in a virtual manner is therefore essentially irrelevant from the perspective of the UK corporation tax. The company *could* use the Internet mechanisms to 'ship' profits overseas into off-shore subsidiaries and so forth; but again, this is a known problem with which the taxation authorities have experience. And with access to published accounts and a 'real-world' presence – the registered office and officers – the problems are no more difficult in the Internet case than in that of any other transnational company.

For companies registered outside the UK but which have virtual sites accessible over the Internet from the UK the situation is slightly more complex. A company registered outside of the UK may be liable for corporation tax on the profits of any local subsidiary or agent. A virtual shop, for example, easily accessible within the UK might be considered as the equivalent of a UK branch; in this situation it might be arguable that the company *is* liable for UK corporation tax.

This might well, however, be overly simplistic. In Chapter 5, we will see that from the perspective of consumer protection, Internet trading is seen within the European Union as being a form of 'distance selling'; that is, the Internet is considered to be a *medium* over which goods are offered for sale. It is therefore considered equivalent to a computerised *Exchange and Mart* magazine even if the Web page is designed to look like a virtual superstore. A company registered overseas and offering goods for sale through a newspaper would not be considered as having a UK agent or branch unless the order is processed through and the goods distributed from such a fixed establishment.

If the Web page for example is resident on a host computer outside of the UK – either in the company's country of registration or anywhere else – then the company could reasonably argue that it has no UK branch. If, however, the Web page is in the UK – eg, 'www.bloggs.co.uk' – then there would be a case for this to be considered as a UK branch if it is seen as being 'fixed' rather than purely temporary.

Internet trading is sufficiently novel for this not yet to have been addressed as an issue. Moreover, the levels of Internet trade are such that no overseas Internet trading company has yet reached the threshold UK profit value at which corporation tax becomes payable; the cost of Internet establishment – estimated by IDC at $1 million *per annum* for a commercial site – still exceeds any revenue benefits and is expected to do so until at least 1998. The arguments have therefore not yet been tested. Applying real-world criteria such as the location of the host computer from which the company trades seems to be the most useful approach – particularly since Internet shoppers can then tell from the page's address whether it does or does not lie within the UK, assuming that the company has made no attempts to disguise such addresses. As discussed in Chapter 5, this is an important question in the context of consumer protection.

This serves as an approach in the case of corporation tax – where companies must be registered and have a 'real-world' presence somewhere. A similar approach can be taken for sole traders, partnerships and smaller companies. Such organisations, while they are not liable for corporation tax or fall below the appropriate thresholds are all liable for UK VAT payments. This is under the responsibilities of HM Customs & Excise, who assess and collect VAT from the 1.5 million VAT-registered traders within the UK.

UK traders *must* register for VAT where they are companies, partnerships or sole traders carrying out their activities within this country. Again, UK virtual companies with existing real-world presences are less of an issue for the authorities than the overseas or unregistered traders might be. Unregistered, fraudulent or otherwise illegal trading will be considered in the following chapter in the context of regulation and legal control. This leaves those organisations that are trading within the UK from overseas and selling goods into the UK market without the payment of VAT. In this case, however, such goods are being *imported*; if not, then the trader is clearly operating *within* the UK and if not registered is doing so illegally. We will consider importation shortly.

Where the goods are professional services – such as the writing of software, provision of advice, etc – there is still assumed to be a deliverable to set against a given invoice, although in this case the importation aspect is more difficult or irrelevant to apply in practice. In this case of course the use to which the purchaser of such deliverables puts them might be liable to VAT, or it might be argued that the trader *is* trading within the UK and should therefore be registered. Again, however, the 'real-world' location of the host computer can be used as an indicator. Where professional services are offered and accepted from overseas via other media and where – for example – a reply to a question is delivered through a telephone conversation, there is no question of VAT being applied in practice, even if strictly it should. Again, the accounts filed by the *customer* companies and audited by qualified accountants would allow such transgressions to be detected in all but the private consumer case.

For Customs & Excise, therefore, as for the Inland Revenue, the registration of a company within the UK acts as the required 'real-world' contact to the organisation. And the physical location of the relevant host computer is also important. This allows the department concerned to ensure that any leakage of revenue into a purely Internet economy is kept to a minimum.

The final category described above was that of duty payable on imports. Assuming that the imported goods have been advertised and purchased over the Internet there are two situations that might arise: firstly, the goods can be imported physically through real-world ports of entry into the country; secondly, the goods can be imported in a digital fashion over the Internet itself, either through 'pure' or 'hybrid' mechanisms. Moreover, those individuals or customers *buying* the goods for importation will either know that the goods are coming from overseas or they might be unaware.

In the case of physical importation, this can reach quite high levels. In the US, for example, even without consideration of Internet shopping, mail-order and telephone shopping across state boundaries has been estimated to leak some $3 billion in unpaid local sales tax. In the UK and elsewhere, while this *does* happen it is a relatively minor problem – beer runs to Calais for example or exploitation of the Channel Tunnel. The introduction and spread of the Internet could extend this further, introducing more people to the prospect of teleshopping on an international basis.

The first point to consider is that of responsibility. *Who* should take responsibility for paying the import duty? In all cases this is of course the *importer*. If goods are bought abroad and carried through the port, the importer is the person carrying them; conversely, if the goods are being shipped from overseas on behalf of a purchaser then it is that purchaser who is responsible for paying the duties; and finally, if the goods are imported from an overseas branch to a local branch of a particular company then it is the local branch that is responsible for paying the duty – although the contract with the purchaser might allow the company to bill them for the monies due.

In most cases therefore where goods are bought over the Internet, responsibility for paying import duty will lie with the purchaser. In some cases, of course, this purchaser might not be aware that the goods *have* been bought from overseas and that they must be paid for. This sort of situation is, however, difficult to construct without considering fraudulent or misleading trading. When a user accesses a Web page for example the page's address is displayed by the browser software. For companies within the UK, the '.co.uk' suffix will be apparent; conversely, where the company is trading from overseas the suffix will be different – '.co.fr' for France, or '.com' for the US, etc. In ordering the goods the user will therefore be able to tell that the company, or rather its host computer, is outside of the UK – and that duty will be payable. Of course a company *could* choose to register a domain name which is misleading – there is no official registrar in any of the Internet-connected countries; arguably, however, such a company doing so with the intent to mislead is trading in a fraudulent manner. These and other issues of regulation will be considered in Chapter 5.

Where the address accurately indicates the company's computer to be within the UK it is reasonable for the purchaser to assume that the goods are coming from within the UK. Where the goods must be imported in this case then the contract between trader and purchaser will apply. That is, if the trader informs the purchaser in advance of duty payable then it is the purchaser's responsibility; if not, the purchaser is protected through consumer rights. In this last case the trader is arguably responsible for paying the duty exactly as though the goods were imported to a local branch or agent – although the purchaser, who will be billed by Customs & Excise, may have to sue for such repayment through the civil courts. Again, however, in the Internet context this has yet to be tested in practice.

In the case of physical imports this is fairly straightforward. In digital importation the situation is less clear. While the same conditions of legality apply it is far easier for a purchaser to import goods inadvertently when they are transmitted electronically, perhaps from overseas 'warehouses' of local companies. Software applications, particularly upgrades, are generally available throughout the Internet. When software is downloaded it becomes eligible for duty – a fact which many Internet users purport not to realise.

While physical goods come into the country through a large but limited number of entry ports – docks and airports – electronic goods flow in through a much larger range of channels. Moreover, digital goods are binary numbers – a stream of 1s and 0s indistinguishable from one another. Although parcels, packages and crates might be distinctive, packets of bytes and bits are far more anonymous. And they might be encrypted, compressed or in an unknown transmission format. The border police task therefore becomes far more difficult – perhaps even impossible. As mentioned above, however, in most cases the purchaser will know that the goods – electronic or physical – have come from overseas. In situations in which traders and purchasers are assumed to act in a legitimate fashion this should be manageable within the existing mechanisms. It is in the *compliance* aspects that the challenges will appear – in checking and preventing illegal activity.

HM Customs and Excise and their colleagues around the world are well experienced in considering the likely impact and implication of technological or scientific development on their activities. New drugs or tricks for smuggling are always under examination. As far back as 1909 in fact, at the time of the merger between HM Customs and HM Excise, the Collector in Dover wrote to the then chairman about the landing of Louis Bleriot's flight from Paris:

> I think that a time may come when this department will have to treat their arrival seriously, and take steps to ensure that no opportunity be given for Revenue interests to suffer through indiscriminate landings of airships in this country.

From a small beginning the world air-travel industry has grown to the point where minute after minute plane loads of passengers, goods – and potential smugglers – arrive at Heathrow, Gatwick and at airports throughout the rest of the world. During this expansion, the Customs authorities within the UK, Europe and elsewhere have fought a long and essentially successful battle against illegal importation. In 1909 the *scale* of that battle was not known but the likelihood had become a realistic expectation; we are at the analogous state with Internet importation, but with many more frontiers to be policed even than there were fields within which the 'airships', planes and so forth of 1909 could land.

DIGITAL CASH

A Cybernation economy is quite obviously strongly dependent on an ability to trade in Cyberspace. As we have explored in Chapter 3, traders and purchasers need to be able to buy and sell goods secure in the knowledge that payment can be effected between them in a reliable, authorised manner. The basic mechanisms that have been developed to support such electronic trading mirror the 'real-world' procedures with which we are already familiar: credit, debit or cash transactions.

The security aspects of managing such transactions in the Internet case have been explored in Chapter 3; in Chapter 5, regulating and detecting fraudulent use of these Internet processes will be considered. In this section we will look at the economic management aspects of Internet transactions but most especially that of electronic cash.

In a credit transaction, goods are ordered by the purchaser but paid for by the credit provider – credit card company or perhaps even the trader if the purchaser has an existing account. This credit provider then in turn requires payment by the purchaser in due course to settle the account; moreover, where the credit provider is a credit card company it is likely also to expect payment for the provision of this service. This payment therefore represents a slightly different economic pattern for the spending than the other cases: at the simplest level, credit transactions involve borrowing, perhaps directly if the card holder's account is overdrawn. On the trader's side, they too are charged a premium for such transactions. Credit card purchases, be they in the Internet or real-world case, therefore inject and move more money through the economy than is represented by the actual price of the goods themselves.

In the debit case, the purchaser has a pre-established quantity of money in an account, usually with a bank or other institution. The purchaser then gives the trader authority to be given some of that money in return for the goods. This can be in the form of a debit card number or a cheque. In the most usual case, the banks do not make a charge to the purchaser for such transactions, unless it also involves a degree of borrowing on an overdrawn account or unless the purchaser is in turn a company. Again, in this case the trader is also charged for debit card transactions, which would be the most usual application of this mechanism in the Internet case. So again there is more than the direct price of the goods involved.

In both of these cases therefore there are more than the immediate two parties involved and the transaction encompasses more than the immediate cost of buying the goods. The credit or debit mechanisms cost money to implement and this is paid for by one or both of the trader and the purchaser. From a perspective of economic management such transactions have further benefits. Most importantly they are audited; because there is a third party involved there is a separate and authoritative account of the flow of money between the various people.

This separate account is important from the terms of ensuring that fraudulent activity has not taken place – or in detecting and prosecuting it where it has. In broader terms, it is also important insofar as it allows monitoring and a direct management of the economy to be established. In each of the industrialised, western economies control of spending, borrowing and investment by both corporate and private individuals is central to the process of government economic policy. While different politicians and parties may have differing views on the processes to be applied there is a broad agreement that such management is essential and that at the very least the levels of such transactions should be monitored. And of course auditable transactions are important in the maintenance of taxation procedures.

In the real world, however, not all of the transactions with which we are familiar involve either credit or debit card use. World-wide over half of purchasing transactions by individuals are carried out by the simple exchange of cash.[129] Of course 'personal transactions' involve purchases ranging from chewing gum and evening papers, through to buying a house; in most cases only the low value transactions are based on cash – credit card transactions do after all come with a degree of consumer protection, insulating the purchaser from fraudulent or unsatisfactory trading; and the quantities of cash required to buy a house are somewhat cumbersome to carry about.

Where they are used, however, cash transactions have several advantages. Firstly, they are private; coins and banknotes do not maintain a record of whose wallets they have passed through unless the parties involved maintain their own records; they are therefore more difficult to audit. Secondly, they are assured; once the trader has the purchaser's cash in his till he can be in no doubt but that the money is his. In the case of credit transactions this doubt persists until such time as the third party actually releases the funds to him. Thirdly, they are rapid; the trader is not required to wait or even to borrow to cover the money owed – it is his immediately and he can then in turn spend it – ie, benefit from it – immediately. And fourthly, cash transactions are cheap; there is no payment to a third party required in order to release the represented funds.

In addition to this of course the transactions have a form of guarantee with them; whereas other forms of transaction will be honoured only if the trader has indeed been dealing with the authorised account holder, in the case of cash there is no doubt (unless the notes are forged) that it will be honoured in future.

From the perspective of the purchaser, these characteristics are slightly more mixed. The privacy and untraceability aspects might well be important, although it is often difficult to see why this might be necessary in legitimate purchases. Cash is of course convenient; but the rapid transference of funds to a trader would not be so convenient in the case where the trader might not deliver the goods as quickly – or even at all.

For the purchaser in the Internet context it is likely that credit transactions will continue to be the preferred option; and while the trader might like the money immediately it is possible that they too will come to prefer Internet-delivered credit card numbers once secure transaction mechanisms to provide guarantees are in place and where the purchasers themselves prefer such schemes. Notwithstanding this, cash transactions *do* have a valid part to play and will become an increasingly important aspect in the Internet case if only because of the low cost of such transactions in the case of low price goods.

The exchange of cash in the Internet context is a particular instance of 'electronic money' – sometimes simply called e-money. While such systems *can* be used over the Internet, they emerged for a variety of other reasons. In the most general case, electronic money is represented by digital impulses stored in an encrypted format on a smart card, often called an electronic purse or wallet. Physical cash is expensive to produce. It must be designed in such a way as to inhibit forgery, which involves special materials, inks and patterns in the case of paper notes. It also needs periodic replacement as forgers become more expert or as notes become damaged or destroyed in use. In addition, it is easily stolen – and the anonymity then implies that the thief is able to spend the funds with impunity. And finally, it is bulky to transport – either in large quantities to banks or in smaller quantities within wallets and purses.

Electronic money has none of these disadvantages. Digital signals are simplicity itself to produce, providing that one has the required software and security codes to allow it. And these signals can be easily transmitted either within physical media such as smart cards or along telephone lines in the Internet case. By using sophisticated security codes and encryption mechanisms the banking authorities can make it very difficult – arguably, even impossible – for forgeries to be produced; and those security measures can also be used to ensure that while the smart card can be stolen the money can only be accessed by the authorised owner of the digital cash.

Moreover, smart cards can hold encoded money in many different formats – ie, different currencies. Given the current high levels of government attention to the prospect of European-wide currencies and the difficulties of establishing and introducing new coinage, smart cards would provide very easy, very flexible means to achieve this. And finally, subject only to any limitations on the smart card itself, the digital wallet can hold any desired quantity of cash.

There are two types of electronic money currently being explored. The first is a 'token' system, in which the digital signal is a one-off representation of a pre-paid quantity of cash. Users buy an amount of tokens at a bank or similar; these tokens are then encoded on the smart card. Once spent, the token is transmitted back to the issuing authority, where it is checked for authenticity and the represented money credited to the trader – rather like a postal order or a gambling chip. In many ways, of course, this scheme falls between the electronic cash and the debit mechanism described above and is the less general of the two e-money mechanisms. Notice that unlike the case with 'real' money a bank or other third party is still required to authenticate – and of course to record – the transaction.

The second system is represented by the Mondex mechanism, whose use has been pioneered by National Westminster and Midland Banks and by BT in an on-going trial in Swindon, Wiltshire and which is expected to form a country-wide roll-out in 1997. This is not the only such trial: from Australia to the US (such as the Olympic Games in Atlanta) and from Denmark to Russia, experiments of varying complexity are being driven by a number of suppliers of competitive products. In some countries this is seen as a means of combating high crime and high inflation rates, such as the case in Russia for example; and in some this is seen as a convenient way of reducing the cost of handling foreign currencies, such as in the European Union.

In the Mondex scheme the signals encoded on the smart card represent real money rather than an encoding of a digital token. The user can 'charge' the card in one of two ways: firstly, by buying digital cash from a bank, in which case the quantity of money – less any commission charged – is securely encrypted and transmitted into the memory of the smart card. Or secondly, the user can receive cash from another Mondex smart card. It is this second case that gives Mondex its great advantages in the e-money stakes.

In the token scheme – and indeed in the credit and debit systems – it is necessary for the bank or other third party to be involved, authenticating and recording the transaction. In the case of card to card transactions – the digital equivalent of moving money from one person's pocket to another's – only the two cards themselves are involved. No outside authentication or authorisation is necessary. Two people can therefore exchange e-money with exactly the same ease with which they could exchange banknotes or coins. Providing that they both enter the correct security codes to access their own smart cards the transaction can be effected easily; and it can be a transaction involving any currency and – subject only to the artificial, smart card induced limits – any quantity of cash, from pennies to hundred of pounds. In practice the Mondex cards are likely to have limits of several hundred pounds although they could support several thousand with the encoding mechanism used.[130] And they can support cash in various currencies, making them ideal for use in a general European context.

To complete the picture, BT have made systems available to allow the Mondex encoded cash to be transmitted over telephone lines, from bank to card or card to card. This of course allows the scheme to be applied in the Internet context, allowing cash – albeit encrypted – to be transmitted around the world; a capability that was formerly the jealously guarded prerogative of banks and national economic managers but is now available to anyone.

Why are such mechanisms important in the context of the economic implications of the Internet?

A basic characteristic of the Internet, to which we have constantly referred, is the essentially global context within which communication – and trading – takes place. Within the Internet realm it is as easy for UK shoppers to browse through US cybershops as it is to browse through the more local ones. In fact, given the strong US bias at present, it is arguably *easier* to browse the American malls.

This means that we can expect Internet shopping to involve the purchase of goods from overseas. In the most usual cases of course such purchasing will be from reputable traders by law-abiding UK citizens who then voluntarily ensure that importation duties are paid promptly and accurately. Even in such a legitimate case, however, there is still the question of the economic management of overseas expenditure – which in large enough amounts has an affect on aspects such as exchange rates.

In the case where the goods are bought using credit mechanisms or other schemes that require third party verification it is a simple extension of current management systems to ensure that such overseas spending is recorded. In each case this spending involves an outflow – or of course in some cases an inflow – from one country to another. Where the banks are involved this is well managed.

However, what if ever more people begin to trade over the Internet on a transnational basis using e-money? As we have said, in the case of the Mondex scheme this e-money is not some form of token, it is the money *itself*. For many years a fundamental plank of UK economic policy has been a knowledge – or at least an estimate – of the money supply. Whether such monetarist schemes are sensible or not is irrelevant; what is important is that we have tried to monitor them. Cash, even in its physical form, is difficult to monitor and trace; hence of course its use by criminals and terrorists. In the digital form it is even harder to monitor since it can flow over the Internet literally anywhere.

Using e-money therefore we have the possibility not only of a global Cybernation, transcending the traditional nation-state boundaries, but of a global cash economy supporting rapid, anonymous and transnational flow of currency. Sterling – in digital form – could flow out of the country, unchecked and untraced, through the millions of Internet connections. Individuals could even be paid, again in untraceable digital cash, from employers overseas. Our economic independence, our ability to manage or at least to monitor our money supply, could be riddled like an electronic colander as ever more people allow cash to slip quietly beyond our reach at the speed of an Internet e-mail message.

Could such a thing happen, with apocalyptic consequences for national economies? In practice it would be very difficult, although even a mild version of a truly separate, electronic cash society would give rise to some management problems. There are a number of factors, however, that mitigate against such consequences – not the least of which are the measures being built into the Mondex cards themselves.

Firstly, the relationship between electronic cash and 'real-world' cash must be understood. If a truly comprehensive electronic economy emerges, with physical notes and coins replaced for all purposes by Mondex-like schemes, then it would be impossible for that economy not to spread so as to include the Internet Cybernation. However, for all practical purposes notes and coins are likely to remain a part of our shopping experience for a long time to come; unless and until a child's pocket money, payment for window-cleaning services – both at home and at busy road junctions! – and purchase of the evening newspaper or shoe-shine can be effected by smart card we will continue to need our coins and notes.

This means that at least in part it will be necessary to translate the e-money into more traditional forms and this will continue to require the services of a bank account. Mondex in fact is structured so as to require such a link to an account – for the sponsoring banks not to have included such a connection would have been irrational. At this junction the e-money, or part of it, must return to the real world. Moreover, each smart card has the pre-programmed limits built in thereby limiting the quantities of cash that can be supported in a given electronic wallet – again, imposing restrictions on its use.

Finally, the most worrying situations are where the e-money is crossing national boundaries. Considering this more deeply it is of course necessary for the e-money to be an encoding of a particular currency. Assuming that the initial encoding is in sterling and the e-money passes out of the UK into France, what happens? There are two cases: either the e-money encoding is traded within France in its sterling form, or it is translated into francs.

If the e-money is traded as sterling, there is still no problem. While the sterling has in principle left the UK it has not yet done so in practice. Provided that the French traders are content to carry out their transactions in sterling there is no real worry. In practice of course they will prefer to have the e-money in their native currency, in the same way that they would be reluctant to trade in UK pound coins. This means that the e-money must be translated: it must be *exchanged*. In turn this means that the sterling e-money must be taken to a bank; the e-money is then exchanged for the quantity of sterling that it represents; and that sterling is then used to buy the appropriate quantity of francs; finally, the francs are used to buy back e-money in turn if this is then required.

Of course these steps might be rapid and automatic; but still it is necessary for some quantity of sterling to be present in the transaction. The French bank must therefore have *bought* that sterling from the UK – or from some other source who in turn bought it from the UK. It was at this point that the quantity of sterling represented by the e-money left our shores – through a real-world, well understood and well managed mechanism.

If the sterling e-money is *not* exchanged then it will ultimately come back into the UK. And because there is a sense in which money is conserved – like energy – then there will remain a basic equation between the e-money *bought* in sterling and the e-money used to trade around the world. Of course it may be that the recipient is happy to leave the e-money in sterling – in which case its utility is dramatically reduced for him unless he can find a sufficiently complete economy happy to trade with the sterling e-money as is. As we said, should a global electronic cash society emerge, content to trade purely in such digital encodings without regard to the currency represented, then the cash will be lost to the UK economy – but this is very unlikely in practice and the effect would be similar to the way in which foreign notes are lost to national economies when holidaymakers bring the 'pretty foreign money' home with them. In the main this has a nuisance value for the economy and nothing more, although some poorer countries can be badly damaged by such measures.

What about in the case where e-money flows *into* the country from abroad? Again, this is either a sterling encoding or it is some other currency. If it is sterling then the appropriate quantity of money must have been bought by the overseas bank in order to exchange into e-money. If the encoding is in some other currency then the recipient must in turn buy the sterling unless they plan to spend the e-money in its home economy.

Internet electronic cash will therefore have some impact on national economies but it will not be 'apocalyptic' in nature. Card limits will act to inhibit their use – even allowing for Internet mechanisms – by transnational drug cartels and the like. Clever encoding and encryption mechanisms will help prevent forgeries, although such things will of course be attempted. And global economic management will help to alleviate any worries about unlimited and unrestricted quantities of cash flowing out of the country without the proper mechanisms for monitoring and adjusting exchange rates to reflect this fact.

If there is any remaining worry about digital cash it must be that an automatic mechanism for translating one currency into another is produced *without* the contingent requirement for an exchange mechanism. In Mondex this automatic mechanism is not present and there are at present no known plans elsewhere to effect such a thing. If it *did* get produced then sterling – and all other currencies – would be able to flow globally without the current economic management in place.

Related to this would be mechanisms to allow files of arbitrary quantities of electronic money to be transferred over the Internet. The current limitations on the smart cards translate into limitations on the amount of cash that can be transferred in a given digital transaction. Again, if these are lifted it will be possible to move greater quantities, perhaps then supporting the sort of money laundering that many authorities unnecessarily fear possible with the existing Mondex scheme.[131]

SUMMARY

The Internet will give rise to a global Cyberspace economy of traders, workers and shoppers in which electronic cash and secure credit transactions can flow around the world, ignoring the real-world frontiers with which existing economic managers have the most experience. While it is true that this will give rise to a series of problems, these will not be problems with which those authorities have had no experience. It is already the case that multinational corporations can move money and goods globally and can employ people in many different countries, perhaps even paying them in many different currencies – at least from the perspective of the corporation's accounts department.

However, the Internet case does introduce the authorities to such behaviour on a far more personal level, perhaps involving very many different people or much smaller companies not already having the required accounting and auditing processes in place. In these cases, however, the basic mechanisms on the authorities' part for ensuring taxation, importation and Treasury management are already established. This is therefore a question of educating those Internet traders, buyers, employers and employees of their responsibilities as well as the advantages.

Internet enthusiasts point to the global and geographically-independent nature of the Internet and argue that such an unprecedented structure – a Cybernation – is implicitly unmanageable. They argue that the emerging Cybernation will fall outside of the ability of national economies to manage and regulate its behaviour. In part this is true – it will be very difficult to control the Internet from the perspective of a single nation state. However, the Internet *does* intersect with existing countries in many different ways, not the least of which is the fact that the very people who inhabit the virtual Cybernation must in practice live somewhere. They must occupy a real-world house, buy vegetables from a real-world grocer, walk along real-world footpaths and spend notes and coins that come from a physical bank.

Because of this it will always be possible to exercise some degree of economic control over the Internet even without global cooperation by the national authorities. Truly virtual companies will certainly emerge and will be able to occupy the digital 'havens' that we have already discussed; while this gives rise to problems of regulation and of ensuring consumer protection, it does not give rise to problems in the managing of national economies.

Workers might be able to receive payment in electronic money, delivered over untraceable Internet connections; and members of Internet-hosted virtual communities might also be able to establish global, token-based economies. But the recipients of electronic money will be unable to spend that money without translating – ie, *exchanging* – it into the local currency, which then exposes it to audit and to effective economic management; and the digital tokens with virtual communities will also fall within existing taxation structures. Of course those workers and citizens of virtual communities could elect to keep the money overseas in foreign bank accounts, or elect not to declare the tokens or e-money credit balances – but if they don't pay tax on such income then they will be acting illegally. Again, this is not a problem for economic management, but for police and for the *compliance* arms of the taxation and customs authorities, a problem to which we now turn.

5

LEGISLATIVE AND REGULATORY ISSUES

Death and taxes: the two eternal aspects of human existence. To this one might also add 'crime'. From the very earliest of civilisations the greedy have attempted to avoid the payment of taxes; and the dishonest have sought ever more sophisticated ways to exploit the loopholes in a complex and ever expanding network of regulations and laws.

Increasing technological sophistication now presents authorities with the means to counter existing illegalities and the fraudsters with the opportunities to develop ever newer techniques. Widespread and cheap printing facilities and then the development of accurate colour photocopiers enabled the forgery of bank notes. And as money becomes more digital in nature 'hackers', 'crackers' and 'phreakers' will become the bank robbers of the future, not with shotguns and dynamite but with laptops and crocodile clips.

In other areas, dishonest trade has been an aspect of society since the very first market stall was erected. *Caveat emptor*: 'let the buyer beware'. The notion that consumers and traders are in a complex, unceasing competition with one another is embodied in our legal and regulatory systems – indeed, without that competition many of the regulations would be unnecessary. Goods might be misrepresented or over-priced; they might not even be the property of the seller. And purchasers might default on payment or pay with forged money, or might copy and then in turn sell the goods.

Regulations have been developed to protect the rights of both consumers and producers and to protect the owners of intellectual property such as trademarks and books; such a legal framework has been developed in each country. Based upon explicit laws, recorded precedent and accepted practices these laws have evolved separately many times over; the politically sensitive issue of legal harmonisation has a long way to go, even within the European Union let alone on a broader basis (see [25] and [26]). And the laws themselves give rise to a requirement to *police* the laws, to ensure that they are not transgressed or that any such transgression is detected, challenged and punished.

These laws, however, are applied according to a complex basis of jurisdiction: the area within which the law applies. Activities which may be legal in one country – ie, one geographic locale – are illegal within another; and vice versa. The question of *where* an act occurred has therefore grown in importance, particularly in the case of buying and selling.

The Internet, however, presents access to a domain ostensibly outside of geography. The application of a legal framework and a regulatory structure therefore becomes a complex issue requiring extensive cooperation between independent countries. Cooperation, moreover, that must be between nations that might have radically different views on the legality – or even the morality – of particular practices.

In the context of Internet-supported activity, the key areas for consideration have been referred to in several of the sections above. These include the general aspects of *civil rights* and other similar rights associated with private individuals; the question of *ownership* of goods that might broadly be considered as digital in nature; and the issue of *regulating* the activities of those trading over the Internet.

The governments throughout the world are therefore presented with a difficult task: in a time of rapid, structural change in the fundamental bases upon which many if not all aspects of our society have been built, the regulating authorities must exercise control that is sensitive to the technological, economic and cultural opportunities presented by the Internet. This means that as well as policing the Internet the authorities might wish to take advantage of the potential it offers – potential that can be exploited to support communication with citizens, to enhance efficiency, or to provide ready access to a broad range of data sources.

Additionally, the regulation and control must be exercised on a global basis involving broad cooperation and agreement to common aims – a *political* issue.

Let me emphasise an important element of the following analysis: this book will *not* present my personal proposal for solutions to any of these issues. The Internet is a relatively recent 'problem'; at best it would be ambitious, at worst arrogant to believe that I had answers to the issues raised. Instead, this chapter discusses the issues and where possible presents those solutions that have occurred to the authorities in question. The rapidity of development of the Internet means, however, that many of these ideas can become unsatisfactory even before they can have time to be adopted. In the main, the regulatory and legal controls have been based on experience with 'real-world' aspects that are at best only loosely analogous to the Internet situation and which do not change particularly quickly. Because of this feature of the regulatory controls, the relatively rapid introduction of what seem like minor advances in the Internet processes can have the effect of dramatically influencing the ability of the various world-wide authorities to control the Internet's use and users. Further, those controls that have been introduced are on a country-specific basis, that being the way in which legal mechanisms work, other than in the case of certain European Union-wide directives to control distance selling and protection of data. The global nature of the Internet, however, means that any and all such local attempts can usually be subverted from elsewhere.

In the main, as with the other chapters of this book, it is the UK perspective that forms the main focus for this examination. However, given that three quarters of the Internet hosts and by far the majority of its users are in the US, this chapter will also describe the American attempts to afford legislative and regulatory protection for its citizens. Furthermore, given the strong US bias to the Internet, it is likely that the US approaches to many of these problems will establish the foundations from which other countries will proceed, making the American perspective of even greater relevance.

FREEDOM OF EXPRESSION

Civil rights are the broad freedoms – and responsibilities – that nation states owe to their individual citizens. These are generally assumed to encompass such diverse aspects as free speech, freedom to associate with groups and individuals of one's own choice and the protection of the law. While civil rights have come to be associated with the various laudable movements throughout the world fighting to protect basic *human* rights, this section will look rather at those rights which can be affected by the Internet. That is not to say that the Internet does not have a part to play in those movements: as we have already discussed, Amnesty International *et al* can all use the Internet as a communication medium to reach those individuals who might support and help them; and the Internet can also be used for communicating with those oppressive governments or regimes where such connections exist.

The specific areas in which the Internet has already been seen to impact on our rights as citizens of democratic nation-states centre broadly on issues of freedom and of privacy. Freedom of access to information about ourselves; and privacy in limiting the access of others to that information. Freedom of expression and a right to say what we want to whom we want; and privacy of maintaining that communication from prying eyes. The privacy aspects in the Internet will be addressed in the following section. In this section, we will look at:

■ defamatory – ie *libellous* – communications about individuals or organisations; and
■ freedom of expression of sexuality or of political opinion.

These contain features which are essentially similar: in the first, newsgroup or Web-page contents are defamatory of individuals or of companies; in the second, the material is offensive – perhaps criminally so – but in a more general, non-personal manner. In the first case, therefore, it would be necessary for the damaged party to complain and pursue a case independently; in the second, either the police, other authorities or some self-appointed public watchdog would have to pursue a complaint.

There are two perspectives that might be taken in this work. The first is that of the Internet 'citizens', challenged by the attentions of the national authorities; the second perspective is that of the national citizens, whose freedoms and civil rights are in turn challenged by aspects of the Internet. Predominantly, this book has taken the second of these and will continue to do so throughout this chapter – although those other aspects will be discussed in passing.

In Chapter 2, the nature of Usenet newsgroup discussions was described. Because of the essentially anonymous personalities involved in such newsgroups, along with the emotional distance that the PC screen and Internet mechanisms provide, many of these discussions can become very heated. So-called 'flamewars' are common in many newsgroups. An initial, often innocuous statement gives rise to an insulting rejoinder which in turn gives rise to ever more offensive communications. Language that would not be considered acceptable in any other form of interaction is commonplace in such flamewars.

In other situations, newsgroups can be established to discuss issues that have a limited scope of interest, such as for a particular town or area. As a simple example, a newsgroup could be established by all those who drive along a certain route to a particular town. The initial reason might be for instance to set up a car-sharing scheme. The discussion has only limited applicability and is probably of no interest whatsoever for anyone outside of the immediate area concerned. Throughout the discussions, however, debate might turn to the state of the road – and from there to the efficiency of the agency responsible for road repairs; and from there to the morality of the chief engineer himself. Newsgroup articles might come to be very insulting about the chief engineer, alleging that he is pocketing the allocated cash; that his efficiency record has always been appalling, etc, etc. Allegations and comments which are globally visible and highly offensive.

This is not a contrived example – although it is fictitious. Newsgroups *have* evolved along this or very similar paths – resulting in a series of discussions and articles that bear a logical but very remote relationship to the original 'thread'. To the users contributing to the newsgroup discussions there comes to be a feeling of 'privacy'; the newsgroup *feels* like a private, bar-room conversation among a close circle of friends and colleagues. In practice of course the newsgroup and the discussion is visible globally and the remarks are recorded.

From this regard the Internet discussion is more like a published account than a real-world conversation. In the case of published comments, such as articles in a newspaper or programmes on TV, an insulting or incorrect statement about an individual would give rise at least to the threat of court action and the expectation of a public apology – from the person who made the statement and those who broadcast or disseminated it. However, in this case there is the assumption that the *publisher* is in some sense responsible for the material – after all, without their involvement the statement remains an essentially private one and not therefore the subject of libel.

In the Internet case, defamatory statements can be made by users who might then be sued on an individual basis by the offended party. However, it is likely that in most cases where punitive damages might be awarded that the offending user will be unable to meet those damages. There is therefore a growing belief that the dissemination of libellous statements is, or should be considered to be the responsibility of the equivalent of a publisher; the Internet Service Provider is assumed to fill this role. This then allows an injured party to have some substantial body against which damages might be sought. Alternatively, the owner of the host computers on which the data file containing the statements is stored is seen as having the responsibility.

In both the US and UK, this situation has been simplified in laws which have been established in early 1996 to cover just these cases. The Defamation Act in the UK and the Communications Decency Act in the US both assign responsibility to the ISPs for what they 'publish', exactly as though they were publishers of print.[132] In these Acts, material which is 'patently offensive' or which contains 'indecent speech' is the responsibility of the ISP. The Acts arise from slightly differing motives in the US and the UK: the US Decency Act was proposed initially with a view to constraining access primarily to pornographic material, which we will consider below; the UK Act as a means of addressing defamation and offensive language under the UK libel laws. Both, however, will come to have a broad range of applicability.

In the UK case, the intention of the Act is that ISPs will be held responsible for the material they distribute. They are held to be *publishers* of the material, rather than *common carriers*. The common carrier defence was suggested for several years in the context of the Internet. In this, the carrier simply transports material sight unseen, without any attempt at examining and guaranteeing the contents – like telephone conversations, rail freight or parcel post.

This then allows the carrier to claim that it has no control over the material carried, and that sole responsibility therefore rests with those putting the material onto the medium. This would then in turn allow the ISP to claim a defence of 'innocent dissemination' in the event of defamatory material appearing in newsgroups and subsequently being adjudged libellous. A by-product of this defence, however, is a reluctance to exercise *any* control, since such a demonstration of *some* editing responsibility undermines a defence based upon having no such capability.

Under the UK Defamation Act, however, while the ISPs are considered to be publishers they are not taken as being 'primary publishers'. Instead, responsibility for the libellous statements will be with the original poster of an article providing that the ISP has taken steps – as yet undefined – to prevent such offensive material from appearing; of course, this does not then address the issue of damages that might be awarded against a 'man of straw' unable to meet such a price. Conversely, under the US Act the ISPs are responsible outright for the material they disseminate. The UK authorities have made it clear that they will not seek to impose excessive regulation on the Internet, preferring a 'self-policing' aspect; the US, on the other hand, are attempting a more stringent degree of control. Under both the US and UK Acts, however, the ISPs are expected to undertake a policing task on the material within newsgroups or Web pages that they host.

The recent Acts therefore simplify the position somewhat, although opponents on both sides of the Atlantic have pointed to the difficulty that will arise in applying them in practice. How can the ISPs police every newsgroup submission and content of every Web page on the Internet? And which ISP is responsible: the ISP that delivers the material to an offended party; the ISP that provides the service to the individual who puts the material in the Internet domain –

who might be outside of the act's jurisdiction; or *all* ISPs who provide access to the host computer or computers on which the material is stored? In fact, it is the ISP who provides the host computer holding the information – although this then leaves unaddressed the situation in which the ISP inadvertently affords access to some other host belonging to a third party and containing the offensive material.

It is also far from clear what constitute reasonable steps for the service providers to adopt. In the case of essentially 'closed' environments such as the CompuServe fora it might be expected that CompuServe could periodically and randomly check the content of their own Special Interest Groups (SIGs) or could hold the SIG moderators individually liable for all of the forum postings. In effect the moderator would become the legal agent of the company in the case of that particular forum. This would provide a mechanism to address both the defamation and the indecent or offensive content situations.

In broader Usenet provision, particularly of unmoderated newsgroups, this would be far more difficult – perhaps even impossible; there are after all many tens of thousands of such newsgroups; to monitor them all would be a Herculean task. Automatic systems *could* be used, scanning for offensive words – but these could be easily fooled and the context would have to be considered. For example, the word 'tit' can be used as an insult or as a description of a small bird; and 'breast' is perfectly acceptable in a debate about mothering or screening for cancer. Moreover, defamatory statements need not be expressed in overtly offensive language and would not therefore be detected.

CompuServe and the other service providers could remove access to those newsgroups which repeatedly publish material which its users find offensive or which contravene the Decency Act or equivalent. This would, however, rely on their *knowing* about the offence, which would only come to light afterwards, at which point the service provider would already be in breach of the law in cases such as child pornography.

One potential approach that has been suggested is for the service providers effectively to pass responsibility back to those actually performing the act of posting the material itself. In the ISP-provided newsgroup software a short reminder message could be displayed *before* the newsgroup article is allowed to be transmitted – many ISPs already implement such a system. This message could advise the user that offensive, insulting or defamatory postings are unacceptable and that Internet access will be withheld from those who transgress the recent Acts.

In the case of newsgroup articles posted by individuals using other ISP services – and perhaps outside the jurisdiction of the UK and US Acts – this is more difficult. To reiterate, expecting ISPs to vet the contents of each and every newsgroup article that users could decide to access is a task of such magnitude as to be essentially impossible. CompuServe *et al* have all expressed their views that such vetting should be the responsibility of those accessing the material rather than those organisations providing them with the communication means.

The US and UK Acts are very new and are expected to evolve throughout 1996; as yet it is not clear the extent to which courts will be able to apply the regulations in practice. The measures that ISPs are able to take in 'self-policing' of the Internet, outlined above are essentially cosmetic; but they *might* prove sufficient to satisfy the courts that the ISP has done everything in its capability – or they might be considered insufficiently stringent. With the capability to access effectively unlimited information sources (and we have considered just the obvious case of newsgroups here) it is very difficult to envisage mechanisms that would allow ISPs effectively to police the content of postings.

In assigning responsibility to the ISP the authorities have attempted to apply 'real-world' and essentially realistic conditions to the Internet – taking TV broadcasters and newspaper publishers as a model. While the Internet is a new type of medium, with different problems, it *is* clear that libel is libel; if a defamatory comment about an individual or a company is made and is published, and damage can be shown, then libel has occurred – whether the statement was carried in the newspapers, on the radio or over the Internet. The authorities have therefore demonstrated that such libel laws as exist in the 'real world' apply equally in our Cybernation and have indicated that responsibility for that libel lies with a specific body or set of bodies: the ISPs are the equivalent of publishers. But yet, the ISPs are *not* publishers; they are a communication medium and what they communicate is driven by users rather than by themselves.

And in practice of course there are many more problems even than these. In the analysis above we have taken the perspective of the authorities. From the perspective of the ISPs or of the users the situation is far more complex than the drafting of the acts would imply. Globally visible statements that might not be considered libellous or offensive in the UK, for example, might be considered highly offensive elsewhere; an Internet version of something like the Salman Rushdie situation, for instance, could easily be imagined.

Existing UK laws make clear where and under what circumstances libel damages can be sought; the Internet, however, is as accessible in countries without those laws or practical experience as it is to those with which we are most familiar. And this does not simply cover the libel situation, it also impacts on many other aspects of our environment – even such things as ownership of property, which has no legal basis in at least some of the countries accessible via the Internet.

Without the experience of having applied these laws in practice – either in the US or the UK – their efficacy cannot be assessed. They do have, however, a number of benefits; it becomes simple for the authorities to assign responsibility and calls upon our existing experience in applying conditions of libel in other media. But they have potentially many more drawbacks, such as the difficulty of applying them in practice. A similar argument applies in conditions of decency.

In late 1995, the German authorities requested – or rather, instructed – that Deutsche Telekom and CompuServe withdraw access to a set of newsgroups and discussion fora containing among other things neo-Nazi and pornographic material. Although this subsequently became a *cause célèbre* within the Internet community the German authorities were plainly well within their rights to request that such offensive material was not made freely available to the citizens they were appointed to protect.

Similarly, in late 1995 the UK police arrested two individuals accused of operating a paedophile bulletin board service offering digitised pornographic images and access to Web pages containing catalogues of obscene material. A number of quite openly pornographic newsgroups exist within the Internet; photographs from celebrity autopsies, sex-line chat groups and information on how to construct home-made bombs can all be found – albeit perhaps with some difficulty.

As well as addressing issues of defamation, the recent US and UK laws, along with laws throughout the rest of the EU and elsewhere, go some way to assigning responsibility for preventing the widespread access to such material. In part, this is driven by a requirement to protect minors and children; in part, by a desire to inhibit terrorist or criminal activities based on the Internet-sourced information; and in part by the legal requirement on organisations such as HM Customs and Excise to prevent offensive material entering the country.

Of course any attempts to prevent such criminal use of the Internet can also be construed as an attempt to inhibit freedom of expression and of speech. Following the US Communications Decency Act opponents immediately began to attack it successfully on the grounds that it inhibits one's freedom to express views. In the US Constitution a basic right of freedom of expression is contained in the First Amendment; this freedom exists without regard to the views themselves – others may find the views sensible, offensive, puerile or distasteful; but this in no way alters one's basic right to express those views. It does not, however, have anything to say in defence of the *way* that one expresses those views.

Those drafting the act wanted to restrict the offensive nature of computer pornography and related material; those opposing it, to uphold the rights of those posting the articles and establishing the Web pages themselves. One party wanted to uphold the rights of citizens to protect their children from exposure to child pornography and 'snuff' video clips; the other, to defend the fundamental right of all users to express their sexual and political views unhindered by authority. An important point to stress, however, is that those leading or coordinating these protests in the US, such as the Electronic Frontier Foundation (EFF), in *no way* support, endorse or approve of the material disseminated; while they *do* defend the rights of Internet 'citizens' to freedom of expression; this is based squarely upon the US Constitution and upon personal philosophies of liberty, rather than upon any belief that what is actually posted is worthy of such support.

While the basic arguments of each party are of interest, however, they are essentially the subject matter of undergraduate Ethics courses. In the context of this book, the interesting aspect is whether or not the regulations can be applied in practice. As with the defamation case, the decency act states that responsibility lies with the Internet Service Provider to prevent access to material that is offensive in nature or to demonstrate that all practical steps have been taken to ensure that such material is not available through them. This differs from the defamation situation, however, in that simple possession, let alone transmission, of certain material – such as child pornography – is a police rather than a civil matter; it is not necessary for an injured or offended party to make and pursue a case independently.

Opponents of the act, such as the EFF, point to the basic nature of the Internet and assert that any constraint upon it is unworkable in practice. The Internet occupies a domain that is separate from that of national, geographic boundaries. The Internet was built, they argue, to survive a nuclear war and to route continuing communication around those parts of the global network that had become radioactive craters. From this perspective, attempts by service providers on behalf of government or other authorities to inhibit communication are doomed to failure – after all, they say, nobody *owns* the Internet and there is no overall regulating body able to impose such restrictions on a world-wide basis. And any system that can route around bomb damage can surely route around attempts to silence parts of itself?

These are all of course valid points; but even without a global regulator it is simply not true to claim that local – that is country specific – laws cannot be applied in practice. After all, the host computers on which the offensive material is stored reside within some country's jurisdiction; those entering the material into the computers live or work within some country's jurisdiction; and those receiving the material are doing so within some country's jurisdiction. What *is* necessary is cooperation between the very many countries within which those computers or users can reside while polluting the Internet – a *political* issue.

That the system can support mechanisms to subvert attempts to isolate and silence users, newsgroups or hosts is also a valid point.

When CompuServe refused access to the set of some 200 newsgroup services banned by the German authorities, so-called 'mirror sites' throughout Canada and elsewhere ensured that the material was still accessible. An important point to recognise, however, was that this was not a case of the 'Internet' ensuring that those people in Germany and other countries continued to have access to the newsgroups. Rather, it was a case of Internet *users* ensuring that the material was accessible. Without the attentions of those 'fighters for free speech' the banned Internet newsgroups would have continued to be inaccessible.

To understand the difficulties involved in this situation we will take a practical example: that of a Web page containing pornographic images. The computer containing the Web page is owned by somebody: a private individual; that individual's employer; or a service provider. Moreover, the computer must occupy a 'real-world' site, either one accessible to – say – the UK authorities, or one which is outside our reach.

'Outside our reach' refers to a particularly special case; existing and long standing legal relationships and experience of cooperation – so-called 'reciprocity' – cover the UK's interaction with most of Europe, the US and Canada, the Commonwealth countries and many others.[133] To be outside our reach the computer must therefore lie outside of these countries, and that country in turn must have access to the Internet. There are such countries – and it is from them that the greatest problems in managing such restrictions in practice will result.

In the cases where the UK has a means, direct or indirect, of gaining regulatory access to the host, policing it is reasonably straightforward. The Web page might be accessible to those Internet users who find it, know about it or are told about it. Given the nature of the Internet, however, it is very unlikely that users will simply 'stumble' over such a page during their random meanderings through the byways of the system; it is far more likely that it will be publicised in some way. Newsgroups or advertisements in magazines can both be used to alert those interested in such material.

Of course, such notification is in the domain within which it can be monitored. In fact in the computer pornography prosecution mentioned above, the UK police were first alerted by newsgroup articles referring to a Web-page catalogue of paedophile material. Newsgroups dedicated to such pursuits are astonishingly easy to locate and then to monitor – both by ISPs and by the authorities. Notice, this is different from the libel case where offensive statements might arise in *any* of the many newsgroups. Advertisements for pornography appear usually in a known or easily identifiable set of newsgroups which can therefore be monitored.

Where the page is *not* publicised through a newsgroup it might be found through a search engine or similar; the ISP and authorities are as free as the Web page 'customers' to run these searches. And the ISP has a range of other mechanisms available to them in locating such material. In a case in early 1996 for example an ISP in the UK, Netcom, noticed an unusually large number of accesses to a previously 'slow' page, leaping from 200 to 50,000. On examination they found that the page contained pornography – and withdrew the user's service.

Once the authorities or the ISP learn about the existence of the Web page within one of their hosts, or a host to which they provide Internet access, it will usually then be straightforward to remove the offending material: the user can have their services withdrawn, the owner of the host system can be threatened with prosecution and the ISP can delete the appropriate files. If the host lies in another country, the authorities can request of their opposite numbers in that country that they carry out such steps on our behalf.

Of course the ISP will not always be able to tell when their services are being used by their customers to disseminate or to access pornographic or other material. In particular a Web page or newsgroup could fall outside of the ISP's immediate control and contain material that continuous searching does not uncover . While it could be argued that such pages which are not found by the ISPs or authorities would not be found by the *users* themselves this would not always be true: the page might have been advertised in some 'underground' publication for example and contain no obvious clues as to its contents in either its title or main text; it might even be encrypted.

Alternatively the Web page can reside on a system which is outside of the UK or US reach, either directly or by means of friendly countries. That is, it could reside in a 'data haven': a country having Internet access and a weaker system of regulatory controls than we are used to seeing. Such havens might emerge in response to the economic imperative to make money from such services – an Internet version of the drug-producing economies. An interesting side point, however: some organisations in the UK have begun to attract the attention of HM Customs and Excise by their offer of gambling services to customers in Japan; an example of a weakly regulated country (the UK) using the Internet to provide a service which is illegal in a more strongly regulated country (Japan). Havens need not therefore be the Internet equivalents of 'cocaine economies'.

Is it possible or even desirable to attempt to exercise control over such havens? In all likelihood not; if a particular haven country were to continue offering an objectionable service then it would have to be isolated and expelled by *all* of the Internet community. This would have to be done by removing the country's computers from the Internet address databases held by the several hundred backbone and several million other host systems. Firstly, there is no legal or practical mechanism in place to allow such a global agreement to be established. Secondly, even such a measure as this would not be fully effective. The country could for example register other Internet addresses, perhaps with misleading domain names; or the country could provide an ordinary telephone connection to a host elsewhere, in say the US, and use that as its channel to the Internet.

As we saw in the case of the German attempts to silence certain newsgroups there is also the question of deliberate subversion by Internet users of attempts to implement self-regulation by the ISPs. From the perspective of the authorities, it is particularly surprising that so mundane an activity as advertising should create a frenzy of outraged responses while such antisocial and even illegal behaviour as the free posting of paedophilia and neo-Nazi propaganda should be supported.

Is it fair for the authorities in the various countries to assign the responsibility for offensive material to the ISPs? CompuServe, Microsoft and many others have argued successfully that it is not; that a better approach would be to target the points at which the material is *accessed*, rather than 'carriers' themselves. In many ways this is perhaps the best approach, since software provided by these ISPs can be used to 'filter' unwanted or undesirable sites *without* the 'big brother' or 'nanny state' impinging on one's right or freedom of access to the information – this being the main objection of many Internet users.

To reprise to an earlier comment, however, such questions are the stuff of Ethics courses and the like; our interest in this book is in whether or not the legislation as currently proposed can work in practice – and we would have to conclude that the nature of the Internet would make it unlikely.

PRIVACY ON THE INTERNET

A further important aspect of Internet civil rights is the question of privacy, particularly with respect to the vast extent of personal information held on databases throughout the world; and also privacy of e-mail communication. With telephone conversations there is the implicit assumption of point-to-point privacy; that is, we assume that the conversation cannot be overheard in any but the most extraordinary of circumstances. In the e-mail case, however, the files containing the written text can be recorded and accessed at several points throughout the system. This gives rise to an obvious requirement for encryption processes so as to maintain the privacy of these messages. Privacy is also afforded by the use of nicknames or aliases in the Internet communication – e-mail, newsgroup and chat.

Taking first the issue of using aliases, this is occasionally cited as an unfortunate aspect of the Internet. By using such misleading names individuals can escape personal responsibility or hide behind anonymity in their communication with others, perhaps with the deliberate intention to mislead. In this, however, there is little or no difference between the real-world and the Internet situations. The key is in the 'intention to mislead'. Actors can use stage names; writers, pen names. When CB was popular, colourful 'handles' were used in place of real names; and anonymity is regularly offered to those writing on sensitive subjects in letters to the papers. Provided that the individual involved has not taken the alias with a deliberate view to disguise their identity for fraudulent or illegal activities then the laws in both the UK and the US protect his or her right to do so.

Nor is it illegal for those involved in Internet discussion groups to withhold personal details – age, race or even sex – again provided that there is no intention to defraud or mislead illegally. The Internet 'urban myths' abound with cases of romantic exchanges between individuals who subsequently discover that they have been fooled into intimacy – albeit keyboard or 'remote' – with a child or even somebody of their same sex. While this is embarrassing, it is not against the law in either the UK, US or Europe provided that one or both parties did not attempt to defraud. And of course in most situations, even where misleading aliases are employed, the ISP account for that person will hold accurate details should the police or other authorities need to locate the 'real-world' body behind a particular Internet persona.

In some cases, however, this might not be possible. There are a number of computer sites which offer an 'anonymous ftp' service; users of the service are allowed access through the computer site without their identity being propagated to other computers within the Internet. Passing through that site therefore ensures that all subsequent sites are unable to trace the access or activity back to a specific individual beyond the anonymity provider; and while some of these maintain records, others don't. If this service is used in conjunction with the encryption mechanisms we discuss below it would give perhaps the ultimate expression of anonymity and privacy in the Internet context. In all but the most contrived of situations, however, it is difficult to construct legitimate uses for such a service – and it is already believed to support many illegitimate ones. Perhaps the only obvious legitimate use of such anonymity would be in the case where privacy is already accepted in the 'real world', such as Samaritan help-lines, crime reporting or similar.

As with so many other features of the Internet, however, this is difficult to regulate since the provision of the service has clearly not been seen as an offence in the operating country, although some – such as the Scandinavian anonymity providers – are under government pressure to police the service more effectively.

Making e-mail private has given rise to some of the more colourful urban myths and conspiracy theories within the Internet. Most e-mail exchanges are mundane, containing material or information that is seldom, if ever, of significant commercial or geo-political relevance. Of course some e-mail messages are private in nature but this is far from the usual case. A persistent myth on the Internet, however, is that the CIA, NSA or SIS are intent on reading the content of any and all e-mail messages. In some cases this may in fact be necessary: spies and increasingly terrorists and crooks have taken to communicating on a global basis and there is at least the potential for them to use the Internet to do so. In the case of paedophile rings, as we have already discussed, they are using the Internet both to communicate and to distribute material. It might therefore be understandable for the various police and security services around the world to wish to access *those* e-mail messages – but it is nonsensical to assume that this also means that communication between undergraduates throughout the US is of interest to the NSA and will be intercepted and read.

In fact, as an aside, the peculiarities of the Internet mean that even 'interception' of communication is a difficult concept to apply. In phone taps for example, the authorities are granted permission to intercept communication which might contain details important for a criminal investigation. In the analogous situation for e-mail on the Internet, however, such interception can occur while the message is being held in a central storage point on a mail server, rather than in the act of transmission itself. In a January 1993 case in Texas, a judge ruled that such reading of e-mail did *not* count as interception; that it was necessary for the act of interception to be simultaneous with that of transmission and reception – by analogy with the telephone case. While this judgement has only limited applicability – it was not a Federal court decision and certainly does not apply to the UK or Europe – it is one of the very few such judgements in this area. It suggests that 'interception' on the Internet is more like seizure of documentary evidence, such as a stored letter which may never in fact be delivered and which must then be handled according to the established evidential procedure for such seizures. In the case of computer-related evidence, however, such procedures have not yet gained acceptance and understanding in *any* of the countries applying such processes, making it particularly difficult to obtain convictions in such cases.

More persuasive as a justification for such privacy requirements is that 'plain-text' e-mail can in fact be read by *anyone* able to get access to the mail files – system operators, hackers or simply the idly curious. Although the e-mail may contain only mundane items, some of this might be of a private or personal nature. By analogy with the real world, while my paper mail – 'snail mail' – might not contain material of commercial or political interest, I still would not like to think that it is read by the Post Office staff or any others. Because of this, for several years there have been attempts to make e-mail increasingly private with the use of encryption technology.

In the case of trading, where credit card details, order details and even the goods themselves require the protection of encryption this is a fairly obvious requirement. Traders and purchasers need to be assured of secure communication, and the various authorities need to be confident that the order details *et al* could not have been 'spoofed' or altered. Applying the technology to e-mail is essentially similar, using a public-key distribution mechanism and strong encryption tools to render the text of the message unreadable.

A particularly popular program for achieving this is the PGP suite which is now available throughout the world. This was developed in the US where such strong encryption tools are considered to be military technology or munitions, and therefore not exportable except under licensed conditions – and even then not to countries from which enemies of the US could obtain them. Unfortunately, 'friends' of the program's creator – Philip Zimmerman – put the software on a publicly accessible Internet host, from which it spread around the world. For four years, Zimmerman lived with the threat of prosecution for illegally exporting munitions, until in early 1996 this threat was lifted. In the intervening years, however, the algorithm was exported repeatedly in other forms which did not count as munitions: written text in a book; even printed on a T-shirt. The conspiracy theorists have even asserted that the prosecution has been dropped purely and simply because the NSA has found a way to break the code. One further point with PGP is that its use is subject to license by the owners of the underlying algorithm – if it is used outside of the US without such a licence, it is being employed illegally. Such unlicensed use arises in the case where Internet users have downloaded the tools from US universities or bulletin board services, sometimes even anonymously.

Because of the military technology restriction in the US even the most sensible uses of encryption to support trade are affected. In the Netscape secure transmission system for example, the length of encryption key – a measure of the algorithm's difficulty to break by exhaustive means – is limited to 40 bits outside of the US and to 128 bits within. Other countries have similarly parochial concerns about encryption. In France it is necessary to have the Prime Minister's permission for transmitting encrypted material in all but the case of credit card numbers and order confirmation.

In the UK the authorities have a more relaxed attitude and impose no limitation on encrypted traffic. In the event that crooks, terrorists or similar *have* used encryption, the UK authorities rely on cooperation from the suspect to provide them with the encryption key. In a paedophilia investigation in 1995 for instance, the material was encrypted but the suspect was found to have written the password key on a note stuck to the side of his terminal. In other situations – such as those involving large-scale fraud, for example – the UK Serious Fraud Office has powers to imprison uncooperative suspects for 6 months if they refuse to grant access to records that are believed to be germane to the investigation.[134] This access to records encompasses encrypted material and so those under investigation must provide the appropriate keys.

With the spread of encryption technology, particularly those tools which form part of the Web browsers, it becomes possible to encrypt *all* communication automatically and simply within the Internet, rendering it essentially private from hackers, snoopers – and from the authorities. Similarly, it becomes possible to encrypt all of the information stored on a local PC or a host system. This would of course allow illegal activities to proceed under cover of such encryption, such as the dissemination of pornography or similar within closed mailgroups and from Web pages that are private to the users around the world. As discussed earlier, however, encryption is a necessary part of trading on the Internet and the private use of such widespread technology would be impossible to restrict. This therefore means that users' privacy can be maintained – but at the expense of providing a refuge for illicit activities, even without the emergence of the data havens discussed above.

One suggested approach to this problem has been that of a general 'key escrow'. In this, the various encryption keys used throughout the Internet community are lodged with a secure escrow service. In the event of the police or security agencies needing access to encrypted communication or data, the escrow agent can be served with a warrant or subpoena to produce the key. Of course, this assumes that those carrying out the communication have indeed lodged their keys – although such failure can be made illegal, it would of course require a change in law; and those involved in illegal activities on the Internet are quite likely to add illicit encryption to their other misdemeanours. Moreover, this change in law would have to be on a world-wide basis so as to avoid the situation in which clandestine data is held outside of the authorities' jurisdiction.

An alternative might be provided by the use of the so-called 'clipper' encryption chip as a standard mechanism for data security. In the clipper scheme – proposed and endorsed by the US government – the keys for *all* individual clipper chips are stored in escrow and again made accessible to the authorities if required. Clipper has not, however, met with general acceptance. Primarily this is because the sponsoring authorities cannot assure the users that the keys might not become accessible to others, thereby losing what privacy it does afford and rendering the technique worthless. Moreover, using the clipper chip scheme would only allow the authorities to decrypt clipper-encrypted data; it would still be easily possible for any user or criminal to encrypt the material further, using an alternative algorithm.

Such 'double encryption' might well be declared illegal, but regulating this in practice would be impossible. Programs to effect such encryption – such as PGP and many others – are now available world-wide; the cat is definitely out of the bag! Further, it would not be possible even to *tell* that the data was encrypted; it might in fact simply be in a format that the authorities do not recognise. In terms. of the basic binary sequence, it is a far from trivial task to determine whether the transmission represents a strongly encrypted e-mail message or a JPEG, MPEG or previously unknown format picture file.

The US authorities in particularly have fought a fierce rearguard action against the widespread introduction and use of strong encryption software. The technology has, however, marched on and over them. As with many other aspects of the Internet, the pace of development and global nature of the system has meant that processes established in more traditional aspects of regulating trade and communication have become essentially useless. While the police can tap phones, eavesdrop on conversations and even intercept postal services, these powers translate only poorly to the emerging Internet community – even without consideration of the EFF arguments calling for the protection of privacy and freedom of speech.

The other aspect of privacy mentioned above – and perhaps the more important – is that of protection of data. Throughout the world, there is a mass of personal information held on a variety of databases: from medical records, through purchasing preferences, to credit ratings and even the balance in one's bank account. Individually, each such database record contains only those personal aspects required by the organisation concerned; with global networks and automatic processing systems, however, it becomes possible to construct a very precise, and very intrusive profile on any individual. To protect against such intrusion, several countries have introduced a variety of regulations to control the access to such information. In the UK, this is embodied in the 1984 Data Protection Act, due to be further extended by 1998.

In the UK, the Act is administered by the Data Protection Registrar. All those who keep information of a personal nature for automatic processing must register that use. Failure to register, or the undertaking of activities outside of those specified in one's registration, can meet with a very heavy fine – unlimited in some cases.

Once registered, there are a set of data handling principles with which the organisation must then comply. Specifically, the data must be obtained and processed legally and only for the purposes registered by the user; it must not be *disclosed* to other people, other than those appropriate for the registered use of the data; and it must be *maintained*, that is it must be kept up to date and continue to reflect a subject's changing status. And finally, the individual who is the subject of the data has a right of access to it and a right of correction in the event that the data is incorrect.

In practice, this means that data held on individuals in the UK – and there are similar regulations throughout the EU and elsewhere

– can only be used for those purposes that the holding company has described. In Chapter 3, we used the example of a car manufacturer able to access personal information about a potential customer. This would only be possible if the individual concerned had given his permission for the several separate databases involved to have been combined into a more general collection of information. Many forms that we now complete, for example, include a specific question asking permission for just this sharing of data – such as in the case of supermarket loyalty cards and so forth.

Where this information *can* be combined – such as by the police authorities in the case of a criminal investigation of a specific suspect – it gives very precise profiles of the individuals. An analysis of spending preferences in supermarkets, bank account details and even an analysis of where and when one bought petrol using a credit card can allow a very detailed understanding of a suspect's movements and habits. Because of the way in which these analyses can give such profiles, the Data Protection Act is to be strengthened to provide a more comprehensive regulation for the maintenance of security around that data, integrating the UK more closely with the European Union regulations, and providing additional levels of confidence.

Privacy of personal data is also afforded in the UK by the Computer Misuse Act of 1990. This makes unauthorised access to computer-held data an offence, especially access intended to facilitate further offences – such as unauthorised disclosure of the data – or to allow the information to be modified. It is this Act, for example, that outlaws computer viruses and the very many headline-grabbing attempts to 'hack' into computer systems holding important information. While this Act provides the *legal* framework for outlawing such attempts, it does not however guarantee that such attempts will not be made, nor even that they will be detected and then reported. Many banks for example are reluctant to 'go public' on successful attacks on their systems, fearing that to do so might undermine public confidence. Police figures suggest in fact that only 5 per cent of successful hacking attempts are *noticed*, let alone reported.

This misuse of computers suffers from two particular features of the Internet world. Firstly, hackers have attracted an outlaw mystique, making their activities attractive – perhaps even heroic –

in the eyes of the more juvenile Internet users. Secondly, and more damagingly, the Internet supports such hacking attempts on a *global* basis – that is, from individuals who are outside of the UK's regulatory control, or who use the anonymity services mentioned above to protect their identity. As with the other such situations, even where their identity can be determined those hackers may well not be within countries with which we have existing agreements to allow cooperative policing. Moreover, with an increasing commercial dependence on Internet structures, such hacking attempts have become increasingly criminal rather than irritating in nature; these could be attempted on a deliberate basis from countries that provide an unwitting refuge – such as certain African states or the former USSR.

Technology – in the form of encryption tools and 'firewall' computers – and the legal frameworks must both develop in tandem to allow the criminal exploitation of the Internet to be constrained. Unfortunately, as with the encryption case, these very technological developments can equally well be exploited by the criminals or terrorist themselves. While this might sound apocalyptic, it is in fact not significantly different from the way in which both criminal and detective can use mobile telephones, high-performance cars and even aircraft.

Crime and detection have always played a game of legal and intellectual leapfrog – or rather, catch-up on the part of the authorities; there is no reason to expect, believe or hope that the Internet or Information Superhighway case will be any different.

DIGITAL OWNERSHIP

In the 'real world' it is relatively easy to know that one *owns* something; a physical object can be one's direct personal property and can be bought outright. It can be traded, damaged or stolen – but it is usually easy to understand when and how one comes to own the thing and how one can subsequently lose or relinquish it. Some real-world entities are less obvious: intellectual property, such as ownership of an idea that might be patented but that might also be shared with friends and colleagues; copyright of a song's lyrics that might be performed by somebody else; or copyright of a CD that might be loaned by a library and subsequently recorded for private use.

In the context of the Internet, these questions of ownership become more complex still. Goods traded within the Internet are digital in nature, and can therefore be duplicated exactly and precisely; and ideas shared among a set of friends might in fact become globally visible, thereby passing into the public domain of general awareness and hence become non-patentable. In this section, therefore, we will consider the concept of owning digital goods, and the issues relating to rights of owners within the Internet. This is most closely bound up with the question of *copyright*; discussion of protection afforded to the owners of company names, tradenames and trademarks will be postponed to the following section on regulating companies.

First impressions might suggest that copyright in the 'information age' is likely to be the most difficult aspect of on-line activity to regulate and to ensure effective protection for citizens of different countries. The goods that are involved – such as software, CD, video and books – can be expressed in a digital format and copied, precisely and exactly at any point of the transmission process. Moreover, when information is issued onto the Internet – perhaps with 'fair use' in mind – it is then effectively published throughout the world. It might be expected that such a development would for all practical purposes prevent any author or copyright owner from ensuring a maintenance of his or her basic rights as the owner of those goods. Furthermore, it might also be thought that the very question of 'ownership' of a digital representation of some entity, being nothing more than a simple sequence of binary numbers stored and transmitted in a file, might also be difficult or impossible to establish.

In fact, the exact opposite is true. Of all the aspects of the Internet discussed in this book, the question of intellectual property rights as protected by copyright mechanisms is perhaps the best developed element of regulatory control – although this is not to say that all aspects of the Internet case can be handled easily. Even without consideration of the Internet, however, copyright law has been established throughout most of the world for very many years – the Berne Convention of 1885 for example first established the basic principles of international copyright; and the high levels of government commitment to the Information Superhighway within the major economies has ensured that copyright laws and regulatory procedures for *digital* ownership have received similarly high levels of attention.

Directorate-General XV of the European Commission, the World Intellectual Property Organisation (WIPO), the Organisation for Economic Co-operation and Development (OECD) and the United Nations Educational, Scientific and Cultural Organisation (UNESCO) are all working to establish a globally effective copyright framework for the Information Society (see reference [26]). In addition to these transnational efforts, individual countries – primarily those that are signatories to the Berne Convention treaty – are working to harmonise their individual approaches to the question. This is not to say that there won't be international differences; not all of the world's economies are signatories to the convention,[135] and there are frequent breaches of copyright even in those countries that are. However, the existence of such international efforts already, and an existing awareness of the likely problems, will ensure that the question of intellectual property in Cyberspace is addressed through agreement by a large number of countries.

The first aspect to be considered in the Internet context is that of *ownership* of digital goods. Does the encoding of some element of property in a digital fashion effect one's ownership of that property? By comparison with other goods it is easy to see that it does not – at least in those countries embracing the notion of private ownership of property. Once the property has been transferred, the receiver owns the entity outright – whether that entity is represented in a digital or an analogue fashion. The comparison might be with an LP versus a CD; one is analogue, the other digital; once bought, however, title to the property transfers to the purchaser. The physical entity of the CD, say, can then be traded in turn, destroyed or retained; it *belongs* to the owner. The same is true with any property, from video cassettes through books to cars and clothes. This is perhaps best expressed in terms of ownership of software, that exists and is traded primarily in its digital form. I have paid for and therefore own my copy of Windows, Word and the various computer games on my computer; this is unaffected by whether one considers the *packaging* or the digital version of those programs; even if I have lost the CD-ROM on which I bought a particular game, the software is still my property.

Books, CDs, software and other entities that are implementations of an *idea* are, however, covered by a number of protections over and above the basic notion of ownership of the physical object itself. Specifically, this book for example is covered by my copyright; this is a continuing – although perhaps time-limited – protection of my rights as the author, and persists even after title of ownership of the specific copy passes to another person. These protected rights cover such aspects as duplication or reuse of the specific text itself in all but a few circumstances of 'fair use': explicit quotation being the most obvious.[136]

What is required to establish a copyright? Recent additions to the Berne Convention and other national and transnational agreements have established a very straightforward aspect to this. Essentially, copyright exists automatically on any composition of an original expression that is fixed in a tangible form. It is no longer necessary in most countries for example to affix a ©-symbol to the work explicitly; provided that the work is an original and fixed expression, it falls within the protection of copyright. In the Internet context, this means that e-mail and Usenet newsgroup postings are automatically the copyright of their author, and that it is incidentally an offence against that author's rights for the e-mail or article to be cross-posted to another newsgroup, published in any other form – such as printout – other than for private use, or for any other than short excerpts to be used in subsequent postings without his or her permission.

As an aside, this also has a bearing on the question of publication of patentable ideas. If an idea is original to a particular person, and represents a process or the implementation of a process that is not already known, or is not a trivial extension of a known thing, then it may be patented. A patent then allows the author – or inventor – to license the use of that idea, perhaps for an industrial production process. If the author allows the idea to pass into the public domain, however, it is not possible for it to be protected under patent. An e-mail exchange does not count as putting the idea in the public domain; the analogy would of course be with written correspondence, and with the author's intentions that the e-mail messages represent a private exchange. Conversely, since a Usenet newsgroup is assumed to be a globally visible publication, a newsgroup article describing the process *would* count as being in the public domain – and thereby prevent the patent from being valid.

If a recipient of a private e-mail cross-posts that message to a newsgroup then the idea has been published, in exactly the same way as a private letter that is copied to the newspapers has been published. An interesting case might be imagined in which a private e-mail is re-posted within a closed mailgroup relevant to the invention. Is that mailgroup the equivalent of a specialist journal or newsletter – in which case the idea has been published – or does it remain a private communication – in which case it hasn't? Again, the Internet is as yet too immature for such a situation to have been decided, although an immediate reaction might well be to say that the closed mailgroup has the same publicity cover as a specialist journal and would therefore count as putting the idea in the 'public domain'.

In these instances that clearly count as publication, however, what recourse does the original author have? As discussed above, the e-mail is protected by the author's copyright, and he or she can therefore sue – within those countries recognising the Berne Convention and its additions – for infringement. The author might not therefore be able to protect the idea by patent, but would still have some form of recourse, although this might well be a cold comfort to them.

A Usenet newsgroup article is therefore afforded the self-same level of copyright protection as is this book. Without a © notice, however, those transgressing the copyright can claim 'innocent infringement', and some countries still require the notice to be present. It is usual therefore to attach such notices where the retention of the copyright is of interest, such as in the case of this book for example.

Copyright therefore gives the author of an 'original expression' certain rights that are violated if the work is treated in a way inconsistent with his interests. Unlawful duplication is the most obvious example of this, but in the case of music, video and even film scripts, unauthorised performance is also a violation of the author's rights. In the context of the Internet, all material distributed represents 'an expression fixed in a tangible form' and is therefore covered by copyright protection, of varying degrees depending upon the use of that material that the copyright owner has *licensed*.

A licence is the means by which a copyright owner allows another party – such as the purchaser of the goods – to use the 'original expression'.[137] In the case of videos for instance, the licence might allow use for home entertainment but not for public broadcast; in the case of books, it might allow anything other than outright duplication. In the case of software, licences can be many and varied. As we discussed in Chapter 2, the licence can support freeware, shareware, loan or rental of the software; it can allow the application to be used freely as a tool for the development of further commercial software applications, or it can stipulate that an additional payment must be made to the owner for each such new copy in this event; and it can allow a game to be played for a limited period before a charge is made.

The information, data and applications within the Internet – ranging from multi-media encyclopaedias, through software applications and games, to electronically published text can all therefore be protected under copyright and their use specified through precisely worded licences. Moreover, while there might be differences between the various countries,[138] there is a broad agreement that world-wide copyright enforcement is a base requirement for the information age. But how can such legal protection as exists actually be enforced in practice?

Rolex watches and Lacoste sweaters are sold quite openly in Hong Kong; pirated video tapes and even CDs are available in car-boot sales throughout the country; and the practice of recording one's own CDs onto tape to be played in the car is near universal. In an age in which goods can be copied precisely and exactly, with a digital-produced fidelity far in advance of that available with even the most sophisticated of analogue devices, how can the protection of copyright be afforded? By a perverse twist of fate, that very digital nature of the Internet-published goods can in fact be used to guarantee that the author's rights are protected in exactly the fashion that their licence stipulates.[139]

Recall from Chapter 3 that it is necessary to protect Internet distributed – and equally, Internet-published – material by means of encryption. This is to ensure that the goods cannot be intercepted (ie, stolen) in the act of transmission to the buyer. The decryption key or keys make sure that the goods can only be accessed by the intended recipient; more than this, however, those self-same keys can be used to further constrain that access by means of encrypted *permission tokens*. In this scheme for example it is possible to use the keys to allow the software, CD or whatever to be used once only, a limited number of times, or for a limited period. Even more usefully, the decrypt/permission key can irrevocably link the goods to a particular PC, or can irreversibly encode the user's details within the file – again, in an encrypted form. In this last case, even if it proves possible to duplicate the material, the original user's name can be recovered from any illicit copies that are discovered and ideally the initial act of illegal dissemination can then be prosecuted.[140]

The digital nature of the goods means that it becomes possible to protect them – and hence the copyright owner's interests – to the same precise degree that the author would like to enjoy. That the goods can be intercepted or duplicated exactly is of no use without an enabling token, and that token can only be obtained by payment to the publisher. As the hybrid distribution examples in Chapter 3 illustrated, it then becomes possible to distribute the basic goods themselves free of charge – perhaps even with certain features already accessible – and then to charge for the enabling key itself. Without that key, the material is simply a useless sequence of binary digits; with the key, it becomes a valuable, tradable and protected instance of the author's expression.

While there are certainly aspects of the Internet's widespread adoption that *will* prove to be a serious concern for the authorities, such as the situation in which physical books or pictures are laboriously copied or scanned, in the case of original, digital goods the technology brings very real, very tangible and very valuable benefits.

POLICING THE INTERNET

While the protection of copyright and of ownership of goods in Cyberspace might be straightforward – or at least, not impossible – to effect, that of policing the Internet is far more difficult. This is particularly the case when we consider 'virtual companies'. The several aspects that must be considered in this context range from the protection of company names, trade names and trademarks in the Internet trading domain; the maintenance of fair trading regimes to protect domestic consumers buying from virtual companies, perhaps from overseas; and regulation of advertising within the Internet. In addition to this company-focused activity, there are also the issues of policing the content of the Internet, and the activities of individuals – involving issues such as taxation and duties evasion.

As we have discussed above, however, the policing of the content of the Internet is essentially resolved by the approach that has been taken in the recent Decency and Defamation Acts, assigning responsibility for offensive material to the ISPs; it then becomes *their* task to ensure that the unwelcome or illegal material is prohibited. While this might not be fair on the ISPs, it does at least mean that the policing task is relatively simple.

In other cases, such as the illicit and unfair use of copyright material, this can be protected by mechanisms that prevent such non-legitimate activities, and pursued by the police, trading standards inspectors or other appropriate authorities in the event of a complaint. Rather than wait for such a complaint, however, some police forces have taken steps to monitor and observe the Internet content for that material which is not simply offensive but illegal – in the case of paedophilia for example, the West Midlands Commercial Vice Squad in Birmingham have run an on-going watch on certain newsgroups and Web sites. This proved successful in allowing them to locate and to prosecute alleged offenders.

For most police forces and authorities, however, the regulation of these activities will be driven and constrained by the scope of their responsibilities. In 'real world' situations with which they have most familiarity, there is an expectation that offences are committed within a specific jurisdiction. That is, not only would one normally expect the UK police force to investigate and prosecute offences in the UK, but more specifically, an offence in Birmingham will be within the jurisdiction of the West Midlands Police. Similarly, in the US the Los Angeles Police Department would not become involved in investigations in New York. In terms of trading-related offences, there is therefore an expectation that the trader has a physical presence in some police force's jurisdiction – or in an area covered by a particular tax office, customs and excise office or whatever authority is relevant to the offence.

Internet-enabled offences are different. This is true whether the offence is the criminal dissemination of paedophilia, the sale of unfit goods, or fraudulent trading. These can all take place from locations which are remote from the jurisdiction of investigative authorities. An offence can be uncovered in one location, but have been initiated elsewhere. Even when both locations are within the UK, this can cause operational difficulties. In the US, offences which cross state boundaries can be handled by the FBI, a *federal* authority rather than a state or city one; in the UK, there is no equivalent body for police matters, other than perhaps to turn to Scotland Yard itself. And of course an Internet offence can cross country and even continent boundaries as easily as state or regional ones. This makes a cooperative approach to such policing a matter of great concern; moreover, this cooperation must be afforded both internationally *and* internally – and both of these will be non-trivial to achieve.

In the case of undeclared Internet imports or a failure to declare income earned or paid through the Internet there is at least an easy allocation of jurisdiction: the appropriate office serving the area within which the offender is resident. In this situation, however, the separate question of *detecting* the offence must be considered.

The first area for consideration is the regulation of names within the Internet. Company names and trade or brand names are a precious and protected resource for the organisations concerned. In most countries, the organisation and its name are associated through the company registration process; the name is a legal device identifying that company in its contracts. In the Internet context, the nearest equivalent to a shop or company name is the *domain* name associated with that organisation's home page. Users wishing to locate a particular company would usually search for reasonably obvious instances of the name as a Web address: 'www.star.co.uk', for example.

This domain name has several elements: the '.co' specifies that this is a *commercial* user of the Internet; in the US, this is written '.com'. Alternatives to the commercial include '.gov', a government user; '.org', a non-profit organisation, such as a charity; and '.ac', an academic user, such as a university. The *country code* element is the '.uk' at the end; in the US, the equivalent '.us' is not necessary – the Internet routers are America-centric and therefore assume that the required host is in the US unless told otherwise. From a trading perspective, however, the important part of the domain name is the '.star' element; this is the name of the organisation owning the target system, and in the commercial context is expected to be the name of the company itself or an obvious variant.

The domain name is a symbolic representation of the physical network address of the machine: the so-called IP address, which is a non-friendly sequence of numbers. To establish a system name it is necessary for the name and IP address to be registered in the routing tables of the many systems within the Internet. This can be done by completing tables in a handful of systems, from which the name and address is disseminated to the Domain Name Server (DNS) systems throughout the Internet world.

This registration is performed by one of several organisations in each country as a voluntary or as a commercial service. A company wishing therefore to establish its Internet presence must use one of these registering services to perform the task. The service will advise on the choice of domain name and will look to check that a particular name has not already been established. In the case of company names in the 'real world' such choice is covered by regulations; in the Internet, there is no *official* registrar. These registration service providers might for example decline to register a name which would clearly offend or which is an obvious attempt to 'steal' an existing company name. In some cases, however, such obvious registrations might not be detected and in any case the registration is covered by the individual organisation's *practice* rather than by set rules established by law.

In attempting to register a domain name, a company might well find that the name has already been taken and is not therefore available. This might occur because the domain name is being used by another company, with or without the same name as the original; it might occur because the company name is also an obvious name for an Internet domain, or at least not obviously associated with another company and has been taken accidentally; or it might occur because somebody has chosen *deliberately* to take the company's name. The first two cases have nuisance value and nothing more. On the 'high street' it is perfectly possible for different shops or businesses to have essentially similar names, differentiated in some way by a logo or other aspect; thus, 'Star Computers', 'Star Interactive', 'Star Internet', 'The Star' restaurant and many, many others might all wish to use the domain name 'www.star.co.uk' – only one of them will manage this (Star Internet, as it happens), the others must use a slightly different version of the name.

The third case is the more worrying. There are a number of immediately obvious reasons why a third party might choose deliberately to take a company name for a domain: they might be a pressure group or similar hoping to discredit the organisation; they might be trading illegally under the company's name; or they might hope to be able to *resell* that name to the company.

In the UK and in very many other countries, because a company name must be registered it is therefore protected. Any third party using that name fraudulently, by claiming to *be* that company or by acting in such a way as to lead an innocent party to believe that they are the company in question, is acting in an illegal manner. Once that activity has been uncovered, by a complaint, by chance or by an attempt to register the domain name legitimately, the offended company can then turn to the law to seek redress.

The simplest case is that of a UK company whose name is being used as a UK domain with the intention to mislead. While it is possible for any IP address to be registered as a UK domain name, it will usually represent a UK-resident computer and will therefore be accessible to the police or other authorities. Alternatively, the domain name might be registered in another country within which the company trades, but with which the UK authorities have a means of undertaking cooperative regulation – such as the US, EU or other established partners. This need not always be the case, however: it is perfectly possible to register any IP address as being within any particular country, rather than the one within which the computer actually sits – although for most registration agencies this would involve completing the registration form in a misleading manner. This would mean, however, that both the computer *and* the offending party can be outside of the UK's jurisdiction, perhaps in a data haven that would prevent any and all countries' authorities from reaching it.

While it is clear that there is a *legal* mechanism whereby the company can seek to prosecute those using its name, the practical aspects of reaching and punishing those using the name for non-legitimate purposes are therefore far from clear. The only way in which this use of the Internet could be acted upon would be for the domain registration agencies to *reverse* that registration when it comes to light as having been effected illicitly, or to re-register the domain but with the legitimate owner's IP address. However, it is not immediately obvious that this could be achieved technically, and the regulatory mechanism that would be required to enforce such a re-registration does not exist at present; moreover, it might well prove difficult to reach an international agreement on such an approach anyway.

The third case described above, of an attempt by somebody to register a company name with a view to subsequently selling it, is an interesting situation. Trading under another company's name is quite clearly illegal; but simply *possessing* that name is not – providing that the person involved is not trying to pass himself off as representing, acting on behalf of, or otherwise associated with the company. What regulations *have* emerged for policing the Internet have been produced by analogy with the real world situations – but the company name/domain name comparison really has no obvious equivalents. In many ways, it is perhaps most similar to the situation where some enterprising person buys or already owns the strip of land providing access to a main road from a new or proposed housing development. In this case, it is the *access rights* that must be purchased; similarly, in our example the company requires or needs the Internet access rights embodied in the domain name.

Is the person holding and selling the domain name acting illegally? Not with the current state of the law surrounding the Internet – nor is he apparently acting against 'netiquette'; by comparison with the real-estate case, he might even be seen as acting in a purely entrepreneurial manner. Many voices have been raised warning companies about this practice and calling for legal clarification in this case. Perhaps the soundest advice would be for the companies actually to register domain names as rapidly as possible so as to provide an immediate protection, rather than rely upon a legal device that may or may not emerge and may or may not be enforceable in practice. And of course all the comments about company names apply with equal force to *brand* names, trademarks and so forth that might equally be used as domain names.

In the case of fair trading within the Internet, this too gives rise to a series of problems mostly concerned with the transnational aspects of the system. As with the copyright case, however, the growth in interest in the Information Society has led to attention at EU, OECD and other transnational bodies. Certainly within Europe, the interest and potential of 'common market' trading has already produced outline agreements on cross-border shopping, even without consideration of the Internet.

The analogy used for establishing fair trading over the Internet is that of mail-order or other forms of 'distance selling'. Buying goods over the telephone or through mail-order world-wide has now become very well established and is governed by local and international regulation and agreements. Distance selling is therefore now very well understood, at least within the EU as a whole and between other countries on the basis of individual agreements. Trading over the Internet counts as a particular form of distance selling, differentiated only by the particular characteristics of the medium: speed and ubiquity of access for example, along with the ability to sell *and* distribute certain goods this way. It is also differentiated by the fact that *all* of the trading communication can take place electronically: there need not therefore be a permanent, written record of the transaction.

These are important aspects in the context of Internet consumer protection. The 'Distance Selling Directive'[141] of the European Union for example stipulates that vendors taking advantage of mail-order – and by implication the Internet – must make relevant information available. This information typically includes details of the service or goods offered; any restrictions or limitations in its use; and address and other details of the company itself. It also includes details of the relevant law under which the transaction takes place – ie, that the contract is drafted within. The directive further stipulates that the information must be made available in a 'durable' form[142]: in 'normal' cases paper records that can be filed and kept. At such an early stage of its development it is not readily apparent how such a stipulation applies in the context of the Internet: while files containing the information can be stored and printed, they can also be modified by one or both parties to their advantage.

From a regulatory perspective the question of maintaining records in the context of Internet trading is a difficult one. While secure, auditable transactions *can* be performed in the open environment of the Internet, the more normal case has seen untracked and untrackable flows of information. In the context of the original use of the Internet – research and general correspondence – this has not been a matter for concern. Where permanent, reliable records of advertised claims or contractual agreements must be recovered this is no longer satisfactory. For example, if an *offer* is made from a trader to a potential customer – usually in the form of an advertisement of some description – then this forms the first part of a contract and the basis upon which the sold goods' suitability will be assessed in the event of a dispute. Where the offer is in an electronic form, such as an e-mail communication, it is entirely possible for either the customer or the trader to alter that text at a later date to their advantage. Unless all parties concerned retain an accredited copy of the original, or use some form of clever encryption as discussed above, then this risk will always be present in such trading.

Where such disputes arise between consumers and suppliers two questions must be considered: under what *law* is the dispute to be adjudicated; and within which *jurisdiction*? That is, whose courts – vendor or consumer – and with what country's protection? These questions have been addressed in the context of certain of the UK's trading relationships within the European Union or related states, and with established trading partners such as the US. In most cases jurisdiction is applied on the basis of the country having the closest association with the establishment of the contract;[143] while the transaction might be presented as having occurred 'within Cyberspace', in fact it has been established and performed within some country and is judged on that basis. Where a consumer therefore receives advertising material in the UK, makes a purchasing selection in the UK, initiates the Internet transaction from the UK and receives the goods or services in the UK, it is clear that UK jurisdiction applies without regard to the country with which the Internet transaction was completed. In most cases for Internet shopping performed by UK residents, UK courts will therefore have jurisdiction in the event of a dispute with the vendor.

The applicable law will similarly be that of the UK in the event that no contractual law is explicitly declared in the text of the contracting order form. Where another country's law *is* stipulated – that is, a Japanese vendor for example, selling over the Internet to a UK consumer explicitly states that the contract is covered by Japanese law – then the UK consumer still retains as a minimum the consumer protection afforded by the UK law. In all cases therefore a UK consumer can expect to enjoy UK levels of consumer protection and the jurisdiction of a UK court. It is important to note, however, that such consumer protection is afforded to the *consumer* of the goods concerned, not to any intermediate purchaser. This means that those companies buying goods from suppliers with a view to trading them are not covered by such automatic protections and must therefore ensure that the contractual arrangements are both explicit and acceptable.

Turning now to the perspective of the *trader*, this places a requirement on suppliers of goods over the Internet to be aware of the many different legal systems within which they might be completing contracts. In 'real world' transnational marketing a company can elect not to do business within a country whose consumer protection regulations might impose a burden which the company may not choose – or may not be *able* – to shoulder. In the case of global Internet trading this will be more difficult to achieve. A simple example: traders in Denmark are not allowed to offer free goods in conjunction with sold goods as an incentive, but yet this is a popular and common trading device elsewhere. Any company offering for example a free copy of sample software with every copy of a particular game would fall foul of Danish regulations.

From the perspective of the legal framework therefore, a consumer of Internet goods in the UK can expect to enjoy high levels of protection. Of course, this might not be of any practical value if the trading company is inaccessible to the UK or other authorities. As we have discussed above, companies could choose to perform Internet trading from poorly regulated 'havens' that provide Internet access to them without imposing restrictions or regulations and without affording access to external authorities. With Internet-enabled payment mechanisms, even where delivery of the goods is effected entirely through traditional distribution channels, it would still be difficult to provide practical methods to protect poorly served consumers when there is no simple way of locating or reaching the entity behind the virtual shop counter. This also of course, as discussed in Chapter 4, would affect the *taxation* authorities' ability to assess and collect corporation, purchase, VAT or any other taxes due from those 'hidden' companies.

For this reason consumers in the UK for example might wish to have the assurance that the company with which they trade over the Internet is either based in the UK, based in the European Union, or established in some state with which the UK has relevant agreements. Similarly, the various taxation authorities would prefer there to be mechanisms allowing them to find and gain access to those organisations. Unfortunately, this might not always be possible. Particularly in the case of fraudulent trading, the use of a UK domain name is no guarantee that the company – or rather, its computer – is indeed within the UK, as we have discussed above. The only way of being sure would be to use the services of Internet shops which are within well established, well regulated digital shopping centres, such as those run by CompuServe or other reputable third parties. In this case, there can be a form of guarantee that the trader does indeed actually *exist* in some 'real-world', accountable sense. This would be like only ever buying from those established shops that have a place within the real-world shopping centres and malls – but even with the availability of such clean, well-lit, well-policed and secure environments, people still choose to buy some of their goods from 'back street' or market stalls. Fair trading regulation has to be able to cover both situations, but the Internet case is far more difficult to effect.

The same situation arises in the case of attempts to regulate Internet advertising, although here it is likely that the antipathy of established Internet users will also need to be considered. As Chapter 3 discussed, UK advertising is performed in an essentially self-regulating environment, with industry watchdogs responding to complaints and criticism. Given that the purpose of advertising is to persuade customers to part with their money, offending their tastes is clearly of no advantage to the industry. Some advertising is of course offensive to some: the most extreme example in the UK might be the striking images used by Benetton (an AIDS victim, a newborn child, etc). However, these images were *not* offensive to the company's target market, although they did give rise to many complaints.

In the context of global Internet advertising, this offensive/acceptable boundary is much harder to establish. Advertising can offend in one country but not in another; furthermore, it can be illegal in one country, but not in another – tobacco advertising, for example. To date, the Internet advertising has been predominantly American and British; as Chapter 3 examined, this advertising appears within specific Web sites dedicated to marketing material, or within the search engines themselves. So far, it has been inoffensive within the majority of Internet-connected countries to all but the most hardened opponents of such activity; and their objection is not to the *content* but to the *fact* of such advertising. Certainly within the UK there has therefore been no attempt – nor any intention – to change the basic 'hands-off' stance of the authorities towards the advertising industry.

And of course, if offensive advertising were to become a part of the Internet, it might well be unnecessary for the authorities to police it anyway . While some Internet 'citizens' have worked hard to ensure that pornographic newsgroups continue to be accessible, offensive advertising could not count on such protection. The 'spamming' approach to advertising gives rise to fierce responses; offensive advertising such as the use of objectionable images and language could expect no less a response. Would this be an example of Internet self regulation or of 'vigilante' activity? Strictly, it is of course vigilante in nature – and arguably some of the potential Internet responses to offensive advertising from the UK would contravene the Computer Misuse Act.

The point remains, however, that since the advertising is intended to encourage purchasing, it is unlikely to become offensive in nature and there are therefore no plans for excessive UK regulation and constraints upon it. That these advertisements are also seen in many other countries means, however, that it is possible for a UK company, projecting a UK message intended for UK audiences, to inadvertently offend against a trading standard regulation within some other country. Even the most anodyne of UK commercial messages might prove offensive in some other culture. An organisation that already trades in that country can of course be expected to be aware of any particular sensitivities; other companies might not. While the UK authorities have no plans therefore to influence UK advertising for the sake of UK audiences, it might prove necessary – or even essential – for such sensitivities to be communicated to all those companies encouraged to trade via the Internet.

The other areas for policing of the Internet are different insofar as they relate to *personal* rather than to *corporate* activities: failure to declare income earned or paid through Internet channels, and failure to declare duty on those goods imported by means of the Internet. The first of these is very straightforward to address: undeclared income is the subject of compliance activity on the part of the taxation authorities in any and all countries. Whether that unearned income comes from the traditional 'hidden economy' of cash payments, unsecured long-term loans or through Internet mechanisms is largely irrelevant. The processes used for detecting undeclared income concentrate not on simply finding the source of such income but rather on consideration of the individual's spending habits and the income that would be required to support them.

The case of undeclared importation duties, however, is much more difficult to handle. In the case where goods are advertised, published and distributed over the Internet, it could prove difficult if not impossible for the customs authorities even to detect that such imports occur. The digital goods are undetectable as such, particularly if encoded or encrypted as would be necessary in practice. In the 'real world', HM Customs & Excise local offices monitor the performance and behaviour of trading establishments and make periodic visits to inspect. The 'customs nose', helped by careful examination of stock, accounts and staff attitude, can often detect illicit activity on the part of such traders; and in real-world ports can usually detect attempts to smuggle prohibited goods or substances.

In the Internet there is no direct equivalent: there are no fixed ports of entry; there are no fixed premises to visit; and perhaps most damagingly, there are no responsible local offices. The detection of illegal digital imports might well therefore be impossible. One suggestion that has been proposed and discussed, although not yet seriously, at senior levels in many authorities – within the UK and elsewhere – would be the introduction of a sweeping 'digital tax': a tax on the bits entering an Internet user's PC without any regard to the content, value or meaning of those bits. However, while this might be technically possible to effect, politically it would give rise to many more problems in return for those compliance issues that it resolves.

POLITICAL CHALLENGES

Much of the current high levels of interest in the Internet have resulted from the enthusiasm of all political parties in the UK, US and elsewhere in favour of the information society. An infrastructure that can help support distance learning, world-wide trading and that plays to the strengths of western economies concentrating on value-add services is clearly of great benefit. The political challenges that result from this enthusiasm are, however, both varied and complex. The political role in the Internet society encompasses aspects such as the establishment of legal frameworks to outlaw offensive practice and content; the establishment of regulating bodies equipped and able to police those very same laws; and associated with this, the establishment of the necessary international agreements to allow those legal and regulatory frameworks to be effective in practice.

Quite apart from these aspects, the politicians in all countries involved in the Internet social experiment face two further, quite fundamental challenges: to benefit from the technology in their own operation; and to ensure that the Internet facilities can be usefully exploited in supporting the mechanisms of democracy. The first of these was addressed in Chapter 3; the second point will be considered in Chapter 6, as we examine the potential of our 'Cybernation' to augment or to supplant the established nation states.

The first aspect of the political challenge lies in the legal frameworks outlawing certain practices. As we have seen throughout the text, the Internet makes a range of activities possible; activities that represent either an obvious development from an existing practice, or wholly new ones.

The Internet can support *inter alia* global chains of pyramid letters, anonymous hate mail, offensive 'graffiti' and a range of other anti-social activities. Just as fraudulent traders are provided with the potential to operate from 'data havens', so too are political agitators and even terrorists afforded havens from which to criticise government policies – either our own or our allies' from within the shelter of the UK, protected by anonymous ftp servers, by complicated cross-posting of articles, or by the use of dial-in access to some other country's machines. In early 1996 for example, plans of the British Army's establishments in Northern Ireland were published on the Internet; a book exposing unsavoury elements of the former French President's life was similarly distributed initially via the Internet; and even the answers to a Scottish mathematics exam have been made available.

More than this, however, the Internet can support terrorist attacks on computers themselves. To date, virus and other attacks on computer systems have been motivated either by juvenile mischief or by greed; as western economies become ever more dependent upon the systems, and as the Internet establishes a role in trading and a self-supporting economy of its own, it might well become a viable target for direct terrorist intervention. While the various UK, other European and US authorities have a range of sweeping powers against bombs, kidnappers and those who trade in or who use guns, similar powers against computer-specific crimes are restricted in the

UK to the Computer Misuse Act and the Data Protection Act. Arguably, the existing terrorist powers might have a sufficiently wide range to encompass this potential, but it is not immediately obvious that this is so.

We have also seen examples of existing Internet practices or activities that might well be deemed illegal as the Internet becomes more widely available. Use of anonymous ftp servers; the application of strong data encryption for other than credit card transactions; preemptive registration of commercial domain names; mail-bombs, flame wars and 'fighting talk' in Usenet newsgroups. The first difficult question that the political challenge gives rise to is that of *legality*: should any of these activities – all of which are recognisable practices within the Internet – be deemed to be illegal?

The current stance, certainly of the UK government, is that the Internet should continue to operate within a self-regulation regime[144] and that excessive legal or regulatory frameworks from Westminster will only act to stifle its use by reputable concerns. By contrast, while US authorities have encouraged the use of the Internet – with which they have had more familiarity than the rest of the world – they have also tended to impose a series of more severe restrictions; as earlier sections discussed, the Computer Decency Act is more stringent than the UK Defamation Act. Even this, however, pales beside the stricter controls introduced by other countries, such as China who have required all Internet users to register with the government, allowing their activity to be monitored or even constrained.

While the UK approach is relaxed at present, ministers have stressed, however, that *without* effective internal policing – primarily by the Internet Service Providers – stricter legal controls might have to be forced upon the industry. This is particularly important given the central role envisaged for the Internet and the Information Superhighway in education.

Of course, such controls need then to be policed; and the transnational aspects of the Internet, which we saw gave rise to the more severe difficulties, would mean that unilateral imposition of new laws by any single country might well simply have the effect of curtailing activity within the originating country but not that of other countries. The most essential political challenge therefore lies in establishing transnational agreements, and in providing a sufficiently flexible policing mechanism, able to operate within a non-geographical jurisdiction. While victim or criminal might well both lie within a particular police force's area, this will become increasingly unlikely as the Internet becomes more popular.

As this chapter described, such transnational agreements have been established in the case of copyright, but even then it is quite possible for those few countries outside the agreement to subvert it. And the transnational agreements must cover many more aspects than this – perhaps including a united approach to those 'data havens' from which fraudulent traders could operate. It is important to recognise, however, that data havens in particular have been identified only as a *potential* source of concern; because they have not yet emerged as a serious practical threat to Internet trading they have not yet been addressed as anything more than a possible worry.

These attempts to establish transnational agreements will also run into a series of problems. Firstly, what are the preferred fora within which such agreements can be reached? There are already a number of international bodies that consider the constituent elements: standards, security, telecommunications, copyright, international trading, cooperative criminal investigations; these bodies are not renowned for the progress they demonstrate and for the sweeping world-wide agreements to which all concerned subsequently comply. Moreover, it is necessary not only for each of the countries involved to reach agreements, it is necessary also for these international bodies themselves to establish frameworks that are consistent.

The second problem is that of timing. It takes a long time to reach an international agreement on all but the most important, urgent and immediate issue.[145] In the case of the basic networking structures for example, the international body formulating such standards is the ISO. Throughout the 1980s, this organisation deliberated over a networking model and several standards proposals before formulating the 'ISO Model', together with a range of specifications. While this deliberation progressed, so too did the technology; few if any computer companies halted their development timetables to wait the several years required. Instead, so-called *de facto* and multilateral standards emerged as the industry produced a series of different practical models, either individually (such as with Microsoft) or in cooperative bodies (such as the OSF). This then resulted in a handful of commercial 'winners' that were subsequently adopted by the other manufacturers. The basic networking structure of the Internet (TCP/IP) is the most obvious example of this, but so too are the other important Internet components: Windows, Java, HTML, SSL, SET and many others.

In practical terms, this means that while the politicians and the various international bodies seek to define, agree and implement an approach to a particular situation, even by the time the first timetabled meeting has completed, the technology will have moved on – giving rise in turn to subsequent and perhaps even more important concerns. While the authorities worried about the legality of seizing and reading 'private' e-mail, encryption technology made such debates irrelevant; while debates about telephone pricing progress, Internet telephony could render standard mechanisms obsolete; while those considering contractual terms in international telephone sales debated the issues, Internet virtual shops appeared; and as the authorities then began to worry about those, the credit card companies proposed and adopted encryption standards to remove as many worries as possible.

The Internet is a global and dynamic environment, driven by economics, technology and curiosity – and it has evolved its own internal regulators. These might not seem relevant or important when set against GATT, OECD and the EU; but arguably, given the relative speeds of each, nor do those bodies to the Internet 'citizens' policing their own digital high streets.

SUMMARY

Central to the concerns of establishing legal and regulatory frameworks for the Internet have been a series of basic characteristics of the technology. Those seeking to establish such frameworks are bound by considerations of jurisdiction and of responsibility; those seeking to exploit the Internet – whether for legitimate or non-legitimate purposes – are not restricted in this way. The Internet transcends the mundane limitations of geography, and this is both its advantage and the threat that it poses to the authorities. In many ways, however, this is in turn a threat that the Internet – or rather, the Internet users – pose for themselves.

Without the establishment of well-managed regulation and a framework within which the Internet can be exploited commercially *it will not survive*. As the various government fundings have been withdrawn, the Internet has become the domain of businesses – those providing connectivity services; those seeking to publish material; and those seeking to advertise and trade. If that domain is polluted by uncontrollable pornography, fraudulent traders and the perception of risk, those commercial concerns that now fund it will in turn withdraw.

The Internet is a unique and interesting experiment; it *does* have the potential to influence our lives and our society, but it is also an unknown frontier. And like many frontiers before, it is home both to the admirable and to the offensive: to vigilante-style self regulation of those things which offend against netiquette; to users who will go to any lengths to help research efforts, or 'flame' the naive questions of the novice; to users who will defend the indefensible and seek to subvert legitimate attempts at regulation; and to a wealth of information resources exceeding that of the most complete library. The establishment of effective controls that allow the Internet to be used profitably – in *all* senses of the word – without imposing such excessive constraints as to make it unusable is one of the greatest challenges that we now face.

6

FUTURE POTENTIAL

The march of technology has, with only a few occasional stumbles, been a steady progression from early, primitive mechanisms, to the most sophisticated of tools; but in most cases the direction of that progression has been difficult in the extreme to predict. In IT and telecommunications, however, the direction is relatively easy to see; the pace, slightly harder; and the implications of that progress almost impossible to assess.

In most cases, the fact that the telecommunications technology would evolve has not been in doubt. An engineer in the mid-war years familiar with the first, primitive attempts at television would not have been able to say *how* it might be achieved but he would certainly have felt confident in predicting the regular transmission of colour pictures. What would have been far more difficult to predict is the nature of that service and the broader implications that would result. Would colour transmissions from 'Wimbledon Fortnight' have been predicted? Probably, yes. Would political protests at televised sports have been predicted? Perhaps, yes. Would 'streaking' have been predicted? Undoubtedly not. Nor would video libraries; 'snuff' movies; televised darts and snooker; sheepdog trials; video-dating; closed-circuit monitoring of car parks; etc, etc.

The evolution in technology through this century is truly staggering to comprehend. In the period of our grandparents' lives, simple copper cables have evolved through complex co-axial bundles to ultra-high capacity fibre optics. This has allowed telecommunications to proceed from a small number of primitive, 'pulse-dialled' mechanisms into a global network of more powerful units. More, it has allowed the development of video-phones, of telephone-driven services, of new industries from telephone banking to explicit sex chat-lines. It has encouraged families to maintain contact around the world. A similar story has occurred with television, evolving into multi-channel, stereo-sound, satellite broadcasting. In the case of computers, the progression is even more staggering. From room-sized machines, to pocket-sized; from bare, single-user monoliths, to brief-case-sized, *personal* computers. These words are typed on a laptop PC which would, only *fifteen* years ago, have been considered one of the most powerful computers in the world.

As these foundation technologies have been combined to form the Internet, however, the implication and potential has become even more striking. The very rapidity with which the system has blazed through our collective lives has led many in fact to doubt that the Internet presents anything more than a brief, albeit dazzling tech-nological comet. The comparison most often used is that of 'Citizens' Band Radio' (CB) that like the Internet enjoyed a relatively long history of use in the US, and a very brief, very quirky exposure in the UK.[146] Is the Internet anything more than the mid-1990s' version of the CB phenomenon?

The answer of course is *yes*; the Internet is far from being another CB. There *are* 'nerds' and 'anoraks' using the Internet, exactly as there were such social misfits using the CB system. And at least in part, CB's very popularity in the UK grew from its initial illegality. In the US, however, it satisfied a very real requirement over and above the obvious 'nerd' aspects, allowing lorry drivers and similar to communicate over the huge and lonely distances of the American interior. In the UK, this more useful aspect was largely irrelevant and was anyway rapidly overtaken by the introduction of mobile telephones. The progression of CB into a more useful form of communication for businesses was therefore stifled by a different technology which gave the benefits of CB but in a familiar package.

The only real points of contact between the CB phenomenon and that of the Internet are therefore in the way in which both have been 'imported' into the UK from America; that both support free-form and idiosyncratic communication; and that both are perceived as being associated with 'nerds' interested in technology and in posturing. A better comparison might be between the Internet and radio itself. Both support communication, idiosyncratic and official; between enthusiasts such as the 'ham radio' users; and between companies, seeking to advertise or to inform. Both require the intervention of authorities to control, monitor and constrain their use for the common good; and both can support legitimate and non-legitimate users. Both are also essentially global – or at least transnational – in their impact and implications.

Of course the most fundamental reason why the Internet should be seen as more than a replay of the rise of CB lies with the attitude of the government itself. In the UK, CB was initially illegal before a reluctant government agreed to provide licences for its use – it subsequently died out. In contrast, the Internet's use forms a key element in the future plans of political parties across the spectrum and in many parts of the world. Companies, schools and individuals are being positively *encouraged* to use the Internet – and while advertisements for CB 'rigs' might have appeared in specialist magazines, those for Internet access appear on roadside hoardings and in the Sunday papers.

As well as the 'nerds' and 'anoraks' who use the Internet, there are grandparents, children, consultants, government departments, car manufacturers, newspaper publishers and many, many millions of others throughout the world. In some countries, the Internet is still the domain of the universities; but in the US and now in the UK, its use has spread far more widely.

This book has examined the way in which the Internet has grown from a basic communication medium, to become a technology capable of supporting publishing, advertising and even the trading of goods. We saw that the foundation stones of a Cybernation have already been placed, and considered the several cultural, economic and regulatory implications that even this underdeveloped form of the Internet society has produced. Beyond this initial state, however, we can expect the Internet technology and application to continue to progress.

The most immediately obvious aspects of this progression lie in the question of communication, trading and legislation. Low-cost, global communication will allow – more, will *encourage* – discussion groups and the exchange of thoughts beyond cultural or geographic boundaries. The first section of this chapter considers the evolution of Internet-supported communities, in which individuals share experiences among a world-wide pool of similar views, tied not by the bounds of geography and accidents of location, but rather by commonality of interests, opinion and a perception of *belonging*.

As the Internet use progresses further and deeper, its use by government members and departments to encourage discussion and communication about politically relevant issues will then lead to a new approach to such debates. Moreover, as digital communities themselves progress, supporting internal debates about their own management, this might well lead in turn to a separate identification of nationhood for those Internet communities. While this won't immediately spell the end of the nation-state, it will of course give rise to interesting identifications of citizenship on the part of such transnational collectives.

Throughout this work, we have constructed a series of visions of the way that the 'Internet Community' can be constructed and experienced. In this chapter, two such visions are presented and explored. One obvious potential future is that of the *collapse* of the Internet before any form of Cybernation can be developed. As the government sponsors of the Internet have gradually withdrawn, the support has been provided by commercial concerns. Without the regulation examined in Chapter 5, however, such organisations might well find the Internet to be a difficult and dangerous place, and might in turn withdraw. Should this happen, the Internet will at best revert to a purely academic device, and at worst will simply disappear.

While this is not *likely* it is certainly *possible*. A more probable future is that of global interconnectedness, on a personal, organisational and corporate level – at least within the developed countries. This in turn gives rise to the potential for information 'haves and have nots' and for discrimination on the basis of technological sophistication. These various scenarios will be explored in the latter part of this chapter.

GROWTH OF DIGITAL COMMUNITIES

A community might be defined as a group of people living together within a specific area, such as a village or small town; or a collection of people sharing some or all aspects of their lives, such as a monastery, artists' collective or similar. In each case there are a number of similar, determinant factors: the people live sufficiently close together to allow frequent communication; they share their goals, passions and disappointments; and they have a sense of membership and commitment to the group. Usually this sense of community can only be fostered in small collections of people, particularly where there is something very specific to share: the common natural resources of a village or a faith in a particular religion, for instance.

In a 'digital community', these various elements are all present with the single exception of physical proximity. In the case of traditional communities, the physical proximity was necessary to allow the sense of sharing and to support communication. In the digital case, this is instead supported by Internet mechanisms such as e-mail, Usenet newsgroups or even more esoteric technologies such as virtual reality environments.

We can consider three instances of such digital communities:

- 'wired' villages;
- Internet-*using* societies; and
- Internet-*supported* societies.

In the first, an existing – or at least a traditional type – of physical community is 'wired' to support Internet communication. In this case, those members of the community might live and interact on a local basis within a village or estate, but their work and other social aspects involve the use of Internet, telecommuting and distance shopping outside of the physical community. Blocks of flats in Singapore have been wired to support this, as have new estates in America and elsewhere; the most obvious instance might be seen within the universities and research institutions themselves. In many ways, however, this is perhaps the 'weakest' example of a digital community.

The second case is slightly stronger, in which distributed communities are supported by means of Internet communication. That is, a community which already exists but which is spread over a wide area, perhaps through several countries, is supported and perhaps enhanced by the use of a communication medium such as the Internet. In this case of course, the communication and sense of community would exist even without the existence of the Internet. Regular telephone or postal services could equally well support such communities. Examples might be the global Jewish population, spread throughout the world but sharing a common identity of beliefs and a sense of belonging. For the world-wide Irish culture, an Internet structure called 'Paddynet' has in fact been established and although it has yet to become widely used, it points to the potential for such a community.

This global community need not be established on the basis of racial or cultural identity; it is equally valid to construe a global society interested in a particular hobby or topic as being a community. Internet interest groups for bird-watching, science fiction or similar are all supported by the Internet Usenet newsgroups and by various chat mechanisms. In all of these cases, communication and a sense of community is *enhanced* by the Internet, but the community itself is not a direct *result* of the Internet's use. Nor do such communities have a political relevance inherited from or enhanced by the use of the Internet; their political weight is determined by the basic *reason* for their existence, rather than by the way in which they express, debate or determine those views. Thus, the global Jewish society has a political importance on the world stage whether it uses the Internet or not; equally, a global bird-watching society has none.

The Internet can provide a mechanism to support *internal* communication for the group, and can hence allow purely internal, group politics to progress. But this does not mean that in this sense the group communication provides a mechanism to influence politics on a broader front.

A more extreme version of these communities would emerge in our third case, in which more general communities having a degree of political relevance arise wholly and completely within the Internet, and within which the actual geographical location of a particular member is not only irrelevant, but perhaps also unknown. It is this last case that would form the basis of a Cybernation.

We have already seen the basic mechanism whereby such a digital community could emerge. In the various Usenet newsgroups or CompuServe SIGs there are global collections of individuals debating or simply discussing items of mutual interest. As Chapter 2 described, in the main these discussion groups might be about trivial issues, but there are certainly some that are discussing topics which the more general society might identify as relevant – such as the car-sharing newsgroup whose descent into libel we considered in Chapter 5. These discussion groups form the kernel from which more community-based discussions might proceed.

Moreover, the CyberCafes described in Chapter 2 have given refuge to users taking part in more general discussion sessions. For those involved in such 'communities', the group dynamics are every bit as real as the more 'standard' situations, and the aspects of digital anonymity introduced by the use of keyboard and terminal do not distract from the validity of the experience. Some of the members might indeed be near to one another, within the same room; or they might be on the other side of the world. The messages might be exchanged in 'real time', through Internet Relay Chat or through a virtual environment; or they might be 'timeslipped' through e-mail messages that cross the globe.

Romances have blossomed – and divorces have resulted – from the keyboard intimacy possible in such communities. More than this, the members of the communities have formed a closed and essentially protective environment. One aspect of Internet discussions and overall culture that was mentioned in the Preface was that of impatience with the new users of the Internet when they ask naive, so-called 'newbie' questions. In many ways this might be seen less as intrinsic bad manners, and perhaps more as the understandable defensiveness of a group 'invaded' by a newcomer.

Newsgroups provide this community aspect with respect to the particular subject of interest. In Victorian times, the middle class would often belong to such discussion clubs, meeting on a regular basis to discuss a given topic: helping the poor, religion, Darwin's theory, politics and so forth. As more general discussion fora develop, through such mechanisms as the CyberCafes, this becomes less like a middle-class discussion group, albeit with bad mannered and occasionally highly abusive language, and much more of a general, open exchange such as might be expected in a friendly and familiar pub or bar.

As the discussion groups move towards more general subjects, and as more people begin to publish, research, trade, shop and telecommute by means of Internet mechanisms, this basic mechanism will grow to provide its members with that sense of belonging required to establish a global, digital community.

Will this happen? It is of course very difficult to predict such a thing; it is quite without precedent. In the weaker, second case described above there are very many people who have maintained a group relationship over time and distance, but this has most usually grown from a desire to retain a group intimacy established in a 'traditional' way: former college room-mates, school-friends or platoon members, for example. In the Internet case, the communication medium *itself* is thought to be capable of fostering that close association that shared exams, history, hardship or danger does in those traditional examples. Traditional pen-friends who have never previously met have sometimes married, and the Internet equivalent has certainly occurred; but this does not mean that a more widespread, *community* identity can equally be fostered by such a mechanism.

In some tightly focused areas, a sense of group identity has certainly begun to emerge; only time will tell, however, whether or not more 'complete' and free-standing communities do indeed evolve. There is in principle no reason why they shouldn't. There is nothing in the Internet mechanisms or practice that would act to *prevent* such developments, and experience to date in America has shown that many users are in fact positively supported in establishing virtual group dynamics. This sense of community, in conjunction with the trading, working and shopping element of the Internet, might then truly be said to give rise to a Cybernation: 'a community of persons ... bound by common descent, language, history, etc' and supported by global, high-speed and inexpensive communication. To evolve fully as such a nation, however, it would be necessary for such a society to evolve a *political* relevance outside of the internal political aspects of the group itself.

GOVERNMENT AND NATIONHOOD

As the Internet-supported digital communities evolve, and assuming that they do indeed grow to incorporate individuals around the world, they present the national governments with a number of challenges beyond those identified in Chapter 5. Government in democratic states is primarily a representative mechanism whereby the selected few debate and enact legislation for and on behalf of the nation-state's citizens. There are several aspects to this that might prove of importance in the Internet context.

Firstly, those elected representatives need access to information and communication resources. It is necessary for them to inform and listen to their constituents; it is necessary for them to communicate with one another; and at the most basic, it is necessary for them to discover and to express the wishes of those who have elected them as *their* representatives. While we elect individuals, we understand and appreciate that they must then balance three sometimes opposing forces: their own conscience; the wishes, commitments or philosophy of their party; and the interests of their constituency itself.

At the simplest level, the Internet can then support this information and communication requirement. E-mail between politicians, and between politicians and departments can be easily established; many politicians in both the US and the UK already have e-mail and Internet facilities – some now even have their own 'home' pages, acting as an Internet constituency newspaper. This then touches on the next aspect, that of communicating with constituents. In addition to the standard channels and mechanisms, the politicians can receive e-mail messages from those wishing to express their views – although the politician must be careful to ensure that the view has come from somebody whom they have been elected to represent; this is an important part of Parliamentary protocol – and a point to which we will return.

In addition to this direct communication with constituents, the Internet provides further communication potential. In many ways, basic e-mail from a disgruntled member of the public is no different from that of a normal letter. The Internet can also, however, provide the politician with access to on-going debates of relevance to their constituency, their professional interests, or the state and performance of their party. Again, the point raised in earlier chapters about the tone and content of such newsgroups needs to be reiterated: on the whole, even when moderated these debates are seldom as well controlled in content or in style as an Oxford Union debate or similar, but they do have the advantage of accessibility and of visibility. Some at least of these newsgroups or fora might present the politician with useful information, even if it might only represent the most vocal minority contributing to such on-line debates believes to be important. And of course, democracy at its most fundamental is about government by the most vocal; at least in newsgroup discussions about politics one needn't raise one's voice in any but the most symbolic of fashions.

To continue the point about Parliamentary protocol raised above, however, it will seldom if ever be the case that *all* of those contributing to the on-line debate are members of the particular constituency. Global visibility and accessibility means just that; contributions can come from all over the world, and while those involved in the debate itself might agree the relevance of comments from overseas, the politicians themselves may not.

The Internet debates, however, raise a second point of relevance for the Internet to 'real-world' political activity. Our democracies are representative simply because it is impractical – even impossible – to allow each and every citizen the chance to speak up on every issue. In the US, Congress is the home of the Representatives; the early settler communities quite explicitly chose their most articulate and best informed members to travel to and speak at those first sessions on their behalf. Politics is about making one's views heard, and it would not be feasible for each and every one of us to stand up in Parliament or Congress and try to shout our opinions. The basic tenets of democracy mean, however, that we all have a *right* to express those opinions, and the mechanisms of elections, newsletters, surgeries and local parties are all intended to provide us with the best chance of achieving this.

So we choose our representatives and allow or encourage them to speak for us. The Internet newsgroups and fora present, however, a foundation from which such a representative Parliament can be replaced by a truly democratic mechanism. All of those able to access a newsgroup could contribute to the debate, and we could jointly move towards truly nation-wide agreements on resolutions, Bills and Acts that govern our country.

This is of course unrealistic to the point of naiveté. Government is about much more than open debate, and much of the work must take place behind 'closed doors' to protect national interests. In the case of the UK, while the subject of many of the Parliamentary debates could indeed be discussed on a more universal basis, in Parliament those presenting, arguing or disputing a case do so from a position of authority: this is *authority* in the sense of knowledge *and* in the sense of responsibility. The anonymity of newsgroups moreover, provides protection for users to say the most outrageous of things; in Parliament, while privilege protects an MP from prosecution should he or she say something offensive or even slanderous, they are unable to hide behind anonymity and must consider their positions carefully in any debate. And finally, Ministers of State are selected from the parliamentarians who demonstrate the best capacity to reason and argue cases, both within and outside the Chamber, and their jobs could not easily be performed by a consensus of Internet 'citizens'.

This is not to say that Parliamentary debates could not be *informed* by debates within the Internet, but rather that the Internet debates will not replace those formal and authoritative sessions carried out by our representatives. The third aspect of the Internet on government, however, centres on the very relevance of those debates. To return to the early years of the American Congress, through the activities of the early settlers, Americans came to owe allegiance to two entities. To a local community or settlement, which of course became the basis of the various states on the eastern seaboard; and to an overarching union of those states, whose primacy was debated for many years and became in fact one of the sparks for the American Civil War. One commentator in fact suggested that the Civil War was effectively fought on the basis of *grammar*: 'the United States *is*' versus 'the United States *are*'.

In Europe, a similar process of 'federalisation' is underway within the European Union, as once fiercely independent nation-states lodge many of their formerly sovereign powers with an equally overarching authority. Certain powers will be passed down to the individual nation-states, a process called 'subsidiarity', but many will remain at the 'higher', European Union level.

In both cases, nation-state citizens are encouraged to see their allegiance as being owed both to a greater power than their individual state, and to that state itself. In America this process has been established for a sufficient length of time that it is no longer thought of as unusual; in Europe, there is still uncertainty. But in each case, it encourages citizens to think of citizenship in two ways: a sense of belonging to a huge and powerful transnational body; and a sense of belonging to a more local and small scale entity.

As government control passes increasingly to a larger and more remote political entity, the activities and decisions of the lesser body can be expected to become increasingly less relevant. As the American Union progressed, state governments moved into the background; as the European Union progresses, in many quarters it is feared that national governments might equally recede. This is by no means definite; as the European debate proceeds through 1996 and beyond it might even be seen as unlikely. There remains, however, the potential for individual nation-states gradually to lose relevance, and to be replaced by a much larger and much less accessible organisation. In this case, the equally transnational but much more accessible Internet might well emerge as the forum of choice for many citizens to formulate and express opinions which have a political 'weight' on the broader stage: in areas of environmental concern, human rights or even transnational economics.

It would be unrealistic to suppose or expect that the very *existence* of the Internet might somehow negate or reduce the political relevance of national government. But other factors could well act to do just this as transnational authorities emerge, and be in turn supported by the Internet communication and the influence of those Internet communities that do evolve. Countries and nation-states retain their identity for both cultural and political reasons: a sense of cultural identity coupled with the central exercise of national political interests. In those countries where either of these aspects have been weakened, the country itself has weakened, splintered and in some unfortunate cases consumed itself. In situations where separate political entities are weakened, and where a cultural identity outside of the nation-state gains in prominence, a separate identity can be expected to emerge.

The Internet will not *destroy* separate countries; but it could certainly make them of much less relevance.

TWO DIGITAL VISIONS

Throughout this book we have built a series of visions of the way in which the Internet is being used and could potentially develop in the immediate future. There are many opportunities associated with the technology, and equally a great number of challenges. We have argued that while there might be *prima facie* similarities between the Internet and more transient phenomena such as CB, the Internet presents a much more complete environment and can therefore be used by many more people for a far wider range of activities.

We have also discussed a number of elements associated with the Internet that could carry it forward as an unprecedented development in the way that communication, trading, publishing and many other topics are perceived. There *are* elements of similarity with the initial development of printing, or of cash trading in place of barter, or of the introduction of TV, radio and telephone. Conversely, the rapid growth of the Internet could easily lead to a structure that topples beneath its own weight of offensive language, pornographic material or support for fraudulent trading and illegal activities. We can therefore envisage two potential futures for the Internet:

■ death, or at least paralysis; or
■ blossom.

These are not strictly utopia *versus* dystopia; to those challenging or attempting to impose regulation on the system, 'death' of the Internet might well seem the preferable alternative. Conversely, to those who see the Internet as a cultural phenomenon of far greater relevance than anything that has gone before, 'blossom' would be a clear favourite – although even this has what one would think of as a 'downside'.

The Internet's continued advance could stumble, be halted or reversed following a number of quite possible developments. This progression of technology is by no means assured. While the Internet is indeed a phenomenon of greater importance than CB, and while it is indeed encouraged by government and commercial organisations, it does still contain the seeds of its own destruction. The three most immediate reasons why the Internet could be forced to withdraw are:

1. insufficient infrastructure investment;
2. excessive and stifling legislation; or
3. legal challenge and prohibition.

Initially, the Internet was a *government* funded activity. In both the US and UK, however, the philosophy of government through the 1980s and 1990s has emphasised a requirement for greater investment from the private sector rather than the spending of public funds. This has lead to private funding roles in the context of infrastructure elements such as roads, bridges, airports – and of course telecommunications. Coupled with this, competition within the private sector has been seen as the most important way of introducing quality and of maintaining a 'value for money' ethos in the provision of infrastructure and utilities.

For the Internet, this has meant the withdrawal or substantial reduction of funding from government bodies such as the NFS in the US or the UK's Science Research Council. Instead, funding for the Internet now comes from the Internet Service Providers themselves and from those private sector, commercial concerns who would wish to make money from the provision or exploitation of the medium.

The Internet must therefore deliver a service that ultimately proves profitable to these commercial concerns, to allow them to continue to justify such investment. As Chapter 4 discussed, only a very few of the larger organisations are making realistic profits from the provision of Internet access; and the establishment of Web marketing and trading is still an expensive and unprofitable exercise. The current numbers of users might be increasing rapidly, but in global terms 30 to 40 million users is only a very small population;[147] to continue to attract ever more users, the Internet must offer a 'clean' environment to those users and a 'secure' environment to the traders and publishers.

Currently, the perception is that those users who are already present on the Internet have the potential to be an important market for the goods, services or information offered. And those users in turn believe that the information and goods will continue to grow in relevance and not be swamped by offensive or illegal postings. While this perception remains, the numbers of users will continue to grow, and with it the numbers of traders and publishers. Throughout 1995 and the early part of 1996, however, there have been very many reports of less palatable material and of less than sensible uses of the medium. Should the Internet continue to get such 'bad press', this growth might be threatened.

If the commercial concerns find that the Internet no longer promises to produce a return on investment – and that investment is currently quite substantial – then they can be expected to withdraw their support for the more open and uncontrolled environment. This could then lead to a diminishing in the popularity of the Internet, reversing or at the least stalling the growth in numbers of users.

This is not to say that the whole of the Internet would die. Internet structures could prove to be of use within companies even without the parallel existence of a global and publicly accessible system; and more private and controlled BBS environments like CompuServe would retain their popularity. Moreover, the requirement for interconnections between universities and similar institutions has also been well established and can be expected to continue. The use of the Internet by private individuals from home would, however, be severely curtailed.

Alternatively, a lack of investment in the fundamental infrastructure itself could equally threaten to stifle the Internet. In Chapter 2, the potential for Internet telephony was discussed; if more and ever more people use this mechanism, there will be little or no incentive for BT or other telecommunication suppliers to improve the capacity of their network. The Internet is ultimately carried over the selfsame cables as the more traditional telephone conversations; if BT loses voice traffic to the Internet, thereby overloading the Internet structures and degrading the already poor network response, BT would be 'cutting their own throats' were they then to improve those network facilities[148] without changing the basis on which such facilities are provided to Internet users.

And this need not be simply associated with *voice* transmission. The capacity requirements for many of the ISPs was calculated on the basis of an essentially character-based network traffic. Increasingly, however, ever more of this traffic has become multimedia in nature, thereby skewing the calculations of capacity requirement per user. Either the ISPs choose to buy more capacity per user – thereby increasing the transmission costs and hence the *price* per user; or they continue with the current capacity – thereby continuing to degrade the apparent performance of the Internet.

The effect will be either to increase the cost of using the Internet to more 'realistic' levels or to stifle the traffic and hence the perceived value of the Internet service. Again, this might have the further effect of reducing or even reversing the public, domestic use of the service.

The second case described above would equally stifle the Internet's use: the introduction of excessively stringent legislation and regulation. As discussed above, the Chinese government's approach to controlling the Internet has been to require each and every user to register; this then allows their use of the Internet to be regulated or even monitored.

Stifling regulation need not in fact be as severe as this. In the early days of radio it was soon perceived that users required licensing so as to ensure that the airwaves weren't soon swamped and thereby unusable. A similar approach could be taken with the Internet in the UK, licensing its use on an individual or corporate basis for a set of specific uses. This is not significantly different from the approach taken in requiring registration of use in the case of the UK Data Protection Act.

This would of course inhibit the free and open use of the Internet by any and all. It need not be entirely negative, however, in that it would provide a controlled and well regulated environment – similar in many ways to the radio and TV environment produced by UK broadcasting regulations. The resulting network would not be as 'exciting' as the current state – but nor would it then be a haven for illicit or objectionable activities. Of course, encryption and the already ubiquitous access to global systems might well mean that such regulation would be difficult to apply in practice without 'tearing out' the current Internet implementations and replacing them wholesale.

The UK government in particular has made it clear that there is no intention to introduce excessive central controls – provided that the Internet is made into a 'cleaner' environment. Others might, however, *force* such measures through legal challenges to the use of the system.

In Chapter 5 we discussed the withdrawal of some 200 newsgroups from the CompuServe services following pressure from the German government. Such legal challenges, associated with illegal material or with the exposure of private or proprietary information represent the third situation described above. Perhaps the most important of these legal challenges to date has come from the Church of Scientology following the unauthorised publication of their religious texts on the Internet. Although this case was subsequently dismissed,[149] the cult attempted to seize Internet published material and even to force the withdrawal or termination of some Internet services.

It has been argued that given the transnational aspects of the Internet, it is essentially proof from legal challenges by offended parties trying to force the Internet – or parts thereof – to be 'switched off'. This is of course not true; it *is* proof from local attempts, as was demonstrated in the German case when users elsewhere continued to provide access. Organisations such as the Church of Scientology are, however, equally transnational; as is the global Jewish population, the Catholic Church and many other religions.

The Church of Scientology case was dismissed not because 'turning off' certain Usenet newsgroups was an unthinkable act, but because the procedures they adopted in seizing material were illegal. If they or another transnational religion were – for whatever reason – to attempt an international prosecution and restraining order on some or all of the Internet newsgroups or practices they might well be able to stifle and kill the Internet.

The Internet might well therefore die, under the weight of its users, under the weight of regulation, or under the weight of restraining orders and similar. Its history, however, has been one of growth, and even in the event of aspects being restricted, it will continue to be of value in many, many areas. This would therefore make the 'blossoming' of the Internet a more likely possibility.

Almost all homes now have access to TV broadcasts and the telephone network. As the Internet grows in use, more and ever more users will then have access to the Internet-delivered services; and these services themselves will grow into a more complete range of home shopping, publishing and educational services. Fixed schedule TV could be replaced by video-on-demand; night school by global Internet classrooms; and daily commuting by teleworking.

This of course then puts a significant premium on *access* to these fundamental services. As the Internet becomes more central to our social and economic wellbeing it would have to become perceived as almost a *utility* provided on an equal basis to all.[150] Subject only to economic pressures, anybody can gain access to the telephone and can benefit from its services. IT, on the other hand, requires higher levels of skill. Currently, many people are not only unskilled in the use of computers, they are positively *frightened* by them. But in the Internet future we have painted, the computer becomes a central requirement in many aspects of social and working life, more so even than the car.

This dependence on computers in the case of a 'blossoming' Internet culture then brings with it a requirement to ensure that citizens do not become 'disenfranchised' by an inability to access the services. This is important within the UK, US and other 'Internet countries', but also on a wider scale. If the western economies come to depend on the Internet – or in turn the Information Superhighway – then those countries *not* having access are at a quite severe disadvantage.

In a world of information and with economies increasingly dependent on value-add, knowledge services, the ubiquitous access to a global computer communication system would have to be seen as a vital priority – for nation-states, organisations and private individuals [7].

CONCLUSION:
TOMORROW'S CHALLENGE TO TODAY

The Internet presents immense challenges – and equally immense opportunities. It can support the most comprehensive range of communication services to date; it challenges our very ideas of 'nationhood'; and it allows government, corporate, educational and entertainment concerns to move – wholly or partially – into a non-physical domain.

Throughout this book I have attempted to give a view of the extent to which the Internet can affect our way of life and the way we view the world. The printing press revolutionised the way individuals gained access to recorded facts and the ideas of other people and remote cultures; the penny post the way we exchange news with our friends and the way we communicate with organisations; the telephone changed the way we carry out conversations and the range of people available for such discussions. The Internet includes and goes beyond these changes.

Powered flight made remote parts of the world more easily accessible; the Internet can allow us to download real-time, immediate pictures from those parts. The car allowed us to work at a greater distance from our homes; the Internet can support us in working for companies anywhere in the world. Our various wars have changed the face of Europe; the Internet could help to remove the very *requirement* for countries.

And it supports facilities that are unprecedented: virtual reality offices; the digital importation of goods; legally empowered, purchasing 'agents' embodied in network-mobile software. The legal, regulatory and cultural frameworks to allow us to control and take advantage of this facility are far from complete.

By comparison with the Internet, at the start of the 20th century the UK had a handful of private automobiles. Travel between cities was supported by trains; within cities by horse-drawn carriage or tram. A few enthusiasts risked life and limb on pedal-cycles and the canal network was beginning to suffer from neglect. Those few cars that *did* exist were noisy, unreliable and slow; they were also expensive to buy and to operate.

That the automobile would become significantly cheaper, faster, more reliable and ubiquitous would then seem to have been a safe prediction: that within a century on average *every* household would have access to their own automobile; that a fortunate few would have the use of more than one – perhaps a visionary would have seen this potential.

If in 1896 at the very birth of the automobile industry one could have presented the authorities with a confident prediction of the automobile's development, what legislative, cultural and political implications could have been foreseen?

Based on an understanding of human nature we might have been able to predict that individuals would prefer *independent* automobile travel to that of the train; and the resulting requirement for paved roads within and between cities. We might even have been able to predict the demise of the railways by comparison with the demise of the canals.

The prediction of millions of automobiles on the roads might have allowed us to guess at traffic jams and the requirement for traffic-flow controls; the growing problems of finding a parking place; a steadily mounting death toll from road accidents; a requirement for traffic regulations such as speed controls and the signposting of bends and of hazards. We might even have been able to predict the requirement for a motorway network and traffic wardens – but perhaps not wheel clamps, breathalysers and airbags.

From a legislative perspective – and by comparison with the horse-drawn and steam-powered world – we might have been able to predict the likelihood of having to prosecute theft of automobiles and the assignment of blame in the case of accidents. We might have been able to predict that unroadworthy automobiles would be sold and that they would be used to transport criminals and stolen goods. We might not have been able to predict motorway patrol cars but we could certainly predict a growing number of car chases; even a requirement for police drivers to be trained in the essential skills.

In the main, our predictions would be based on experience with the existing means of travel, perhaps informed slightly by the limited experience to date with the automobile.

We are at the analogous state with respect to the Internet and the so-called 'Information Age'. Our legislative and regulatory structures are based on experience and practice from an earlier age – the IT equivalent of the 'steam' age. We have trade and consumer regulations based on high street shops and experience of mail order; we have importation and duty controls based on the continued presumption of 'real-world' frontiers across which goods must pass. In common with the 1896 state of automobile regulation, we are waiting for the problems and the solutions to evolve.

Yet the true comparison lies *not* with the state of play at 1896 but rather more with the world of 1946. We have a far greater number of PCs and telecommunication connections than there were automobiles in 1896. In 1946, we had the expectation of motorways and larger highways; we had traffic regulations and a growing set of criteria of roadworthiness. The growth towards ubiquitous automobile provision was well established – exactly analogous to the penetration and trends with respect to the Internet today.

In the case of automobiles, the growth was steady – impressive but not dazzling. The legislative framework and the cultural norms – abhorrence of drunk-drivers for example – both evolved slowly throughout the century. In the case of the Internet, however, the growth is not just dazzling; it is *staggering*. Careful, informed – but above all *imaginative* processes to develop this framework are urgently required.

It is all too easy to present a 'science fiction' view of the future we all face in the context of the Internet. In many ways, however, it is not necessary: the most modest prediction of possible trends present us with sufficiently challenging prospects; prospects for which we are woefully unprepared. For a technologist, the future is rosy; for private citizens and those who can trade or work over the Internet, it is probably equally rosy, but with a few difficult aspects. But for politicians, policemen, tax and customs authorities, the Cybernation presents a challenging picture.

Tomorrow's challenge to today is one which we *must* face today; by the time tomorrow comes, it may be too late.

APPENDIX

NOTE ON REFERENCES

The material from which this book was compiled comes from several sources. Most immediately, from conversations with those working in the various fields: those in the UK's Trade and Industry, Customs and Excise, Inland Revenue, Police, Serious Fraud Office and Office of Fair Trading departments responsible for establishing and implementing policy towards the challenges and opportunities of the Internet; those companies seeking to use, exploit or benefit from the Internet; and those advising such people and trying to sell goods and services to the emerging Internet market, such as the CCTA, British Telecom, computer manufacturer and consultancy organisations. These conversations allowed me to collect and to digest a wealth of opinions, suggestions and proposals for the direction in which the Internet regulation and implications would proceed.

I also managed to collect specific source material, in the form of publications which are listed below; conference papers which I have sought to reflect within the text; but most interestingly, publications *within* the Internet itself. As the text of the book has made clear, the Internet presents the most comprehensive, complete and accessible source of information for *any* research project. The material that I collected came from three types of Internet sources:

1. Electronic newspapers and magazines;
2. Corporate home pages; and
3. On-line directories.

The on-line versions of *The Economist* or *The Times*, for example; the home pages of Vauxhall cars, of Netscape Communications, or of Corbis; or the on-line directories of the Electronic Frontier Foundation, or of the search engines themselves. This of course means that it is easy for any reader to retrace or to supplement the research that I undertook. For any particular topic within the book, from transaction security to Internet lingerie catalogues, it is simply necessary either to look for appropriate organisations' home pages (eg 'http://www.vauxhall.co.uk' or 'http://www.corbis.com') for information on the companies; to search the archives of on-line publications for stories of interest or relevance – such as the current state of the UK Defamation Act, for example; or to enter a series of key words for the search engines to retrieve any and all appropriate references.

The presents the reader with several benefits; most obviously, the Internet content is current – it is perpetually revised and therefore will not suffer from being out of date. As the Preface made clear, the Internet changes and develops so rapidly that some of the book's content will already be superseded by new events, announcements and even inventions. This will also introduce the reader to the interesting – and yes, exciting – process of 'surfing' page after page of Internet information.

REFERENCES AND BIBLIOGRAPHY

[1] Tanenbaum, Andrew (1989) *Computer Networks*, 2nd ed, Prentice-Hall
[2] Gates, Bill (1995) *The Road Ahead*, Viking
[3] Bridges, William (1995) *Jobshift*, Nicholas Brealey Publishing
[4] Negroponte, Nicholas (1995) *Being Digital*, Hodder & Stoughton
[5] Womack, James *et al.* (1990) *The Machine That Changed The World*, Rawson Associates
[6] Hutton, Will (1995) *The State We're In*, Jonathon Cape
[7] McRae, Hamish (1995) *The World in 2020*, Harper Collins
[8] Morin, Gavino and Cavazos, Edward (1994) *Cyberspace and the Law*, The MIT Press
[9] Levinson, Jay Conrad and Rubin, Charles (1995) *Guerrilla Marketing on the Internet*, Piatkus
[10] Haslop, Brent and Angell, David (1995) *The Internet Business Companion*, Addison Wesley
[11] Giddens, Anthony (1994) *Beyond Left and Right*, Polity
[12] 'The Death of Distance', Economist Survey of Telecommunications, *The Economist*, 30 September 1995
[13] 'The Accidental Superhighway', Economist Survey of the Internet, *The Economist*, 1 July 1995
[14] Heath, William (1995) 'Close Encounters of the Digital Kind' *Demos Quarterly*, no. 7
[15] 'Information Superhighways: Opportunities for Public Sector Applications in the UK', *CCTA*, May 1994

[16] 'Electronic Commerce', CCTA *Technology Update*, July/August 1995

[17] Buck, Peter (1995) 'Making Payments on the Internet', Hyperian Systems

[18] Arnold, Stephen (1994) 'Internet 2000: The Path to the Total Network', Infonortics

[19] 'The Information Society: the Way Ahead', *European Commission I & T Magazine*, Winter 1994–5

[20] Bouthors, Vincent (1995) 'Evolution of the World-Wide Web and the Internet', *The Journal of Technical Information for the Distributed Computing Model*, vol. 5, no. 5, Bull Information Systems Ltd, December

[21] Tabizel, David and Rosen, Nick (1996) 'The Internet in 1996: An Investment Perspective' Durchlacher Multimedia Ltd, January

[22] 'Information Superhighway', CCTA *Technology Update*, January 1995

[23] 'Falling Through the Net: A Survey of the "Have Nots" in Rural and Urban America', US Department of Commerce, July 1995

[24] Wilcox, David (ed) (1996) 'Inventing the Future: Communities in the Information Society', *Partnerships for Tomorrow*

[25] 'Regulating the Internet', Office of Fair Trading, International Marketing Supervision Network conference, Vienna, November 1995

[26] 'Copyright and Related Rights in the Information Society', Green Paper, Commission of the European Communities, July 1995

[27] 'Internet vs Intranet: Markets, Opportunities and Trends', Zona Research, January 1996

[28] 'A New Computing Paradigm', Gartner Group, Research Note T–140–135, 28 September 1995

[29] Hawes, Ursula (1993) 'Teleworking in Britain', The Employment Department, *Analytica*, October

[30] Cochrane, Peter (1995) 'Communications, Care & Cure', BT Laboratories

[31] 'IT in Schools', BCS, Computer Bulletin Special Supplement, Spring 1996

ENDNOTES

1. In [18], the Internet is defined as 'a code word for making education available to everyone [. . .] and a litany of benefits that baffles and bedazzles'.
2. While there are a number of committees and societies associated with the Internet, such as the Internet Society and InterNIC, these are not governing bodies in the usual sense of the term; they are essentially voluntary organisations or collections of Internet vendors, including universities and so forth. They have no *executive* power, however, beyond that of trying to advise others.
3. Zona Research's report [27], gives more detailed figures for this. Some observers have suggested that as much as 90 per cent of the e-mail and related communication is in English.
4. See, for example, Durlacher [21], for a more detailed breakdown of host systems and projected numbers.
5. Netiquette was originally used to describe acceptable behaviour associated with the submission of e-mail and newsgroup postings. With the more commercial aspects of the Internet it has come to have a broader applicability for aspects such as advertising, covered in more detail in Chapter 3.
6. The Electronic Frontier Foundation (accessible on the Internet at 'http://www.eff.org') gives a number of links to such 'declarations' and 'constitutions'. In the main, the arguments of each appear to be that since the Internet encompasses more than one single nation state, it is impossible for a single nation state

to impose regulations to manage it. Therefore, such attempts should not be made, and the Internet community should be left to regulate itself. While there is a germ of truth in this, we will show that this is not the whole story.

7. Gartner Group were quoted in a January 1995 CCTA 'Technology Update' as assigning an 80 per cent probability that the Internet would be the primary Information Superhighway for the public sector, but a 90 per cent probability that individual private sector organisations would have their own individual 'superhighways'; these *Intranets* are discussed in Chapter 3.

8. The 'Information Superhighway' was first pushed strongly by the American Vice President Al Gore in 1993/4 as a key plank of the Clinton Administration's policy. While all previous discussions had centred on the technological opportunities, the US initiatives made clear the political and legislative requirements and outlined the key components that would be required. These centred on 'open access', private investment and measures to ensure that all citizens would have equal opportunities to benefit from the services. These have subsequently been adopted to a greater or lesser extent throughout the world.

9. The word was first popularised by William Gibson in his now classic science fiction novel *Neuromancer*, set in a nightmarish near-future of ubiquitous computer dependency.

10. Bulletin Board Services are strictly speaking distinct from the Internet in that they involve the provision of services to end-users who dial-in to the computer systems via ordinary telephone lines. Access is then restricted to just those host computers on which the BBS runs and is therefore an 'island community'. In the Internet, the access is via computer networks running the TCP/IP protocols, although such access can be provided from home computers using PPP (Point to Point Protocol) or SLIP (Serial Line Interface Protocol) dial-in services to a host computer provider. To the end-user, however, this distinction is broadly irrelevant as BBS services are gradually merged with the Internet as a whole.

11. CIX, Prodigy, America on Line, Europe on Line or many others could equally have been chosen. Since CompuServe has the

largest share of the UK market I chose to use it as my example.

12. This was TCP/IP – two interacting protocol levels: Transmission Control Protocol and Internet Protocol. IP is the lower level, referred to as the 'Network Layer', which controls transmission over the physical network. TCP is the 'Transport Layer' which breaks the original message into packets for subsequent transmission. In the initial Internet implementations, this service was provided by a less reliable version (NCP – 'Network Control Protocol') which assumed a perfect network and could not therefore manage under less than ideal circumstances.

13. Standards can be *de jure*, meaning that they have been issued by an authoritative body following an extensive period of consultation; or they can be *de facto*, which means that they emerged through practice and agreement on 'the way to do something'. These last are the more common in a rapidly changing computer marketplace, in which the protracted consultation periods are damaging to the commercial success of a given product, and are therefore most often ignored as suppliers instead rush to satisfy customers with a non-standard but nonetheless successful offering.

14. This in fact required a change in the US law which had until then refused permission for the Internet to be used for commercial purposes.

15. See [1] for an excellent introduction to the more technical aspects of the ARPA Internet and other networks.

16. These are then in turn supported by protocols that run over the TCP/IP stack – such as SMTP (Simple Mail Transfer Protocol) for resolving e-mail addresses.

17. Viruses are often classified further, as 'Trojan horses', 'worms' and so forth. For the sake of simplicity, I've chosen to use the word 'virus' to refer to all categories of malicious program that might be introduced in a clandestine manner onto a local computer.

18. Developed at the nuclear research facility CERN in order to support projects, but distributed free of charge around the Internet.

19. The original Web server software was developed and distributed freely by CERN; the original client software was called

Mosaic and was developed by the National Centre for Supercomputer Applications in Illinois. NCSA Mosaic lead the way in developing 'standards' for the client software, but has subsequently been overtaken by Netscape Corporation's *Navigator* program. This is currently estimated to have a 75 per cent market share, but Microsoft's *Explorer* browser is expected rapidly to gain on it. Each is roughly similar, giving a mouse-driven interface to the text, pictures and other content of the Web pages. In researching this book, I used Mosaic for the browser interface to CompuServe's Internet connection, and Netscape Navigator for direct access.

20. The Web page is expressed in a language known as HTML – Hypertext Mark-up Language, an implementation of OSI's SGML; the format for transmitting these pages through the Internet is HTTP – Hypertext Transfer Protocol. In the case of HTTP and HTML, because of the absence of standards, these have been modified and evolved by the browser producers to allow them to support a variety of further facilities, including aspects such as transmission security. Netscape, for example, have made a number of extensions to the basic HTML 2.0 which form a part of HTML 3.0.

21. This address is referred to as a URL – Unique Resource Locator, and has a format like 'www.bloggs.co.uk'. This is a symbolic representation of the more basic Internet address, which is called an IP number. These are described in more detail in Chapter 5.

22. 'Killer application' is an often-used phrased in the computer industry. It refers to an implementation or aspect of using a particular technology that allows it to become more than a toy. In the case of lasers, for example, audio CDs were the killer application; in the case of polymer strands, nylon stockings!

23. Developed by Sun Microsystems, but gaining acceptance in many areas – Microsoft, for example, have licensed Java for use in their Explorer browser. Perversely, the browser developed initially by Sun to exploit Java (called *HotJava*) has gained very little ground.

24. The Java interpreter constrains the access that a Java program can have to system resources – including computer memory

that lies outside of the interpreter's control. Despite this careful system monitoring, however, there have been rumours and fears of more malicious viruses spreading by means of Java; these have been addressed in the most up to date versions.

25. Pushed most obviously by Oracle's Larry Ellison; a UK constructed device featuring up to 8 Mbyte flash-RAM memory and a built-in 28.8 kbps modem, retailing at £400 to £500 was the first, launched by Oracle in April 1996. Sun Microsystems also have a prototype device and even Microsoft are working actively in this area.

26. N-ISDN can support such high data rates, although figures of 64 or 128 kbps for ISDN 2 are the more normal case.

27. Experiments on a 'normal' laptop showed disk accesses of between 1 and 2 Mbytes per second; ie 8 to 16 mega *bits* per second. I have therefore averaged this at being of the order of 10 mbps, although of course this will vary dramatically depending on the type of disk and on computer activity.

28. As [30] explains, advances in ISDN could support transmission speeds of some 155 Mbps by the end of the century – sufficient for most purposes.

29. In [25] the UK Office of Fair Trading put the number of users at 100 million; other estimates range from 20 million in [18], 70 million in [31], 33.4 million [21] and 38 million [10]. A figure of 30 million would seem a reasonable current estimate, although by early 1997 this might have risen beyond 40 million users world-wide.

30. The original material is found in Everett M Rogers, *Diffusion of Innovation*, 4th edition, Free Press, November 1995.

31. Pamela Anderson; Kylie Minogue; Uri Geller. Geller in fact has a home page (accessible at 'http://www.urigeller.com').

32. Reference [21].

33. Mike Moore of D'Arcy Masius Benton & Bowles at the Federal Trade Commission, November 16 1995. He quoted estimates that 'by the year 2000, the percentage of US homes with access to the Internet will grow from 9 per cent to 30 per cent'.

34. Part of the Henley Centre for Forecasting's strategic analysis services for the telecommunications market, also presented at a CCTA-hosted IT-2000 event in 1995.

35. Or more importantly, the Information Superhighway. In a speech by the Secretary of State for Education in January 1995 at Olympia, an annual IT expenditure of £250 million in schools alone was quoted, and the speech made clear the importance of e-mail, multi-media and broadband communication over and above the Internet facilities already used.

36. The UK's CCTA – a government organisation – have produced just such a booth; separately, so too have BT themselves.

37. France has also been somewhat restricted by the cost of Internet services, although these have fallen quite dramatically through 1995 and 1996; in the February 1996 edition (p 48), the *Internet* magazine quoted a drop in hourly connection charges from £13 to 31p! The other issue for the French in particular is the jealously guarded quota system for French language content in French-accessible media; a requirement which is insupportable in the current Internet bias towards English – and has in fact now been dropped for the Internet.

38. Some analysts – such as Zona Research [27] – have effectively dismissed this aspect, suggesting instead that *internal* company use (Intranets, discussed in Chapter 3) will form the most important elements of the Internet in the 21st century. Unless the security systems described in Chapter 3 are implemented successfully and the reductions in telecommunications prices described in Chapter 2 become a reality, this may very well be proved to be true.

39. Many of these are the Internet equivalent of 'Urban Myths'. There are rumours of an American student who provides a direct picture feed from a miniature camera in the bowl of his toilet directly onto the Internet; there is a similar feed from a camera monitoring another user's goldfish bowl, and yet another monitoring what the user is currently watching on TV! Some pointers to such live Internet camera feeds can be found at 'http//in.net/~chucka/index.htm'.

40. ;-) is a wink; :-(is sad; :-() is a gasp of shock, etc, etc.

41. The most obvious places are at the host system that sends and the host system that receives the complete file. In each of these, the e-mail message is stored in a directory and is available to at least the system operator and to any others who can manage

to access those directories.

42. Cyberia and Cafe Internet in London, for example, and many, many more throughout America.

43. Or at least their application must be accepted, although this is seldom if ever more than a formality in the CompuServe case; in more specialist 'interest groups' – such as those for the medical profession – this might be more difficult.

44. This cartoon is copyright of the *New Yorker* magazine and was drawn by Peter Steiner. It is reproduced in [2], p 93, and shows two dogs at an Internet-connected terminal.

45. It is not clear from where the phrase came, although it does have the pleasing imagery of lighting a flame-thrower before hurling abusive text over the ether.

46. The Durlacher analysis [21] in fact quotes sex as by far the most popular content within the Internet. A Carnegie-Mellon research project of 1995 claimed that 83.5 per cent of pictures available through newsgroups were pornographic; this figure – and indeed the research – has subsequently been discredited, but the mud has already stuck to the Internet.

47. After the US terrorist strikes in 1995, it was primarily the terrorist and pornographic material that lead to widespread congressional support for the US Communications Decency Act.

48. Not the least because the information is visible in all those countries accessing the Internet, not just the country concerned in the posting or the offence itself; this means of course that there is not a single authority to which one could turn.

49. Which was also undermined by activities undertaken in foreign countries – Australia in this case – not immediately under UK control.

50. Moreover, unlike encyclopaedia and dictionaries, the information has little or no structure or tagging to allow easy analysis.

51. Some of these are in fact already available; some of them are not, but there is no practical reason why they shouldn't be: they simply have yet to be added.

52. UK government estimates show that an estimated 50 per cent of schoolchildren have access to a PC at home. At school, there have been a large number of initiatives to provide Internet or broadband communications access: Energis and Research

Machines, for example, have agreed to provide local call rate ISDN access to schools and estimate that 70 per cent will be connected by 2000. In November 1995, the then Education Department launched a £10 million sponsorship for over twenty Internet and related projects for schools. See reference [31].

53. The usual mechanism would be to enter the relevant keywords at the browser's search tool – eg, 'Yahoo' for CompuServe's Mosaic – and then to begin following and recording the increasingly complex trail of relevant and interesting pages. Some will be essentially trivial, but others will lead rapidly to the most fascinating of topics.

54. HOS is a doctors-only BBS and so is not strictly the open environment of the Internet; given the privacy of data involved it would be impractical for it to be so open. In fact, it uses the self-same network and Internet protocols, but privacy and exclusivity is ensured through encryption technology; HOS is the only non-US system to have been awarded an export licence for the strongest of encryption software, using a massive 786 byte key to ensure confidentiality.

55. This of course works *against* the Internet as well; in their April 1996 'Network World 500' study of the top 500 US networking users, IDC's report 'Networking in the Cyber Age' reports that 70 per cent of the organisations believe that their employees are using the Internet for entertainment at the company's expense.

56. In the UK, £1 billion per annum[31].

57. This was exactly the mechanism used to push Netscape's *Navigator* Web browser, for example.

58. This was the original idea behind *The Times'* Web site for example, and is embodied in a daily search routine in their 'Interactive Times' pages that builds a personal newspaper from the daily published material. This also gives access to an archive of *The Times* and *Sunday Times* published material. In many ways, this is the more ideal way of building information sources within the Internet since, unlike the other cases, this material has been checked and verified by a reputable editing process.

59. And of course are dedicated to a single newspaper source; more interesting would be agents that construct news from a variety of sources.

60. This is not to say that such vanity publishing cannot be of value. Pressure groups with only minimal resources, for example, could benefit from such services. But the point remains, with paper publishing the costs are much higher; Internet publishing is sufficiently cheap to encourage a much broader range of publishing ventures.

61. An 80,000-word book without illustrations is of the order of 0.5 Mbytes. This can be downloaded in a matter of some ten minutes at even the slowest periods of the day.

62. A typical 15 track music CD requires 500 to 600 Mbytes; depending upon the encoding and compression mechanisms used, a 2 hour feature film will require of the order of 1 Gbytes. By comparison, a packed, compressed computer game of 5 Mbytes takes anywhere from 40 to 90 minutes to download depending on the time of day (and hence the loading on the network).

63. Fibre-optic cabling already forms the basis of much of the backbone network of the Internet, supporting transmission speeds of 32 Mbps; the current bottlenecks lie on the 'local loop' between these and the home or office. Advances in signal compression, transmission media and processing power will all combine to improve this, but will require – according to Gartner Group and other analysts – some twenty years to complete. In the UK, BT are already investing some £15 billion on this upgrade, and the cable TV providers are ensuring that fibre optic is introduced as rapidly as possible to many cities.

64. Although it will of course lead to an increase in the loading placed on the Internet backbone provision.

65. There are of course programmes that are *sponsored* in an explicit way already, or that feature product placement or similar. In the main, however, the advertisements are quite separate from the programme, and in fact are different in different regions.

66. Bill Gates's company *Corbis* for example provides a complete and quite excellent gallery of pictures, sculptures and so forth from many periods. The home page is 'http://www. corbis.com'.

67. [3] describes this change in jobs over the centuries and the

implications of technology on existing workplaces and employment.

68. For example, for a listing of Welsh telecottages 'http://www.netwales.co.uk/tcw'.

69. Developed by Silicon Graphics. Perhaps as one might expect, it requires very performant machines for most implementations.

70. This is particularly useful given the environmental damage being caused to many of these sites. The Valley of the Kings in Egypt for example has had to be closed because of damage from visitors' breath and sweat.

71. *Doom* by iD is an excellent example of just such a virtual reality game. Users can define their own environments, and throughout the Internet there are realistic implementations of Silicon Valley offices, Cambridge College quads, and even home towns.

72. [16] p 3 *et seq* presents a summary of the most immediate challenges to be faced in the context of so-called 'Electronic Commerce' in general, and the Internet in particular.

73. To set this in context, in early 1996 a market research firm, International Data Group, surveyed a set of technology-oriented companies, who might have been expected to use the Internet. Only 10 per cent planned to use the Internet for selling goods, while 75 per cent planned to use it for communicating marketing information. Moreover, a 1996 report by IDC ('The Marketer's Internet: Motivation, Cost and Customisation') put the cost of a commercial Internet site at $1 million per annum.

74. In many ways, of course, this should not be surprising, since these are exactly the goods that have more traditionally found acceptance in telephone shopping.

75. Note, this is a *perception* issue; the shopping itself is entirely safe – or at least, it is as safe as the telephone or mail order case which has already been accepted by shoppers.

76. Most of the Web pages providing advertising fall into this trap. Very intricately designed pages of dense pictures and pointers to games, puzzles etc. At work, with fast access speeds these are usually accessible; at home, with slower speeds (and with a requirement to *pay* for the telephone call) few people have

the patience. Some, however, are quite excellent: 'http://www.thespot.com' for example.

77. As one would expect, such on-line lingerie catalogues already exist! A search on the key word 'lingerie' will produce an embarrassment (!) of such sites.

78. There are very many of these: *Excite, Yahoo, Magellan, InfoSeek,* etc, etc. The browsers support access to several of these; Netscape provides access randomly to a selection; CompuServe Mosaic defaults to Yahoo. These are best used as a 'launch pad' to further investigation.

79. The search engines work by constructing directories. Software agents are despatched from the host system of the search engine company; these trawl through the Internet, constructing directories for the material on each host within the network. The browsers then provide a connection to the search engines' host computer, which in turn provides a front-end program to support queries. Funding for this service comes from two sources: from the browser vendors and from the advertisements displayed, estimated to cost the advertisers $10–20,000 per month. Because the users' search terms are known, the search engine software knows the users' interests; the advertisements are therefore chosen appropriately and are usually well targeted – other than the US bias.

80. See my own article in *New Scientist*, 17 March, 1996.

81. This might well, however, be used by pressure groups wanting no more than to express a particular message.

82. At the time of writing, this particular development has not evolved; discussion with advertising companies, however, suggests that it might well be imminent and widespread by 1997.

83. Try the various Guinness links, accessible through 'http://www.itl.net/guinness'; further contacts, and access to the infamous screen saver, is through the Irish-culture connection: 'http://www.paddynet.ie.guinness'.

84. Other than in the case where the most obvious of company names can be collected, based on the 'real-world' company name.

85. These are the established shopping sites, such as 'http://www.cybershop.com' or the Internet Shopping Network 'http://www.internet.net'.

86. HTTP is said to be a 'stateless' protocol, meaning that no record of the progression of a particular transaction is built-in. Extensions to the basic protocol have been developed to allow this information to be stored in so-called 'Cookies', state information variables that are established and set on the client machines.

87. In establishing my own CompuServe account, I suffered from a faulty modem. This would allow the dialogue between my own and the CompuServe host to get only so far before failing; this meant that I was able to establish *four* CompuServe user accounts – as far as the remote host was concerned – before that host was able to succeed in confirming account details to my local PC. I was left with the four accounts until CompuServe's customer service team noticed (very rapidly, following the weekend) that I had suffered from these difficulties. Had I been ordering goods and dictating my credit card number to a third party I would have been even more concerned.

88. HTTP is the protocol for transmitting the Web pages themselves; these pages are actually turned into packets by TCP for transmission by the IP layer over whatever physical network is in place – such as X.25 or Ethernet. Secure HTTP (SHTTP) applies the encryption processes between the HTTP and the TCP layers; Secure Socket Layer (SSL) applies the encryption between the TCP and the IP layers. A mediation period is employed between sender and recipient to establish the specific encryption type and encryption key to be used.

89. PGP applies the encryption *before* whatever application-level process – such as the mail transfer protocol – is used to pass the information to TCP for 'packetising'. It can therefore be used in place of or in addition to any other security processes required. It is also referred to as a 'strong encryption' tool, meaning that a brute-force, trial-and-error attempt to produce an exhaustive list of possible keywords is impossible (or at least, would take a cosmic time period).

90. Through a security Application Programming Interface (API) that will allow *any* application to operate without regard to the particular security software to be used over the network –

a general and elegant approach to the problem of differing sensitivities between various countries.

91. These are based on the RSA algorithm that now forms a near-universal standard. In 'normal' encryption, the same key is used to encode and to decode a transmission. In the RSA scheme, two different (and not obviously related) keys are used. One is kept secret, the other made public. If A and B then wish to communicate entirely privately, A uses first *his* private and then B's public key to encode the message. To decode, B must use first his own private, followed by A's public keys. By using this mechanism, *only* A and B can access the message. In practice, RSA encryption is time consuming and so the most common method is to generate a single key (a 'one-time' key) and then use the RSA scheme to transmit *that* between the two parties; thereafter, the simpler and faster mechanism of 'standard' encryption programs is used. For additional security, a table of many hundred such one-time keys could be transmitted, and used in a known but private sequence for each of the transmitted packets. The SET scheme uses public keys, but provides for two different encryptions: the order is communicated to the trader, but the credit card details may only be decrypted by the bank; this provides additional levels of security.

92. Quoted in Computing in March 1996, Lorna Harris, head of fraud prevention for APACS ('Association for Payment and Clearing Services'), said 'the advice we would give to card holders would be not to put full card details on the system'.

93. That is, instead of presenting evidence giving details of the precise encryption methodology used, the parties involved can say simply 'we used the accepted standard'. In the same way that judges and juries don't need to be geneticists to accept DNA evidence, they then don't need to be computer scientists or cryptologists to accept arguments around encryption.

94. Almost all of the credit card, e-money or shopping ventures on the Internet or associated BBS have some form of security inbuilt. These have varying characteristics and strengths – measured by length of encryption key – depending upon the application or even the country within which they are being used.

95. These are referred to as EARMS – Electronic Authors' Rights Management Systems. [19] has a good summary of these systems on p 21 *et seq*.

96. The extent of compression depends primarily on the contents of the file. Some information is held in a significantly compressed format anyway, such as picture files. In the case of text files, the redundancy is such as to allow quite substantial levels of encryption.

97. And of course, this key could be 'imported' digitally from overseas, but without obviously attracting importation duty.

98. Or, one can act as one's own travel agent, using the Internet to access the carriers directly. One of the best examples of such direct carrier access is to the UK's British Midlands, accessible at 'http://www.iflybritishmidland.com'. This runs a reservation and information service called *CyberSeat*.

99. Although some have begun to offer their services through dial-in services like a private BBS. This is maintained quite separately from the Internet itself, however.

100. NOP surveys in early 1996, however, suggest that such Internet shopping will treble throughout 1996.

101. £83.3 million was lost through credit and/or debit card frauds in 1995 according to APACS.

102. Conversely, it is of course *visible* on a perpetual basis – embarrassing should the host system crash or the Web page contain incorrect information.

103. [23] makes clear that the US telecommunications policy is for 'Universal Service' – on this basis, the telephone at least should be seen as a *utility* in the sense of being a service that should be available to all.

104. In most cases of course, such virtual companies will be using the Internet to establish an initial presence in a particular country *before* undertaking to set up a physical, real-world shop. The Internet would allow the 'toe-in-the-water' approach with only minimal outlay, important for smaller, ambitious concerns.

105. Most importantly, perhaps, this allows such companies to be established and run from 'back bedrooms' on a shoe-string, without the expense and hassle of a physical office. In the ideal

case, this might allow an employment agent (say) to work from home. In this case, the costs of such Web sites are assumed to be lower than the equivalent cost of office sites – currently this is the case, but the IDC report referenced above made clear that the cost of Web sites is more substantial than many users first assumed.

106. Forrester Research for example predict a world-wide market of $1 billion for the internal Internet servers alone.

107. Observers such as Zona Research show intranet sales growing three times faster than Internet ones, topping $7.9 billion by 1998. And all of the major industry players, from Microsoft to Netscape, from Digital to IBM, have established plans to address this important field through 1996 and 1997. An IDC report, 'Networking in the Cyber Age', 1996, surveyed the top 500 US networking users (having networking expenditure exceeding $5 million and more than 1,000 employees). 89 per cent of these had or planned to implement an intranet strategy and 73 per cent already had Web servers in place to support their *internal* operations. Equivalent figures for much smaller enterprises have not yet been acquired, but they can be expected to follow such a strongly marked trend.

108. This is a 'gate-keeper' that prevents unauthorised access to the internal information services. While these provide a degree of security, they are not the complete answer. The BSI security standard BS7799 defines further requirements, such as control of access to files or services even once the user has been admitted 'within' the system.

109. Of course, there was a commercial issue associated with this, in that Mosaic was developed and distributed initially free of charge. Netscape Communications was established by the original Mosaic developers with the express intention of profiting from their expertise. In 1995, its second full year, Netscape's sales were a massive $80 million

110. Or even from an established vendor: Microsoft's *Explorer*; Sun Microsystems' *HotJava*.

111. [15] lists the CCTA-identified opportunities of the Information Superhighway for government; and [14] gives a 'vision' of potential future uses across several departments.

112. At the time of writing (April 1996), the Parliamentary Information Committee had just made the decision to begin introducing such free of charge information access. Prior to this, it had been necessary to order such information via Internet connection to the HMSO. By contrast, information in the US has been available this way for much longer.

113. As [14] discusses, IT expenditure in the civil service alone for the financial year 1995/6 was expected to be some £2.3 billion; if local government, schools, police and health service expenditure is included, this rises to £10 billion *per annum*.

114. This is referred to as the 'Communication Link-Up' scheme in Labour publications.

115. Worth some $500 billion world-wide.

116. Over 70 per cent in fact. Much of the information about PIPEX *et al* can be found on their home pages: 'http://www.pipex.com' for example.

117. PIPEX saw growth at 5–10 per cent per *month* throughout 1995, for example. Moreover, stock market valuations of these companies currently run at over ten times their annual turnover.

118. This is taking the domestic end-user perspective. For companies, of course, there is a requirement to pay for such software if it is to be used for commercial purposes (and if it isn't, one must ask whether or not it is simply being used as a toy!). The most successful of the browser companies is Netscape themselves, who had a very profitable stock market flotation following superb sales to companies. Throughout 1996, however, they have found themselves in an increasingly bitter contest with Microsoft as the former PC giant repositions itself as an 'Internet Company'.

119. In the *Sunday Times* of 14 April 1996, Meta Group were quoted as stating that 'nearly all' of the world's 2000 biggest companies were already using Netscape for browsers and servers on their internal, Intranet services. By 1998, Zona Research expect intranet business to be worth nearly $8 billion.

120. See for example, *The Economist*, 2 March 1996, p 77 on the $10.8 billion merger of Continental Cablevision and US West.

As the article explains, a change in federal law in January 1996 allows free competition within national communications markets, thereby encouraging such massive mergers and allowing broad approaches to the content market to be made.

121. See *The Economist*'s survey on telecommunications, reference [12].

122. Planet Internet, established by the Dutch post office. There is, however, a limit of 5 hours a month on this service.

123. *The Economist*'s Survey on the Internet, reference [13] describes just such a 'balkanisation' of the Internet, dividing into a dis-organised, general network and a more structured, business network.

124. [11] p 4 defines this globalisation as 'action at a distance', intensifying as a direct result of rapid, world-wide transporta-tion and 'instantaneous global communication'.

125. The trends and figures in this section were taken from the Henley Centre for Forecasting's Policy for Social Change and on-going monitoring services, and from the Warwick Institute for Employment Research's 1995 'Review of the Economy and Employment'.

126. The UK government's £35 million 'Information Society Initiative' managed by the Department for Trade and Industry (DTI) provides Web pages, helplines and a roadshow to help small and medium enterprises to get on-line with the Internet so as to maintain or to establish competitive advantages. Particular encouragement is given for marketing over the Internet, although it is expected that broader use of the system will then result.

127. Although this has not met with complete acceptance within the accountancy profession. As far back as April 1994, for example, the *Accountancy Age* magazine was carrying articles critical of the initiative.

128. The Henley Centre for Forecasting provide the most compre-hensive study of this phenomenon in the UK, described in their 1996 'Planning for Social Change' report.

129. *The Economist*, 30 March 1996, p 89, quote cash transactions accounting for $8.1 trillion of the total world personal spending of $14 trillion in 1993; figures from Visa.

130. In fact, the limit on the Mondex cards is expected to be set at £500, although they could theoretically support around £10,000.

131. Money laundering is currently worth almost £500 billion world-wide and is strongly dependent upon computerised schemes, usually involving 'hacking' the existing, private banking networks.

132. In April 1996, the UK Defamation Act had passed through its first reading but is not yet law. By contrast, while the US Computer Decency Act has already been signed by President Clinton, it was successfully challenged by the ISPs in June 1996. The US government is now planning its appeal.

133. These are referred to as 'Mutual Legal Aid Treaties' MLATs and demand that the countries concerned perform investigations exactly as though they were their own.

134. This power comes under Section 2 of the 1977 Criminal Justice Act, unfairly referred to as the 'Draconian Powers'. In fact, the actual information demanded under these powers cannot subsequently be used as evidence. The encryption key itself, however, which is demanded would never be used as evidence itself; rather, it would be used as a pointer to the actual evidence. The situation is analogous with demanding the code for a safe, for example.

135. The United States of America for example only became signatories to the convention in 1989 ([8] p 48).

136. Although this of course allows only a reasonable fragment of the work to be so quoted.

137. Strictly, it is this *licence* that one buys when purchasing a video or software, rather than the item itself [2].

138. Such as the 'fair use' aspect of taping CDs for playing in the car, which is acceptable in the US but still not so in the UK [8].

139. This ignores the case in which a user deliberately and expressly copies the physical text of a book or scans a 'real world' picture and subsequently releases it onto the Internet. Even with the protection mechanisms discussed, this infringement will remain a worry [26].

140. Section IX of [26] presents this as one of the most important

elements, but makes the valid point that software and systems to encode and to decode such digital 'tattoos' would need to be introduced very rapidly. Reference [19] also discusses the central importance of such 'Electronic Rights Management' processes, and both [2] and [4] provide an additional 'vision' on the implications of such approaches.

141. "Directive of the European Parliament and of the Council on the protection of consumers in respect of distance contracts" 7623/2/95.

142. See Article 5, p 10 'Written confirmation of information' in the Distance Selling Directive mentioned in the previous note.

143. See reference [25] and [8], together with comments in [9] and [10].

144. That is, be regulated primarily by the Internet Service Providers or by those organisations – such as advertisers – who would wish to use the medium. ISPA (the Internet Service Providers Association) have a code of practice, and certainly within the UK the Science and Technology minister at the DTI has expressed hope that this will be sufficient.

145. A Henley Centre for Forecasting report 'The Social and Economic Consequences of a Labour Government', 1995, quoted the chairman of the *Guardian* Media Group, Tony Roche: 'it takes at least two years to draft, pass and implement a piece of legislation addressing [. . .] media content and ownership. Yet computers [. . .] double in power (or halve in cost) every two years." He was referring, moreover, to UK-centric and not even international legislation in this case.

146. See for example 'The Shape of Nets to Come', in [13].

147. That having been said, the Soviet Union's Communist Party numbered only 20 million full members at its largest; and if the number of users is indeed 100 million by 1998, it will exceed the population of the UK.

148. BT currently expect to spend some £15 billion on upgrading the 'local loop' to support fibre-optic; in Japan, the necessary investment is a staggering $400 billion. And the UK is in the best position, with already some 1.5 per cent of local loop services supported by fibre-optic, versus only 0.25 per cent for

the US and less than 0.1 per cent elsewhere in the world. The 3 million km of fibre optic cable provide for 90 per cent of the UK telephone requirements – and was built from silica from just 90 tonnes of sand [30].

149. The most comprehensive source of information on this case has been collected by the Electronic Frontier Foundation itself, with a multitude of links to newspaper articles, comments and even transcriptions from the judge's comments. This is all accessible at 'http://www.eff.org'.

150. This was a key cornerstone of Al Gore's vision of the Information Superhighway, Principle 4, stating 'Take action to avoid creating information "haves" and "have nots".' An analysis of what is involved is given in [23].

INDEX